CW01431965

BAKE YOUR SWEET TIME

FOR EUAN, HAL AND PETER.
(HAVE YOU SEEN MY PHONE?)

BAKE YOUR SWEET TIME

TAT EFFBY

Different takes on classic bakes to fit the time you have

murdoch books
London | Sydney

CONTENTS

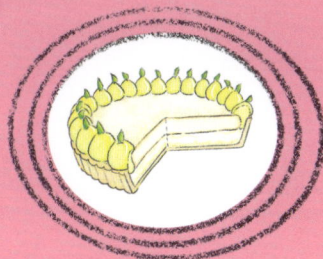

I'LL KEEP THIS QUICK... (OR MEDIUM, OR LONG)

As someone who has baked to avoid everything from doing the dishes to writing a will, I'm an expert in baking my time whether it's 15 minutes or all chocolate-fudging day. But this book is not designed to stop you getting on with your to-do list, in fact it's meant to do the opposite.

Each chapter is based on a classic bake or flavour combination and I've used its building blocks to offer you different recipes depending on how much time and effort is needed to create them. So there are quick bakes for a quick fix in a 15-minute lull, there are medium-timed foolproof recipes for a 90-minute interlude and there are multi-step, big-wow bakes for when you're lucky enough to be able to take your sweet time over straining, proofing, chilling or tempering.

My entire career as a baker, and indeed this book, is the happy result of being an arch procrasti-baker, but I'm not going to recommend it as a life choice: my house is a mess and my mum is furious I never call her. So I'm not here to drag you down to my level, rather I hope to raise you up on my flour-dusted shoulders, sharing recipes to fit around filing your tax return and mowing the lawn, not instead of. Think of it as my toxic avoidance morphing into your baking joy. And one of the best things about doing what I say, not what I do, is you don't have to dust them all with the guilt of knowing you should really be doing something else. Like I do.

If you're really pushed for time, of course you could just buy a packet of Jaffa Cakes. But if you're reading this I'm going to assume that, like me, you're the sort of person who never asks 'What shall I do?', you ask 'What shall I bake?' And you know all this isn't just about the result, it's about the sweet, sticky, bowl-licky process of baking: the sugar highs; the sunken lows; the triumphs and the tragedies of the cake tin. We few, we happy few, we band of bakers know – it's not just the Jaffa, it's the journey.

So the only thing to do before donning our pinnies is to ask: what do you want to bake and how long have you got?

HOUSEKEEPING

CUPS ARE FOR BRAS

OVENS

All ovens heat differently; some have hot spots, and thermostats tend not to be terribly accurate. Mine always burns the biscuit unlucky enough to be sitting in the back left corner. Some are really well insulated so stay hotter for longer, some are just as good at heating the kitchen as they are at baking a loaf. So, to eliminate the guess work, the recipes in this book include instructions on what to look for to tell if your bake is ready.

DIGITAL SCALES

A digital scale for weighing ingredients is essential for many of these recipes, particularly for small amounts of something that will not register on an analogue scale – cornflour (cornstarch), for example. My digital scale is just a cheap one from the supermarket that measures down to 1 gram; there's no need for a set of scales that registers milligrams, none of my recipes qualify as molecular gastronomy.

WEIGH EVERYTHING

No, that's not a typo. All measurements, be they dry, wet, or somewhere in between, are listed in grams. Weighing liquids is far more accurate than measuring them in a jug (pitcher) against a vague line, and could mean the difference between a recipe working and being a complete disgrace. As 1g of water equals 1ml of water, so a 15ml tablespoon of water is the same as 15g of water. For watery liquids, such as juice, it's pretty much the same, however 15ml of syrup is 20g and 15ml of oil is 13g because sugar is denser than water and fat is less dense. But you don't need to do any maths, just follow the recipe. I devise all my recipes with ingredients measured by weight, but other bakers don't, so I'm not suggesting you start converting someone else's millilitres into grams because that might potentially screw their recipe up. What I'm kindly asking of you is to trust me. At least as far as weighing liquids goes.

CUPS

For me, measuring in cups doesn't provide enough accuracy for consistent, successful baking. Particularly if some ingredients have to be tightly packed or lightly scooped, the margin for error is just too great. And the maths involved. Fractions? No thanks. I want these recipes to work for you and the best way to achieve that is for you to use digital scales for accuracy.

DIGITAL THERMOMETER

My digital thermometer is actually a meat probe, but it's perfect for baking. You can stick the probe into a bun to test whether the dough has reached a high enough temperature to be fully baked, and you can slot a skewer through its back clip and rest it in a pan of heating sugar. A thermometer is essential for some recipes on the fancier end of the spectrum, like Italian meringue (page 218), but is also useful for many of the easier ones. Mine, like my digital weighing scales, is not an expensive or fancy one, so if it's possible, I encourage you to have one to hand.

CAKE TINS

Using good-quality cake tins (pans) will help you make better cakes. They diffuse the heat more effectively than cheaper thin ones, so cakes rise more evenly and the edges don't over-brown. The circular cakes in this book are all baked in two 18-cm (7-inch) anodised aluminium tins with 7-cm (2¾-inch) tall sides. A taller tin means you can bake a deeper cake in a single tin, but also that the tops of shallower cakes are slightly protected from direct heat.

SPLITTING A CAKE INTO TWO LAYERS

There are loads of ways to split a cake: using wire contraptions, garrotting with dental floss, jabbing in cocktail sticks until it looks like it's cosplaying Hellraiser. This is my preferred method. It's quick and delivers good results.

Put your cake on a lipless cake plate or turntable. Measure halfway up the side of the cake – use a ruler if you want to be really accurate, otherwise just eye it – then using a serrated knife, make a horizontal cut into the side of the cake about 3cm (1 inch) deep. A bread knife is ideal as it needs to be at least as long as the cake is wide. Rotate the plate a little at a time to continue the shallow cut at the same height around the cake until you get back to the start.

Starting at one side, sit the knife blade in the shallow cut and gently saw horizontally through the body of the cake. Keep the knife blade sitting in the shallow cuts on both sides of the cake to achieve even layers.

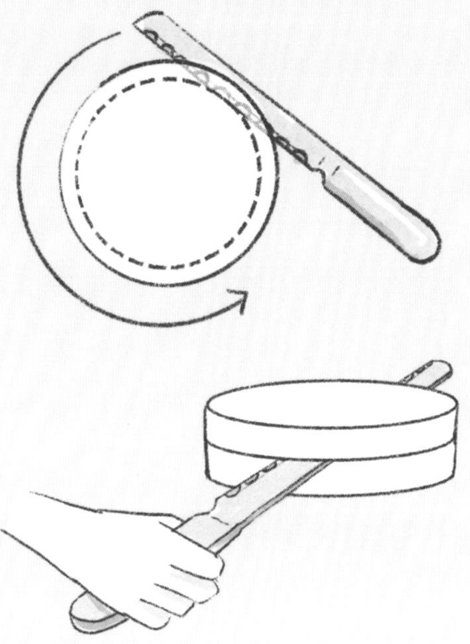

PIPING NOZZLES FOR FILLING CHOUX

Don't waste money on elongated, needle-like nozzles that, in a different setting, look like they might be used to artificially inseminate livestock. Even with the most biddable, soft filling, I've never successfully filled anything with the finer ones; I've managed nothing more than to explode the piping (pastry) bag due to a build up of pressure. Even the larger gauge nozzles put up such a fight that I now only use their pointy end to pierce holes in choux buns or the opposite end as a circular cutter for decorations. Instead, what I recommend is a plain 6-mm (1/4-inch) nozzle, small enough to fill a discreet choux hole but large enough for the filling to be squeezed through.

GLUTEN-FREE

For cookies and cakes, I've offered a gluten-free alternative wherever minimal adjustments and additions make the option possible. Look for the gluten-free option listed alongside the other ingredients. Gluten-free bread is out of my wheelhouse so I haven't offered alternatives to wheat flour for those recipes. However, if you want to convert any of my ideas to gluten-free, there is no better starting point than Katarina 'The Loopy Whisk' Cermelj's book, *The Elements of Baking*. It's quite simply a work of genius.

PLANT-BASED

Almost half of the recipes in this book don't use eggs – in fact, the entire Sticky Toffee Pudding chapter (pages 184–195) is egg-free – so by swapping dairy butter and cream for readily available plant-based alternatives, they can be easily veganised.

CHOCOLATE FUDGE CAKE

Between the ages of 8 up to about 25, if I was lucky enough to eat out, ordering chocolate fudge cake served hot with cream was my knee-jerk response to being handed the pudding menu. Choosing to have it warmed, or more likely, nuked in a catering microwave, was my stab at sophisticated decision making. Admirable, but futile, because chocolate fudge cake is no place for sophistication. Just like this chapter, it's simply a celebration of all things unashamedly chocolatey and wantonly sweet – at least, that's how I've treated these bakes. Chocolate is represented in various cake forms: brownie squares; layer cake; bundt mountain. The fudge appears as literal fudge as well as frosting and sauce. Writing this chapter has made me wonder why I ever moved on from CFC when it never, ever let me down. I hope these incarnations will prove as reliable at shielding you from disappointment as chocolate fudge cake was for me for those 17 precious years.

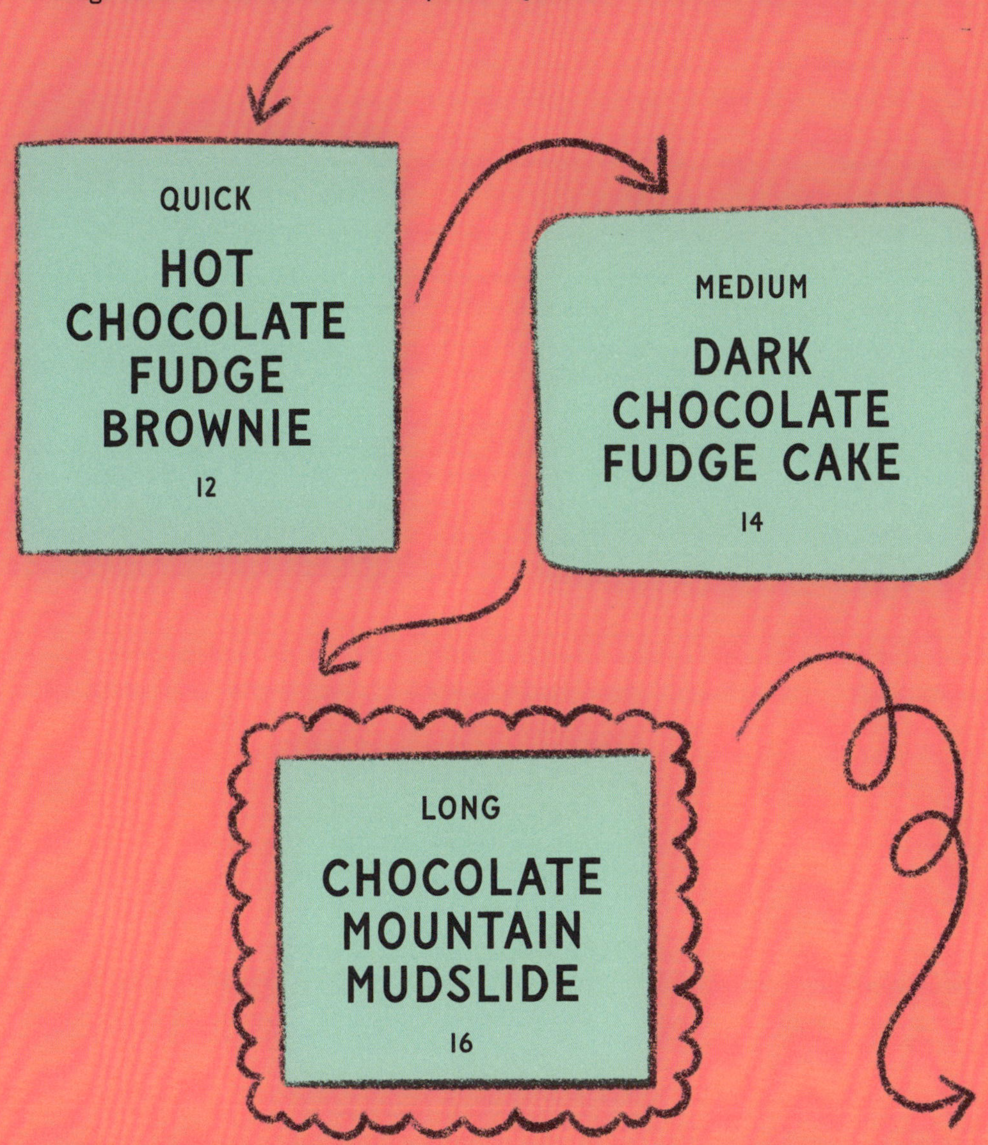

HOT CHOCOLATE FUDGE BROWNIE

Hands on **5 minutes**
Ready in **30 minutes**

MAKES
2 very generous, 4 slightly more responsible or 8 very restrained portions

EQUIPMENT
1-kg (2-lb) loaf tin (pan)

This quick chocolate brownie, designed to be eaten hot from the oven with ice cream, is the second answer* to the age-old question, 'What shall I do with this leftover condensed milk?' It's a fudge brownie because it's supremely fudgy *and* because it's made with the same primary ingredients of a quick fudge. So if you need a really quick fix, just melt the chocolate with the condensed milk, chill it and cut it into squares. But we're here for the baking, so chuck in a bit of water, flour and heat and bam! We're pastry chefs.

50g (1¾ oz) milk chocolate

50g (1¾ oz) dark (bittersweet) chocolate (70% cocoa)

100g (3½ oz) sweetened condensed milk

30g (1 oz) / 2 tbsp boiling water

Pinch of salt

30g (1 oz) plain (all-purpose) flour or gluten-free plain (all-purpose) flour

½ tsp baking powder

TO SERVE

Vanilla ice cream

1. Set the oven to 175°C fan (375°F/gas 5). Line your loaf tin with baking paper brushed with a little oil or melted butter.
2. Break both the milk and dark chocolate into a microwave-safe bowl, then microwave in short bursts to melt. If you don't have a microwave, put the chocolate in a heatproof bowl set over a pan of hot water to melt.
3. When the chocolate is completely melted with no remaining lumps, stir in the condensed milk and boiling water.
4. Once you have a smooth liquid, add the salt, flour and baking powder, then mix well until no dry pockets of flour remain.
5. Scrape the batter into the lined tin and bake in the middle of the oven for 17–19 minutes or 20–23 minutes if using gluten-free flour. For a fudgy brownie, test by poking a table knife into the centre of the batter. As soon as it comes out clean, remove the tin from the oven.
6. Leave the brownies to cool in the tin for 3 minutes before lifting out using the ends of the paper. Cut the brownies into portions and serve with scoops of vanilla ice cream.

*The first answer is spoon. There's actually a third one, but it's a bit more sensible: decant it into an airtight tub and freeze it. Yawn.

If using all 70% dark (bittersweet) chocolate, use 20g (¾ oz) of flour. If using all milk chocolate, use 40g (1⅓ oz) of flour.

DARK CHOCOLATE FUDGE CAKE

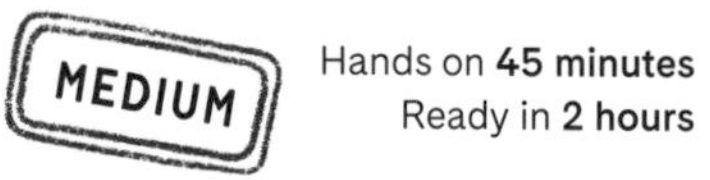

Hands on **45 minutes**
Ready in **2 hours**

SERVES 10–12

EQUIPMENT
Two 18-cm (7-inch) round cake tins (pans)

Not dark in a brooding Dark Knight sort of a way, just deeply chocolatey. In fact, a slice or two of this (ironically) light-in-texture cake might have cheered Bruce Wayne up a bit. That and maybe a cuddle. Packed with chocolate flavour but not too sugary, it's perfect for layering and covering with a chocolate fudge frosting that kicks your recommended daily intake into next week.

70g (2½ oz) unsweetened cocoa powder

1 tsp instant coffee powder

¼ tsp salt

180g (6⅓ oz) boiling water

4 large (US extra-large) eggs

160g (5⅔ oz) light brown soft sugar

1 tbsp vanilla extract

120g (4¼ oz) sunflower oil or any other flavourless oil

35g (1¼ oz) dark (bittersweet) chocolate (70% cocoa)

65g (2⅓ oz) milk chocolate

100g (3½ oz) plain (all-purpose) flour or gluten-free plain (all-purpose) flour + ½ tsp xanthan gum

4 tsp baking powder

Full quantity of Chocolate Fudge Frosting (page 225)

1. Set the oven to 160°C fan (350°F/gas 4) and line the base of each cake tin with a disc of baking paper.
2. To a large mixing bowl, add the cocoa powder, coffee powder and salt. Pour over the boiling water and mix by hand with a balloon whisk until smooth. Leave for 5 minutes to allow the cocoa to bloom.
3. Add the eggs, sugar, vanilla and oil, then whisk until combined.
4. Break both the dark and milk chocolate into a microwave-safe bowl, then microwave in short bursts to melt. If you don't have a microwave, put the chocolate in a heatproof bowl set over a pan of hot water to melt. Whisk into the batter until evenly blended.
5. Add the flour and baking powder, then whisk in until no dry pockets of flour remain and the batter is smooth. If using gluten-free flour, mix the flour, baking powder and xanthan gum together before whisking into the batter.
6. Divide the batter between the lined tins and bake in the middle of the oven for 28–30 minutes or until a metal skewer comes out clean. (Use a metal skewer, rather than a wooden one, as the batter sticks to wood and gives a false impression of being underdone.)
7. While the cakes are baking, make the chocolate fudge frosting following the instructions on page 225.
8. Leave the cakes in their tins for 10 minutes before turning out onto a wire rack to cool.
9. When completely cooled, split each cake in two so you have four layers (page 9). Sandwich each layer with up to 90g (3 oz) of the chocolate fudge frosting. Using a large palette knife, spread a thin coating of frosting over the top and sides of the cake to trap the crumbs, then chill for 10 minutes to set that layer. Finally, use the remaining frosting to thickly coat the cake. With chocolate fudge frosting, I take a relaxed approach to the end result, preferring to see the strokes of the palette knife. If you want a smooth, sharp finish use a large, wide cake scraper and a turntable.

CHOCOLATE MOUNTAIN MUDSLIDE

Hands on **1 hour 20 minutes**
Ready in **2 hours**
plus 6–24 hours for freezing

SERVES 12–14

EQUIPMENT
1.2-litre (5-cup) bundt tin (pan)

Flat baking sheet

I think of this ridiculous ice-cream cake as 'dessert-meets-disaster movie'. Salted caramel ice cream fills the core and caps a rich chocolate bundt cake, the whole cake 'mountain' is coated in snowy folds of whipped mascarpone cream, which is then destroyed by twin torrents of butterscotch and chocolate sauce. It's got drama, it's got jeopardy and no one's coming out of the experience unchanged.

SALTED CARAMEL ICE CREAM

275g (9¾oz) Salted Caramel Sauce (page 230)

320g (11¼oz) double (heavy) cream

CHOCOLATE BUNDT CAKE

40g (1⅓oz) unsweetened cocoa powder

1 tsp instant coffee powder

¼ tsp salt

75g (2⅔oz) boiling water

150g (5¼oz) granulated sugar

125g (4½oz) mascarpone

50g (1¾oz) sunflower oil or any other flavourless oil

2 large (US extra-large) eggs

2 tsp vanilla extract

125g (4½oz) plain (all-purpose) flour or gluten-free plain (all-purpose) flour + ½ tsp xanthan gum

2 tsp baking powder

MASCARPONE CREAM

10g (⅓oz) granulated sugar

2 tsp vanilla extract

200g (7oz) mascarpone

300g (10½oz) double (heavy) cream

TO DECORATE (OPTIONAL)

150g (5¼oz) dark (bittersweet) chocolate (70% cocoa)

BUTTERSCOTCH SAUCE

20g (¾oz) dark brown soft sugar

20g (¾oz) light brown soft sugar

10g (⅓oz) cornflour (cornstarch)

200g (7oz) milk (any)

50g (1¾oz) cold salted butter

CHOCOLATE SAUCE

10g (⅓oz) unsweetened cocoa powder

100g (3½oz) light brown soft sugar

200g (7oz) water

50g (1¾oz) double (heavy) cream

MAKE THE SALTED CARAMEL ICE CREAM

1. Make the ice cream at least 6 hours before assembling the cake.
2. To a large mixing bowl, add the salted caramel sauce and half the cream. Gently stir together until evenly blended. Stir in the rest of the cream and beat until thick and holding stable peaks.

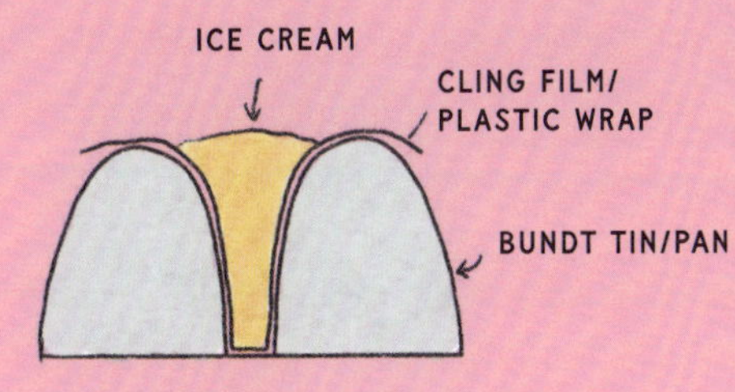

3. You now need to form the ice cream mixture into a 'plug' to fit inside the eventual cake. With the base of the bundt tin facing up, lay a large piece of cling film (plastic wrap) loosely over it. Spoon the ice cream mixture into the middle of the cling film and push it into the central void of the tin. Keep adding the mixture until the void is filled, then fold the excess cling film over the 'plug'. If your freezer has space, freeze the bundt tin with the ice cream in situ, otherwise carefully tip out the ice-cream column and freeze it separately, but make sure it doesn't get squashed out of shape or it won't fit later.

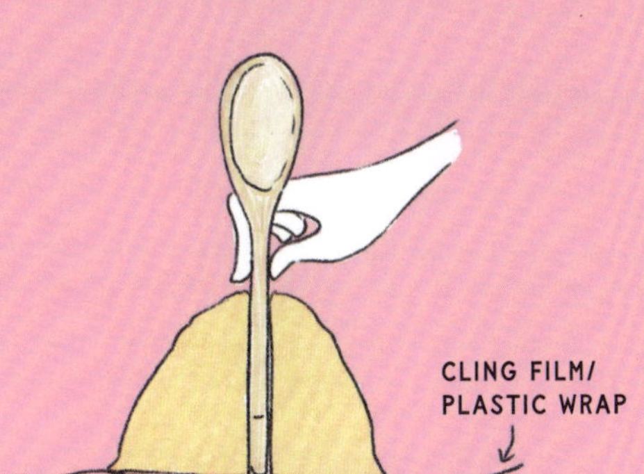

4. On another sheet of cling film, pile up the remaining unfrozen ice cream into a mound to form the mountain's 'peak'; it should be stable enough to hold its shape. Wet the handle of a wooden spoon and push it down into the mound, wiggle it around a bit then pull it out to create a clear channel from top to bottom. You may have to repeat this a couple of times. This central cavity will be filled with hot sauce when poured over later. Wrap the ice-cream 'peak' in the excess cling film and freeze it.

MAKE THE CHOCOLATE BUNDT CAKE

5. Set the oven to 150°C fan (325°F/gas 3). Spray or brush the inside of the bundt tin with cake release.
6. To a large mixing bowl, add the cocoa powder, coffee powder and salt. Pour over the boiling water and mix by hand with a balloon whisk until it forms a smooth paste. Leave for 5 minutes to allow the cocoa to bloom.
7. Add the sugar and mascarpone. Using a spatula to loosen the cheese so it blends more evenly, squish everything into the cocoa paste. Add the oil, eggs and vanilla. Whisk by hand to bring all the ingredients together in a smooth, even batter. Add the flour and baking powder (and xanthan gum, if gluten-free), then whisk until all the dry ingredients are mixed in.
8. Scrape the batter into the bundt tin and bake in the middle of the oven for 35 minutes or until a metal skewer comes out clean. Leave the cake in the tin for 10 minutes before turning out onto a wire rack to cool.

Continued overleaf

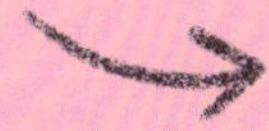

MAKE THE MASCARPONE CREAM

The mascarpone cream can be made while the cake is baking, then sit in the fridge until needed.

9. To a large mixing bowl, add the sugar, vanilla and mascarpone. Using a spatula, loosen the cheese and mix everything together. Add the cream a little at a time, mixing it into the mascarpone so there are no lumps. When all the cream has been incorporated, beat until just thick and spreadable. Cover and chill until ready to assemble the cake.

MAKE THE TREE DECORATIONS

10. If making the tree decorations, temper the chocolate (page 226) and scrape it into a disposable piping (pastry) bag. Line a flat baking sheet with non-stick baking paper.

11. Snip 2mm (1⁄16 inch) from the tip of the piping bag. Pipe several overlapping lines up and down to form the trunk between 6–8cm (2–3 inches) high. Zigzag more lines across the trunk for the branches, starting narrow at the top and widening the lower they go. Don't pipe any branches at the base of the trunk. Create a variety of tree sizes from about 6–8cm (2–3 inches) high. Leave the trees to set on the paper until assembling the cake.

MAKE THE BUTTERSCOTCH SAUCE

12. To a heavy-bottomed pan, add both sugars and the cornflour. Gradually stir in the milk, a little at a time, until you have a smooth paste. Pour in the rest of the milk, put the pan on a medium heat and stir continuously until the sauce thickens. Remove from the heat and stir in the cold butter, then decant into a serving jug (pitcher) for later.

MAKE THE CHOCOLATE SAUCE

13. To a heavy-bottomed pan, add the cocoa powder and sugar. Slowly whisk in the water to avoid lumps forming, then add the cream. Put the pan on a medium heat and bring to an even boil. Keep the sauce at this heat for 5 minutes; the bubbles will get smaller as the sauce thickens. Remove from the heat, then decant into a serving jug (pitcher) for later.

ASSEMBLE THE CAKE

Assemble the cake no more than 20 minutes before serving and eating.

14. If using, carefully peel the chocolate tree decorations off their baking paper and keep them to hand.
15. Set the cooled cake on a large serving plate, ideally with a lip to catch the sauce. Leaving the central cavity bare, cover the sides and top of the cake with a thin coating of the mascarpone cream to trap the crumbs.
16. Unwrap the column of ice cream and slot it into the central cavity. Unwrap the ice-cream 'peak' and sit that on top. Working swiftly, cover the ice cream with mascarpone cream. Next, work down the sides of the cake to coat them in a thicker layer of mascarpone cream so no dark shows through. When your 'mountain' is completely covered in 'snow', stick the chocolate trees upright into the mascarpone cream layer over the cake.
17. Heat the sauces. Trickle both sauces simultaneously (as best as you can) over the peak of the mountain. Some sauce will pool in the mountain peak and soften the ice cream; this helps to cut neat slices of the ice cream-topped cake. But this is a mudslide after all, and just how neat can one of those really be? Serve with extra sauce, if needed.

BAKEWELL TART

How have I only just noticed this chapter title reads like an impertinent question? Bake well, tart? Well, yes, actually I do and I happen to like this shade of lipstick, so keep your moral judgment to yourself. Tart shaming aside, Bakewell tart flavours are predominantly fragrant almond and sharp raspberry, with the sometime, but always welcome, additions of cherry and water icing. A crisp pastry is an essential element, which is represented in these bakes as both shortcrust and choux. Almond does a lot of heavy lifting, featuring as flaked nuts, crumble, frangipane, craquelin and an Amaretto-flavoured pastry cream. Raspberry puts in the work as jam, curd and fresh fruit. Pearly white water icing is an optional flourish for one recipe and an essential for another. Cherry has the easiest gig, arriving when all the hard work has been done, plonking itself down as decoration, turning a Bakewell into a Cherry Bakewell. Cherry bake well? I don't know, she's never let me try any.

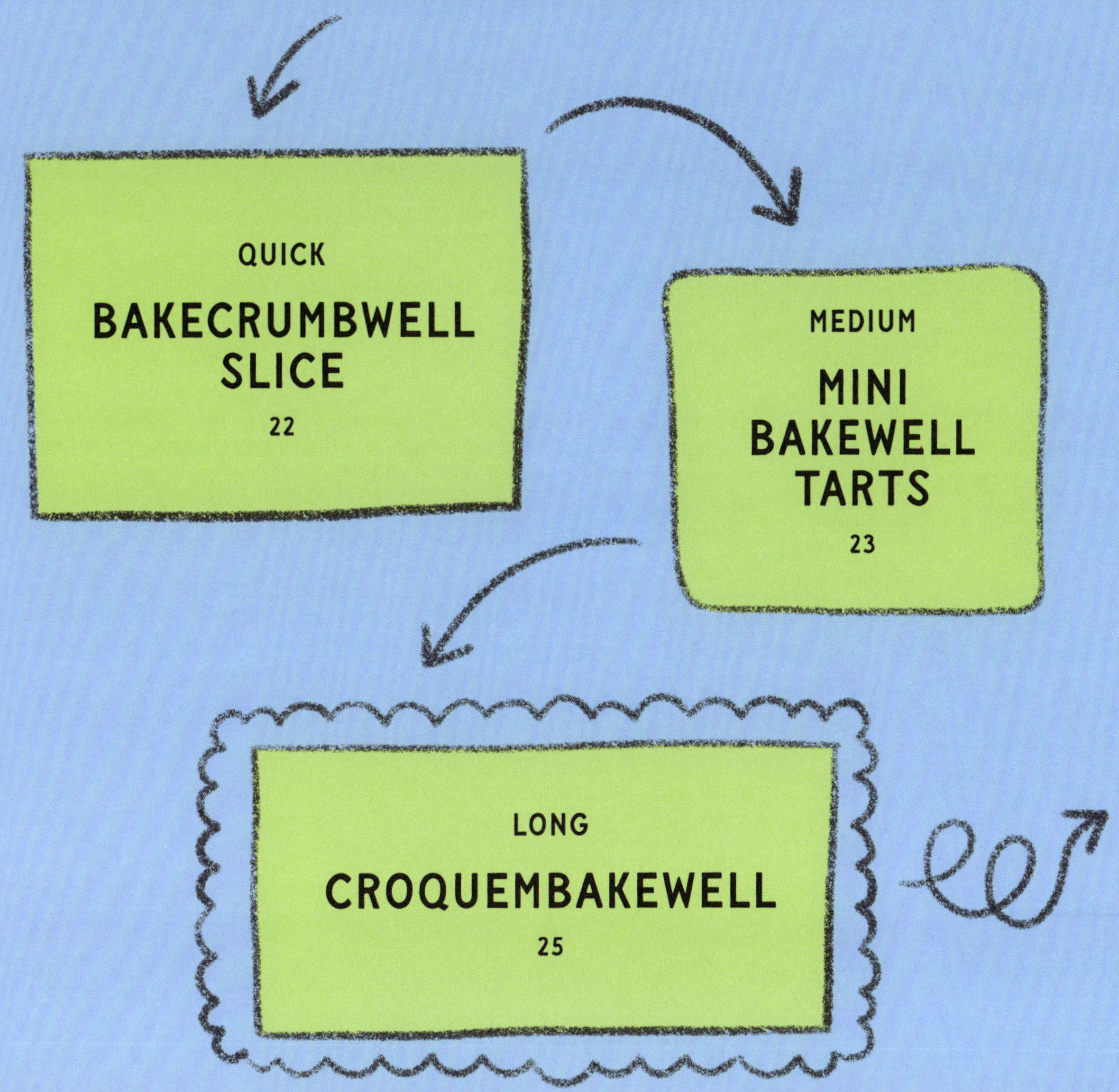

BAKECRUMBWELL SLICE

Hands on **10 minutes**
Ready in **40 minutes**

MAKES
16 slices

EQUIPMENT
20 x 30-cm (8 x 12-inch) brownie tin (pan)

Sorry about the recipe title, I couldn't help it. A Bakewell-flavoured slice covered in crumble: I was powerless to call it anything else. Word play aside, these simple treats have a lot to recommend them: a shortcrust base scattered with almonds, raspberries and a marzipan crumble. If you're a hater, don't let the marzipan put you off. It's there to add extra almond flavour and a delicious chew to the whole moreish jumble of tastes and textures. You may be turned. If not, I'll have your slice.

PASTRY BASE

250g (9 oz) ready-rolled shortcrust pastry (sweet or plain)

OR

Half quantity of Sweet Shortcrust Pastry (page 210)

OR

Half quantity of Gluten-Free Sweet Shortcrust Pastry (page 210)

CRUMBLE TOPPING

150g (5¼ oz) plain (all-purpose) flour or gluten-free plain (all-purpose) flour

50g (1¾ oz) granulated sugar

100g (3½ oz) cold salted butter

100g (3½ oz) marzipan

30g (1 oz) flaked or chopped almonds

RASPBERRY FILLING

60g (2 oz) raspberry jam (preserve)

150g (5¼ oz) frozen or fresh raspberries

1. Set the oven to 200°C fan (425°F/gas 7). Line the brownie tin with baking paper, leaving an overhang for lifting the bake out later.
2. If making your own shortcrust pastry, follow the instructions on page 210. Roll out the pastry to a thickness of 4mm (⅛ inch).
3. Cut the pastry slightly larger than the tin's base to allow for shrinkage, then lay it in the tin with the excess sitting up the sides. Prick the pastry all over with a fork. Bake for 10 minutes on the second rung in the oven.
4. Meanwhile, make the crumble topping. In a large bowl, combine the flour and sugar. Coarsely grate the butter into the bowl and, using your fingertips, roughly rub it into the mix. Grate the marzipan into the bowl and rub it in to make a rough, damp crumble. Stir through the almonds.
5. Remove the pastry base from the oven and drop the temperature to 185°C fan (400°F/gas 6). Spread the jam over the hot pastry and scatter half the crumble topping over that. Dot the raspberries over so they're evenly distributed, then top with the remaining crumble topping. Return to the oven for 20 minutes or until the crumble is a light, even golden brown.
6. Once baked, remove from the tin straight away, sliding everything off the baking paper onto a wire rack so the pastry crisps as it cools.
7. When completely cool, cut into 16 slices. When stored in an airtight container at room temperature, leftovers will keep well for 2 or 3 days.

MINI BAKEWELL TARTS

Hands on **30 minutes**
Ready in **1 hour**
plus 30 minutes chilling for wheat pastry

MAKES
12 tarts

EQUIPMENT
12-cup muffin tin (pan)

These individual tarts, filled with jam, use ground rice instead of almonds in the topping. That makes them thriftier but every bit as delicious as a traditional frangipane topping. The almond flavour is present and correct thanks to the natural extract. What I love about these – apart from how fun it is to fit a whole one in my mouth – is you just line the tin with pastry, add the fillings and get them in the oven. No blind bak(well)ing required.

PASTRY BASE

Full quantity of Sweet Shortcrust Pastry (page 210)

OR

Full quantity of Gluten-Free Sweet Shortcrust Pastry (page 210)

FILLING

120g (4¼ oz) raspberry or cherry jam (preserve)

140g (5 oz) salted butter, melted

140g (5 oz) granulated sugar

140g (5 oz) ground rice

½ tsp almond extract

2 large (US extra-large) eggs (or 1 large egg plus whatever is left over from pastry making)

50g (1¾ oz) flaked almonds

TO DECORATE (OPTIONAL)

50g (1¾ oz) icing (confectioners') sugar

1 tsp water

6 glacé cherries, halved

1. Very lightly oil the cups of the muffin tin. Cut 2-cm (¾-inch) wide strips of baking paper, 15cm (6 inches) long. Before adding the pastry, lay a strip in each cup to hoist the tarts out of the tin once baked.
2. Make the pastry following the instructions on page 210. Wheat-based pastry needs to be chilled for 30 minutes before rolling out; gluten-free can be used straight away.
3. Set the oven to 185°C fan (400°F/gas 6).
4. Sit the pastry on a large, flour-dusted piece of baking paper. Dust the pastry, cover with another large piece of paper and roll to 3mm (⅛ inch) thick. Using a 9-cm (3½-inch) round cookie cutter, press out 12 discs.
5. Carefully lift the pastry discs into the muffin tin. Using a lump of spare pastry to prevent tearing, press them into the cups. Drop 10g (⅓ oz) of jam (a slightly rounded teaspoon) into each tart case.
6. To a large jug (pitcher), add the melted butter, sugar, ground rice and almond extract, then mix. Add the eggs and mix in until blended.
7. Divide the batter equally between the tart cases, filling them to just below the top. Scatter a few flaked almonds over the top of each one.
8. Bake in the middle of the oven for 15 minutes. These tarts are best when the filling retains some squidginess. As soon as they go from wet to set, give the filling a gentle prod; if it feels slightly soft under the set top, they are ready. Leave to cool in the tin for 5 minutes and then lift out the tarts using the paper strips onto a wire rack to cool completely.
9. While the tarts are cooling, if icing the tarts mix the icing sugar with the water to make a thick icing. Scrape the icing into a disposable piping (pastry) bag.
10. When the tarts are completely cool, snip a small tip from the end of the piping bag. Pipe a zigzag of icing over the top of each tart. If using, finish each tart with half a glacé cherry.

CROQUEMBAKEWELL

Hands on **1 hour 45 minutes**
Ready in **3 hours**

MAKES
One 35-cm (14-inch) tall croquembouche

EQUIPMENT
Two flat baking sheets

Straight-sided pint glass

This Bakewell-inspired croquembouche is an undertaking, so make sure you're fully committed otherwise it may end up a towering embodiment of resentment. With almond craquelin-covered choux buns, filled with Amaretto pastry cream and raspberry curd, piled high with caramel, there's plenty to keep you busy. You could just make a fraction of the buns, fill them and eat them without bothering to stack them up, but if you've got this far, you're probably up for a delicious challenge.

AMARETTO PASTRY CREAM

40g (1⅓ oz) cornflour (cornstarch)

50g (1¾ oz) granulated sugar

2 large (US extra-large) eggs

½ tbsp vanilla extract

350g (12⅓ oz) whole (full-fat) milk

50g (1¾ oz) Amaretto (for alcohol-free, use 400g/14 oz milk and ½ tsp almond extract)

80g (2¾ oz) unsalted butter

RASPBERRY CURD

350g (12⅓ oz) frozen or fresh raspberries (sieved for 250g/ 9oz of pulp and juice)

20g (¾ oz) cornflour (cornstarch)

60g (2 oz) granulated sugar, plus extra if needed

90g (3¼ oz) unsalted butter

Micro pinch of salt

CRAQUELIN

55g (2 oz) ground almonds (almond meal)

45g (1½ oz) plain (all-purpose) flour or 65g (2⅓ oz) gluten-free plain (all-purpose) flour

55g (2 oz) granulated sugar

65g (2⅓ oz) salted butter, softened

Ingredients continued overleaf

MAKE THE AMARETTO PASTRY CREAM

1. Using the quantities given here, make the Amaretto pastry cream following the instructions on page 220, adding the Amaretto in step 3 once the hot milk and egg have been poured back into the pan. Leave the pastry cream to cool while you make the raspberry curd.

MAKE THE RASPBERRY CURD

2. If using frozen berries, defrost the raspberries, then push the fruit through a sieve (strainer) to remove the seeds. If there's not quite enough pulp and juice to give 250g (9 oz), add enough water to make up the weight.
3. To a heavy-bottomed pan, add the cornflour and sugar. Add a little of the raspberry pulp to make a lump-free mix. Stir in the remaining pulp and juice.
4. Put the pan on a medium heat and keep stirring to mix out any lumps. When the curd thickens, taste it. If there's any chalkiness from the cornflour, heat for a further minute or so until it fully cooks out. If the fruit is too sour, add more sugar. Remove from the heat. Stir in the butter and a tiny pinch of salt.
5. Pour the curd into a bowl and sit a piece of baking paper or cling film (plastic wrap) directly on the surface to stop a skin forming, then chill.

MAKE THE CRAQUELIN

6. To a large bowl, add all the ingredients for the craquelin and mix together to make a dough – the butter should be soft enough to do this with a spatula.
7. Roll out the dough between two sheets of baking paper to a thickness of 2mm (1⁄16 inch). Freeze the craquelin flat while you make the choux buns.

Continued overleaf

CHOUX BUNS (MAKES 52)

140g (5 oz) plain (all-purpose) flour or 80g (2¾ oz) gluten-free plain (all-purpose) flour + 60g (2 oz) gluten-free self-raising flour

200g (7 oz) boiling water

70g (2½ oz) salted butter

4 large (US extra-large) eggs

CARAMEL (TO ASSEMBLE)

150g (5¼ oz) granulated sugar

50g (1¾ oz) water

1 tbsp golden syrup or glucose syrup

TO DECORATE

100g (3½ oz) icing (confectioners') sugar

15g (½ oz) / 1 tbsp water

50g (1¾ oz) flaked almonds

50g (1¾ oz) slivered pistachios (optional)

200g (7 oz) fresh raspberries

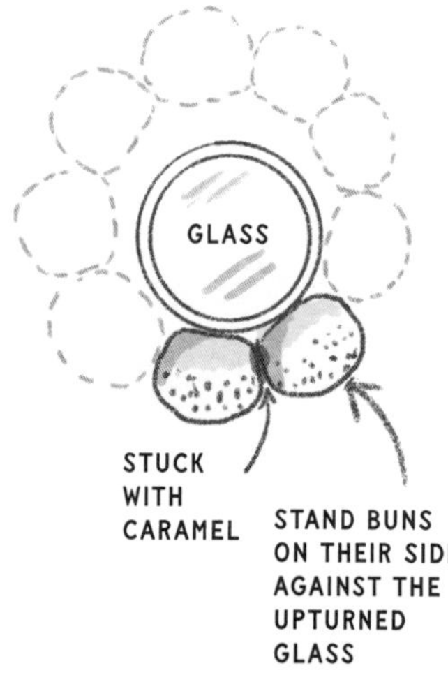
GLASS
STUCK WITH CARAMEL
STAND BUNS ON THEIR SIDE AGAINST THE UPTURNED GLASS

MAKE THE CHOUX BUNS

8. Set the oven to 175°C fan (375°F/gas 5) and line two baking sheets with non-stick baking paper.

9. Using the quantities given here, make the choux pastry following the instructions on page 208. Scrape the dough into a piping (pastry) bag fitted with a 1-cm (⅓-inch) nozzle. Onto the baking sheets, pipe 3.5-cm (1⅓-inch) blobs of dough (each bun uses 8g/¼ oz), leaving 3cm (1 inch) in between. Pipe 52 buns – you need 43 for the tower, but spares are very useful. For even buns, pipe directly down onto the baking sheet and don't lift the nozzle until the circle of dough is 3.5cm (1⅓ inch) wide.

10. From the frozen craquelin, press out 3.5-cm (1⅓-inch) discs. The wide end of a large piping nozzle makes an excellent circular cutter. Lightly press the craquelin discs onto the choux buns – don't squash the choux wider than it has been piped. Re-form, re-roll and re-freeze the offcuts of craquelin, if needed.

11. Bake the choux buns in the middle of the oven for 20 minutes, then drop the temperature to 150°C fan (325°F/gas 3) for a further 8–10 minutes or until the craquelin is evenly golden. Once baked, poke a small hole in the base of each bun with the pointy end of a chopstick. Sit the buns on the sheets, hole side up, and return to the oven with the heat turned off but the fan on. (If you don't have a fan oven, prop the door open with a wooden spoon handle.) Leave the buns to dry out in the residual heat for 20 minutes, then remove and leave to cool completely.

FILL THE CHOUX BUNS

12. When the buns are cool, scrape the pastry cream into a piping bag fitted with a 6-mm (¼-inch) nozzle. The bag may take only half the pastry cream, so refill when it runs out. Scrape the raspberry curd into a separate piping bag with a 6-mm (¼-inch) nozzle. Fill all the buns (including any spares) via the hole in the base with half curd, half pastry cream.

MAKE THE CARAMEL

13. Using the quantities given here, make a wet caramel in a heavy-bottomed pan following the instructions on page 228. Only let the caramel turn a pale straw colour. Leave to cool so the caramel thickens slightly.

ASSEMBLE THE CROQUEMBAKEWELL

The croquembouche is formed from seven rings of choux buns (plus a single bun) assembled separately and then stacked.

14. Lightly oil the outside of the top of a straight-sided pint glass and place it upside down on the centre of your serving plate. Wearing heatproof gloves, new washing-up gloves or just being very careful with bare hands, take a bun in each hand. Dip the edge of one bun into the caramel and then stick it to the other bun at a slight angle, resting the pair against the glass to prop them up. Hold the buns together until the caramel hardens. Continue, one bun at a time, dipping an edge in the caramel and sticking to one of the propped-up buns. The glass is only there to support the buns if needed – don't try to follow its exact curve as it will be too small. After sticking four or five buns together, they should be free standing, so remove the glass and complete the nine-bun ring. You can

trickle extra caramel over the joins to strengthen them, just be careful to run it down the back of the buns so it doesn't spoil the craquelin. If the caramel hardens in the pan, reheat it gently to make it liquid and usable.

15. On a large sheet of non-stick baking paper, construct the next six rings of buns as illustrated. Use a smaller oiled glass as a prop, if needed. Leave the last-constructed ring for 5 minutes so its caramel hardens completely before stacking the rings. You can hide any surplus buns within the tower as you assemble it. Gravity will hold the rings in place, the water icing decoration will help secure them.

16. Make up the icing. In a small bowl, mix the icing sugar with enough water to make a thick but pipable icing. Scrape into a piping bag fitted with a 2-mm (1⁄16-inch) nozzle. Pipe a little icing where the choux buns join and use it as glue to stud the croquembouche with almond flakes, pistachios (if using) and raspberries. Finally, spoon 1 tablespoon of icing sugar into a fine-mesh sieve (strainer) and lightly dust the tower to finish.

17. Serve within 3 hours. Any leftovers can be refrigerated but the choux buns will lose some of their crispness.

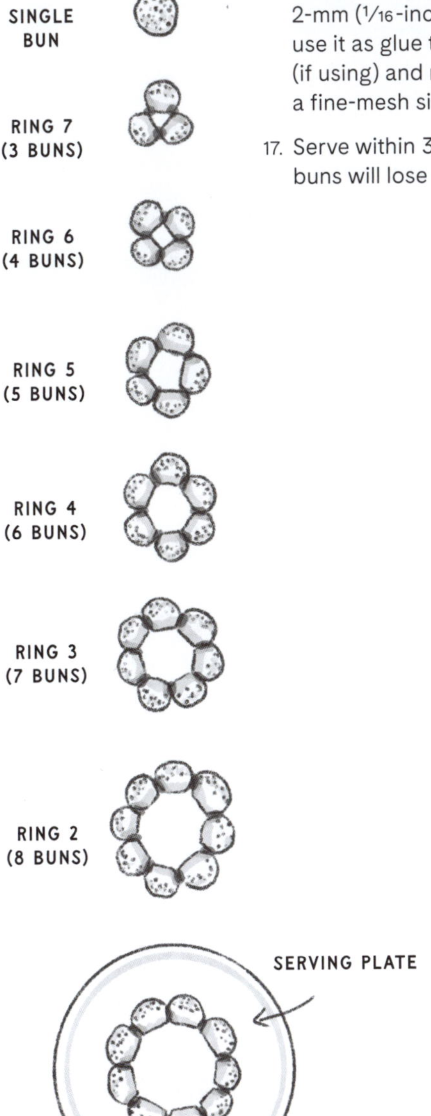

* GLACÉ CHERRY OPTIONAL

BAKLAVA

For this chapter I would be nowhere without my friend Anna Christoforou acting as baklava adviser / taster / intimacy co-ordinator and lending me *Greece: the Cookbook* by Vefa Alexiadou, whose traditional Greek recipe provided an invaluable starting point. Of course, baklava is not exclusively Greek. Said to have originated within the Ottoman empire, it didn't put its feet up, spreading its sticky way into dessert cultures throughout the Mediterranean, the Middle East, the Balkans and North Africa, picking up variations in ingredients and spellings along the way. My offerings are all the things I like in a baklava with no claim to authenticity or specific geography. For the crisp golden layers, there's puff pastry as well as traditional filo (phyllo) to sandwich a mixture of spiced nuts, based mostly on what I can afford. To soak the layers, there's both pure honey and syrup flavoured with rosewater and lemon. If you're not convinced about rosewater, try it with something sharp to balance its floral fragrance; I promise you'll never look bak(lava).

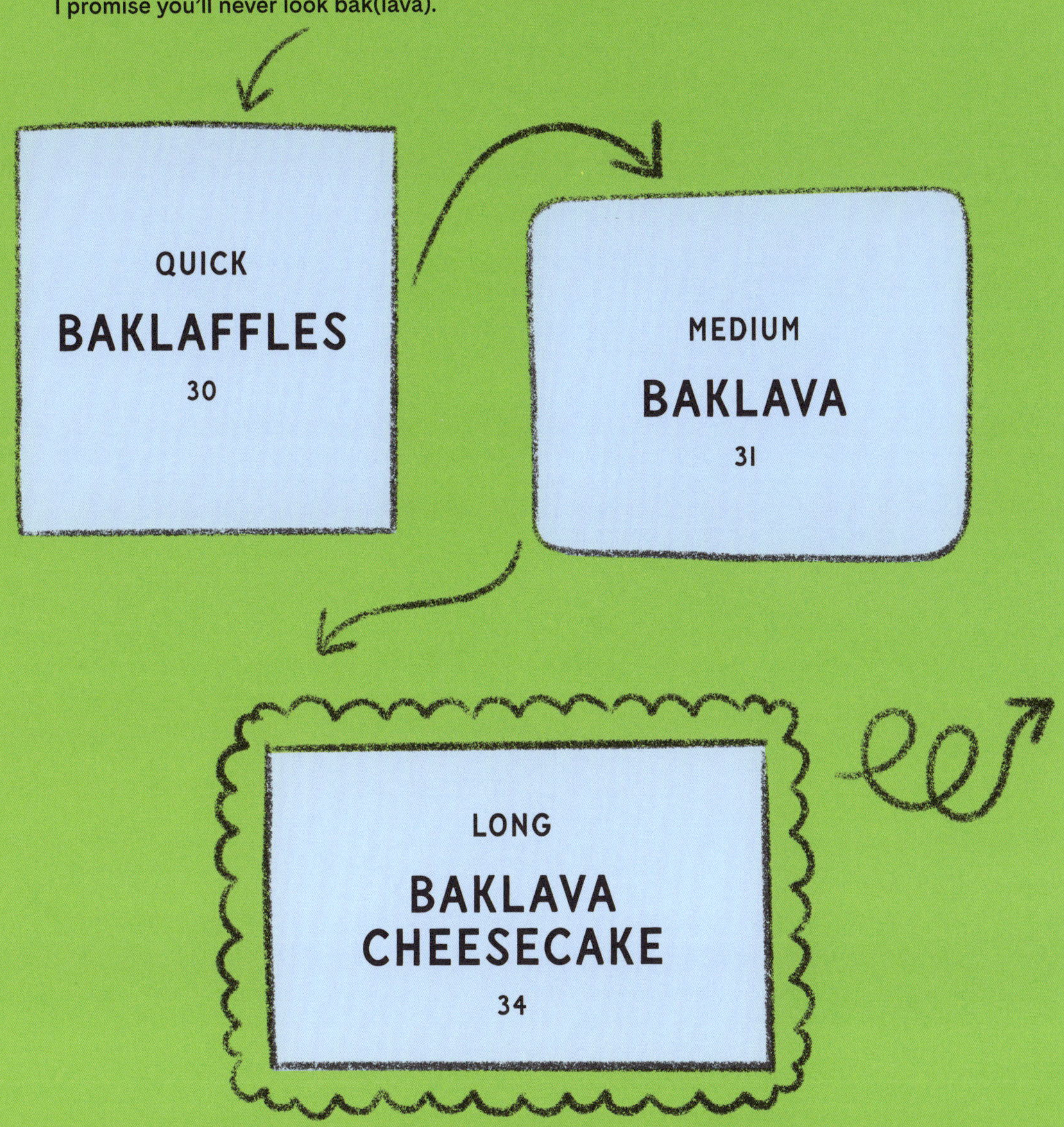

BAKLAFFLES

Hands on **15 minutes**
Ready in **20 minutes**

SERVES 4

EQUIPMENT
Waffle maker

Spiced nut-filled squares of puff pastry, crisped golden in a waffle maker and soaked in honey, lemon and rosewater syrup. When I waffled these super-quick baklava-inspired delights in a video I was braced to be cancelled but, mercifully, the majority were ok with it. Possibly because they make no claim to be authentic and possibly because they are delicious enough for the audacity to be overlooked. The only real point of contention was the inclusion of rosewater, which seemed to be based as much on personal taste as on heritage. With or without rosewater, I think you'll enjoy these.

FILLING

40g (1⅓ oz) nuts – walnuts, almonds, pistachios, cashews or a mix of your choice

¼ tsp ground cinnamon

Pinch of ground cloves

Pinch of ground cardamom

5g (⅕ oz) / 1 tsp granulated sugar

10g (⅓ oz) salted butter, softened

PASTRY

320-g (11 oz) packet of ready-rolled puff pastry

SYRUP

75g (2⅔ oz) runny honey (or use 60g/2 oz icing/confectioners' sugar mixed with 15g/½ oz hot water)

20g (¾ oz) lemon juice (approximately juice of ½ lemon)

1 tsp rosewater

1. Switch on your waffle maker to preheat, if using an electric machine.
2. In a food processor, blitz the nuts with the ground spices to a fine, sandy texture. Tip the spiced nuts into a small bowl.
3. Add the sugar and softened butter to the bowl with the nuts. Using a spoon, work everything together.
4. Unroll the pastry and cut it into eight 10-cm (4-inch) squares or the correct size to fit your waffle maker. You should get six full squares from one sheet of pastry, then you can form two more by pressing the offcuts together. (The pastry offcuts will fuse together when pressed in the waffle maker, so you won't notice the difference.)
5. Spoon a quarter of the filling onto one of the pastry squares, spreading it out but leaving a clear 1-cm (⅓-inch) border all the way round. Sit another pastry square over the filling and lightly press the pastry edges together – there's no need to crimp the pastry, the waffle maker will do that for you. Repeat with the remaining filling and pastry squares.
6. Carefully sit the sandwiched pastry squares into your waffle maker, press the top closed and cook until they are puffed, crisp and golden.
7. While the pastry cooks, make the soaking syrup. In a small bowl, stir together the honey, lemon juice and rosewater.
8. As soon as the baklaffles are out of the waffle maker, sit them on a plate with a lip. Spoon over half of the soaking syrup so that it pools in the waffle pockets. Once the warm pastry has absorbed plenty of syrup on one side, turn the baklaffles over and soak the other side with more syrup.
9. Once cooled, serve the baklaffles with a scoop of vanilla ice cream or a dollop of sour cream and an extra drizzle of any leftover syrup.

BAKLAVA

Hands on **35 minutes**
Ready in **2 hours**

MAKES
One 20-cm (8-inch) baklava, 18–24 pieces

EQUIPMENT
20-cm (8-inch) round cake tin (pan)

Sheets of butter-brushed filo, layered with spiced, finely ground nuts, baked and soaked in syrup hot from the oven. This version sticks to the rules right up until the cutting. Due to my lack of skill and overwhelming impatience to get to the eating, I usually go with a simple diamond, but for those with more resolve there are instructions on how to cut a star pattern. The layering pattern, interleaving the filling with single sheets of filo to keep the portions neatly intact, is entirely based on Vefa Alexiadou's recipe. I'm forever grateful to it because now I can deftly crane a diamond of baklava into my mouth without fear of losing a single crumb.

250g (9 oz) nuts – walnuts, almonds, pistachios

1 tsp ground cinnamon

Pinch of ground cloves

3 cardamom pods or ¼ tsp crushed cardamom seeds

100g (3½ oz) salted butter

270-g (9½ oz) packet of ready-made filo (phyllo) pastry (7 sheets) or 1 full quantity of Filo Pastry (page 211)

SYRUP

150g (5¼ oz) granulated sugar

75g (2⅔ oz) runny honey (or use an extra 60g/2 oz sugar + 15g/½ oz / 1 tbsp boiling water)

150g (5¼ oz) boiling water

40g (1⅓ oz) lemon juice

1 tsp rosewater (or to taste)

1. Set the oven to 175°C fan (375°F/gas 5) and line the cake tin with a single piece of baking paper that overhangs the sides.
2. In a food processor, blitz the nuts and ground spices to a fine, sandy texture, stopping before they turn to nut butter.
3. Melt the butter in a microwave-safe bowl or in a pan on low heat.
4. For ready-made filo, unfold the sheets, long sides running left to right. Cut down the middle so you have two square stacks. Sit one stack on top of the other, so you have 14 square layers of pastry. Sit the cake tin on top and cut round it through all the layers. For homemade filo, cut your stack of 15 circular sheets in the same way. Keep the offcuts in an airtight container and use them to make Filo Crisps (page 32).
5. Brush the top disc of the filo stack with melted butter and lay it, buttered side down, in the tin. Repeat with the next four discs, so the pastry base is five layers thick. Scatter over 50g (1¾ oz) of the nuts in an even layer. Cover with another buttered filo disc, then cover that with 50g (1¾ oz) of nuts. Repeat with three more discs of pastry and three layers of nuts.
6. Using a skewer, pierce holes in the pastry, passing through all the layers in the tin. (This helps the syrup soak into the layers.) Brush the remaining discs of filo with the last of the melted butter and layer them in the tin.
7. Using a very sharp knife, cut through the top layers of pastry in a diamond pattern – don't cut all the way down to the base as you don't want to risk slicing the baking paper or damaging the cake tin.

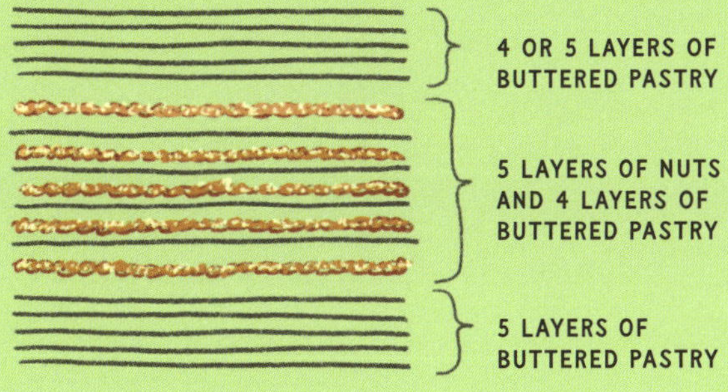

8. Bake in the middle of the oven for 30–35 minutes. The pastry should be rich and golden, but not too dark.
9. While the baklava bakes, make the syrup. To a heavy-bottomed pan, add the sugar, honey and boiling water and put on a high heat. Stir until the sugar grains have dissolved, then boil for 5 minutes. Remove from the heat. When the bubbles have died down, stir in the lemon juice and rosewater.
10. Pour half the syrup over the baklava and let it soak in for a few minutes. Repeat with the remaining syrup and leave to cool completely.
11. Using the paper, lift the baklava out of the tin. Following the lines and cutting through all the layers, slice the baklava into 18 diamond portions.

FILO CRISPS

Make a tray of filo (phyllo) crisps while your baklava bakes. Tear the saved pastry offcuts into bite-sized pieces, toss in any leftover melted butter and bake on the oven shelf below the baklava for 10–15 minutes or until golden brown. You can turn them halfway through, so they bake evenly. Tip the hot filo crisps into a bowl and sprinkle with a little salt for savoury or sift over some icing (confectioners') sugar as well as a pinch of salt for a sweet-and-salty popcorn vibe. Store in an airtight container or simply tuck in while you wait for the baklava to cool..

BOOZY BAKLAVA

Swap out the lemon juice for any liqueur of your choice. Something spritely and citrus based works nicely with the rosewater: Cointreau, Grand Marnier, Limoncello, etc. Or leave out both the rosewater and lemon juice and replace them with Amaretto, Baileys or a coffee-flavoured liqueur, such as Kahlua, Tia Maria, etc. Chin, chin.

STAR CUTTING PATTERN FOR A 20-CM (8-INCH) BAKLAVA

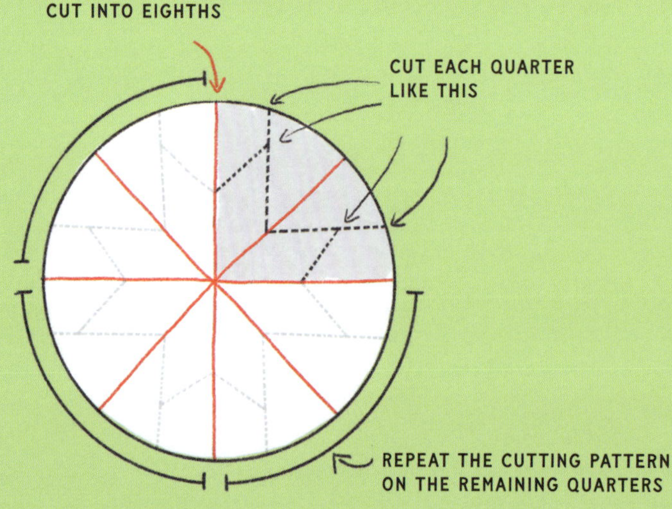
CUT INTO EIGHTHS
CUT EACH QUARTER LIKE THIS
REPEAT THE CUTTING PATTERN ON THE REMAINING QUARTERS

BAKLAVA CHEESECAKE

Hands on **1 hour 10 minutes**
Ready in **2 hours 50 minutes**

SERVES 16–18

EQUIPMENT

20-cm (8-inch) round springform cake tin (pan)

Small roasting tin (sheet pan)

Flat baking sheet

In short, this is a sort-of-baklava topped with a no-bake cheesecake and it is *fire*. In long, saragli (filo sheets rolled with a spiced nut filling into cigar-like cylinders) are cut into slices, then set on their ends on a puff-pastry base. The filo spirals are perfect traps for the rose-flavoured syrup, while the puff acts as a platform for serving neat slices and a syrup-catching backstop. The filling is made with feta for sharpness and depth, which contrasts the sweet intensity of the syrup-soaked pastry. My friend (yes, Anna, that's you) described eating this as an erotic experience. I can tell you, making one is more than a labour of love, but it's definitely worth the sticky fingers.

PASTRY BASE

275g (9¾ oz) nuts – walnuts, almonds, pistachios, cashews or a mix of your choice

1½ tsp ground cinnamon

½ tsp crushed cardamom seeds

Pinch of ground cloves

200g (7 oz) salted butter

160g (5⅔ oz) puff pastry (half a 320-g/11-oz packet of ready-rolled)

270g (9½ oz) ready-rolled filo (phyllo) pastry – 7 sheets

TO DECORATE

100g (3½ oz) grapes – your choice of colour

½ lemon

3 tsp icing (confectioners') sugar

2 rosemary sprigs

Small pinch of salt

SYRUP

150g (5¼ oz) granulated sugar

75g (2⅔ oz) runny honey (or use an extra 60g/2 oz sugar + 15g/½ oz/1 tbsp boiling water)

150g (5¼ oz) boiling water

40g (1⅓ oz) lemon juice

1 tsp rosewater

1. Line the springform cake tin with one large piece of baking paper so it extends above the sides.
2. In a food processor, blitz the nuts and ground spices to a fine, sandy texture, stopping before they turn to nut butter.
3. Melt the butter in a microwave-safe bowl or in a pan on a low heat.
4. Unroll the puff pastry sheet. Sit the springform tin on top of the pastry and, using it as a template, cut round the tin. Lay this pastry disc in the base of the tin. Freeze the offcuts for Baklaffles (page 30).
5. Unroll the filo. Brush the top layer with 2 tablespoons of the melted butter, then scatter 65g (2⅓ oz) of the spiced nuts over the sheet – go to the edges with both butter and nuts. Starting at one short edge, roll the sheet into a tight cylinder. Cut the cylinder into 2-cm (¾-inch) slices – you should get 12 out of one roll. Arrange the slices, spiral side up, on the puff pastry base so they fit snugly together with no gaps. Repeat with two or three more filo sheets until the tin is filled and the puff pastry is covered. (You can bake any leftover spirals separately.) Scatter any spare nuts over the base. Save three filo sheets and the remaining melted butter for the decoration. Any remaining sheets can be used for Filo Crisps (page 32).
6. Set the oven to 175°C fan (375°F/gas 5).
7. Using the pointy end of a chopstick, poke a hole in the centre of each spiral, without piercing the puff pastry base. (This helps the syrup soak in.)
8. Bake in the oven on the second rung down for 40 minutes. The top of the spirals should be golden, but not too dark.
9. Meanwhile, prepare the grapes. Cut in half and add to the small roasting tin. Squeeze over a little lemon juice and sprinkle on 1 teaspoon of the icing sugar. Roast the grapes on the middle shelf, while the baklava bakes above, for 20 minutes. Remove the tin from the oven, turn the grapes so they don't catch, tuck the rosemary under the fruit and bake for a further 10 minutes. Leave the grapes to cool and macerate in their juices.

CHEESECAKE FILLING

400g (14 oz) feta cheese

Grated zest of 2 lemons

125g (4½ oz) icing (confectioners') sugar

75g (2⅔ oz) unsalted butter, softened

280g (10 oz) full-fat cream cheese

150g (5¼ oz) sour cream

10. While the grapes bake, make the decoration. Line a baking sheet with baking paper. Roll the three reserved filo sheets into a cylinder. Shred the filo into 2-mm (1/16-inch) strands with a sharp knife, then unravel the strands on the baking sheet. Drizzle over the remaining butter and toss together until all the strands are well coated. Bake on a baking sheet in the bottom of the oven for 15–20 minutes until crisp and golden. Remove them from the oven, then dust with 1 teaspoon of icing sugar and a pinch of salt. Leave to cool on their sheet.
11. While everything bakes, make the syrup. To a heavy-bottomed pan, add the sugar, honey and boiling water and put on a high heat. Stir until all the sugar grains have dissolved, then boil for 5 minutes. Remove the pan from the heat. When the bubbles have died down, stir in the lemon juice (save the zest for the filling) and rosewater. Spoon 3 tablespoons of the syrup over the roasted grapes once baked.
12. Once the base is out of the oven, re-open the central holes in the spirals with the chopstick. Spoon over 250g (9 oz) of the syrup, directing it into the holes. (Save a little syrup for serving.) Leave the base to cool completely and the syrup to soak in before starting the cheesecake filling.
13. Add the feta, lemon zest, icing sugar and butter to a food processor. Pulse to blend, stopping as soon as it's smooth, so the feta doesn't over-whip.
14. To a large bowl, add the cream cheese and sour cream. Work the two together with a spatula, folding rather than beating, until fully combined. Scrape the feta mixture onto the cream cheese and fold together.
15. Spread the cheesecake filling onto the cooled baklava base, level the top and chill in the fridge for at least 30 minutes.
16. Remove the cake from the tin, pile the golden filo strands on top of the cheesecake layer and spoon over the roast grapes and their juices. Serve the slices with a drizzle of the reserved syrup. Keep any leftovers in an airtight container in the fridge for 3–4 days.

BANOFFEE PIE

Banoffi Pie, to give it its original spelling, was invented (although he would say evolved) by Ian Dowding, in 1971. Its crowd-pleasing combination of crunchy base, toffee filling, fresh banana, whipped cream and the sometimes overlooked second 'offee', coffee, hasn't really evolved since. Why would it? It's everyone's natural selection from the dessert trolley... *sigh* First iterations of the pie were contained in a pastry case, but I've gone with what is the now more common biscuit base and interpreted that throughout these recipes. The original's filling was a toffee, made by cooking a tin of condensed milk for 4 hours, but I've gone for caramel. Choosing between toffee and caramel isn't exactly a rock and a hard place, but caramel edges it taste-wise for me and it only takes 20 minutes to make. As I hope this book demonstrates, I'm all for taking your time, but 4 hours for a banoffee pie might be pushing it.

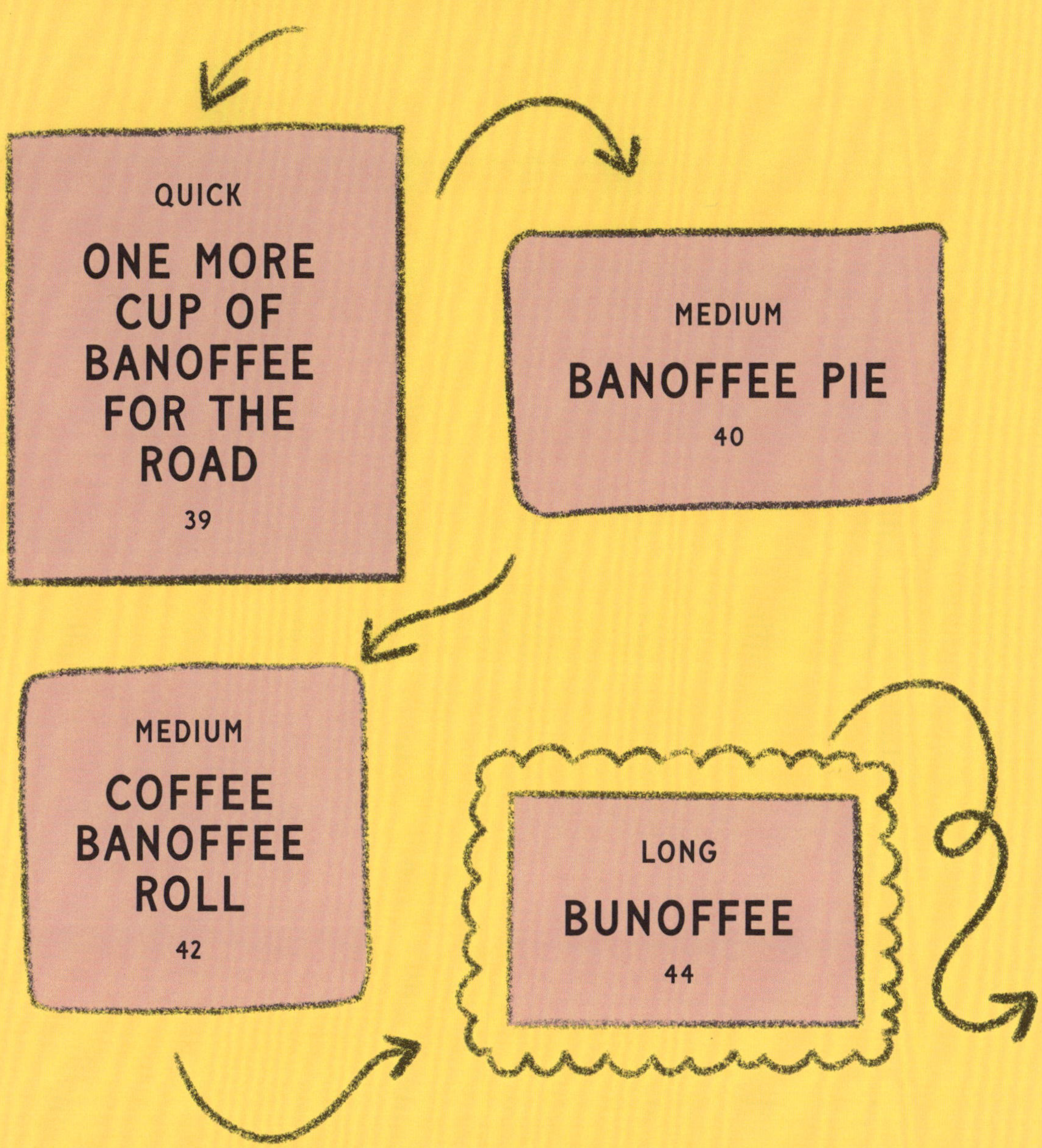

ONE MORE CUP OF BANOFFEE FOR THE ROAD

Hands on **15 minutes**
Ready in **15 minutes**

SERVES 4

EQUIPMENT
Four 250-ml (8½-fl oz) wine glasses or cups

120g (4¼ oz) digestive biscuits (graham crackers), approximately 8 biscuits OR make your own gluten-free digestives (page 215)

100g (3½ oz) Salted Caramel Sauce (dairy or plant-based, page 230) OR ready-made OR use canned caramel condensed milk with a pinch of salt

200g (7 oz) double (heavy) cream (dairy or plant-based)

2 large bananas

10g (⅓ oz) milk or dark (bittersweet) chocolate

It will probably take longer to describe what banoffee in a cup is than it will take you to make it. It contains all the component parts of a banoffee pie: fresh banana, caramel, crumbed biscuit, whipped cream and a bit of chocolate layered in a cup. Actually, that was a bit quicker than it takes to make it. But not by much.

1. To a medium bowl, add the digestive biscuits and crush to crumbs; a mix of fine and larger, gravelly pieces is good. My favourite method is to put them in a bowl and press them under the base of a sturdy glass, or you can seal them in a strong plastic food bag and roll a rolling pin over them.
2. Gently warm the salted caramel sauce, in the microwave or in a pan on a low heat, to make it slightly runnier, and pour about two-thirds over the biscuit crumbs. If using canned caramel condensed milk, stir in a pinch of salt before pouring over the biscuit crumbs. Using the back of a dessert spoon, work the caramel into the biscuit crumbs.
3. To a large bowl, add the cream and whip to soft folds*.
4. Save a dessert spoonful of caramel biscuit crumbs for decoration then divide what's left between the four glasses. Top each cup or glass with half a banana cut into 1-cm (⅓-inch) thick slices and drizzle with a generous teaspoon of the remaining caramel sauce.
5. Divide the whipped cream between the four glasses, over the banana, then top with a sprinkle of caramel biscuit crumbs and an extra drizzle of caramel sauce. Finally, draw a vegetable peeler along the side of the chocolate block to create curls of chocolate to decorate the top.
6. Serve straight away or store in the fridge until ready to serve. These cups can be assembled several hours before being served.

***WHIPPING CREAM**

As cream continues to thicken after it's beaten, stop whipping before it reaches the consistency you need. Wait 15 seconds to see whether it becomes the consistency you're looking for; if not, give it a few more beats and check again. If the cream is overbeaten to the point the water and fat separate, your only option is to make it into butter. If it's just a little bit too stiff, there is a fix. Add a little cold tap water, 1 or 2 tablespoons at a time, and fold through the stiff cream until it relaxes to the consistency you need. It's not always perfect but it might save you having to buy more cream.

BANOFFEE PIE

Hands on **25 minutes**
Ready in **55 minutes**

SERVES 8–10
Makes one 21-cm (8½-inch) pie

EQUIPMENT
21-cm (8½-inch) loose-bottomed tart tin (pan)

I could spend hours making something with a boundary-nudging flavour profile when all my family really want is banoffee pie. In fairness, for all my tamarind virtue signalling, I love banoffee too. So, here we are. The salted caramel sauce is chilled and then whipped so it forms a thick yet light layer, which holds its form when cut. Making your own caramel ensures the right consistency to achieve this, but if that's not feasible, look for a spreadable sauce in a jar rather than a runny sauce in a squeezy bottle. Canned caramel condensed milk doesn't whip, so if that's all you can get, simply spread a thinner amount over the base. And if anyone complains, threaten them with a beetroot and lavender pie.

300g (10½ oz) Salted Caramel Sauce (dairy or plant-based, page 230) OR ready-made (see note in introduction above)

250g (9 oz) digestive biscuits (graham crackers) OR make your own gluten-free digestives (page 215)

125g (4½ oz) salted butter (dairy or plant-based), melted

300g (10½ oz) bananas (approximately 2 large or 3 medium bananas)

½ tsp instant coffee powder

1 tsp boiling water

300g (10½ oz) double (heavy) cream (dairy or plant-based)

15g (½ oz) granulated sugar

10g (⅓ oz) milk or dark (bittersweet) chocolate

1. Into the bowl of a stand mixer or large bowl, add the salted caramel sauce and chill in the fridge for 40 minutes.
2. Meanwhile, break the biscuits into a food processor, add the melted butter and blitz to damp, sandy crumbs. If you don't have a processor, seal the biscuits in a strong plastic food bag and crush them to fine crumbs by rolling a rolling pin over them or put them in a large bowl and crush them with the base of a sturdy glass, then mix in the melted butter.
3. Using the back of a spoon, press the buttery biscuit crumbs firmly into the base and up the sides of the tart tin so they are well compacted and not crumbly. Chill in the freezer for 30 minutes.
4. Once the salted caramel sauce is firm and cold, whip with the beater attachments for 1 minute until pale and thick, then spread this over the chilled biscuit base.
5. Cut the bananas into 1-cm (⅓-inch) slices and arrange them over the whipped caramel layer.
6. To a large bowl, add the instant coffee powder and pour over the boiling water, mixing to dissolve the granules. Stir in the cream and the sugar. Don't worry if there are coffee granules still visible – they will dissolve as you whip everything to soft folds.
7. Spread the coffee cream over the bananas. Make chocolate curls by drawing a vegetable peeler along the side of the chocolate block, then tumble them over the cream to decorate the top.
8. Serve straight away or store in the fridge for up to 24 hours.

COFFEE BANOFFEE ROLL

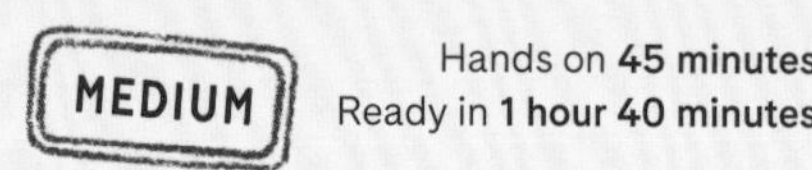

Hands on **45 minutes**
Ready in **1 hour 40 minutes**

MAKES
One 20-cm (8-inch) long cake

EQUIPMENT
33 x 25-cm (13 x 10-inch) Swiss roll tin (jelly roll pan)

Flat baking sheet

With a coffee roulade cake enrobed in a dark chocolate glaze, this variation borders on sophistication. But don't worry, it doesn't fully commit. It's still packed with caramel biscuit crumbs, whipped cream and banana slices. One important note about banana ripeness: this is an egg-free batter and it relies on really yellow bananas to give the cake its miraculous structure and flexibility (even in its gluten-free form). Riper bananas mash down to a runnier consistency and you won't get the same results. You can, however, use them for the filling. Or wear them as a hat to prove how sophisticated you really aren't.

CAKE

150g (5¼ oz) plain (all-purpose) flour or gluten-free self-raising mix

1½ tsp baking powder (omit if using gluten-free flour)

¼ tsp bicarbonate of soda (baking soda)

165g (5¾ oz) just-ripe bananas (very yellow but without any black spots)

1½ tsp instant coffee powder

75g (2⅔ oz) light brown soft sugar

Large pinch of salt

50g (1¾ oz) sunflower oil or any other flavourless oil

1 tsp white wine vinegar or cider vinegar

1 tsp vanilla extract

FILLING

60g (2 oz) digestive biscuits (graham crackers), ready-made or make your own (page 215)

100g (3½ oz) salted caramel sauce (dairy or plant-based), ready-made OR make your own (page 230), OR use canned caramel condensed milk with a pinch of salt

125g (4½ oz) double (heavy) cream (dairy or plant-based)

1 large yellow banana (optional)

1. Set the oven to 160°C fan (350°F/gas 4) and line the Swiss roll tin with baking paper.
2. In a bowl, combine the flour, baking powder and bicarbonate of soda.
3. To the bowl of a stand mixer or large bowl, add the banana and coffee and roughly mash with a fork. Add the sugar and salt and beat with a whisk attachment, for about a minute, or until the mixture becomes pale and thick and there are no lumps of fruit visible.
4. Add the oil, vinegar and vanilla, then give it a brief mix. Fold in the flour mixture. As soon as the wet and dry ingredients are evenly blended, scrape the batter into the lined Swiss roll tin. Level the batter in the tin with a palette knife, but don't overwork it or knock all the air out. It will seem like a thin layer, but it will rise once baked.
5. Bake in the middle of the oven for 11 minutes. The top will lose its wet look, the edges will shrink slightly from the sides and a metal skewer will come out clean when the cake is ready.
6. While the cake bakes, cut a piece of baking paper slightly bigger than the tin. As soon as the cake is out of the oven, lay the paper over the top and cover that with the flat baking sheet. Hold the two trays together (with gloved hands or a dish towel) and flip everything upside down so the cake is lying on the flat baking sheet. Carefully peel away the paper, then lay it loosely over the cake so it doesn't dry out while it cools.
7. Now, make the filling. To a medium bowl, add the digestive biscuits and crush to crumbs. Gently warm 30g (1 oz) of the salted caramel sauce, pour over the crumbs and mix together. If using canned caramel condensed milk, add a pinch of salt. If you can't source gluten-free digestive biscuits, make them yourself (page 215) or omit them and spread the cake with the full amount of salted caramel sauce in step 10.
8. Into a large bowl, pour the filling cream and whip to firm peaks.
9. After about 30 minutes the cake should be cool. Using the same method as before, flip the cake back over and remove the top paper; the bumpy top you're looking at will be the interior of the roll and the neat, flat underside will be the exterior.

GANACHE GLAZE

50g (1¾ oz) dark (bittersweet) chocolate (70% cocoa)

100g (3½ oz) double (heavy) cream (dairy or plant-based)

10. Warm the remaining caramel sauce to the point it's spreadable. Spread over the surface of the cake, cover with the whipped cream then, saving 1 tablespoon for decoration, scatter over the caramel biscuit crumbs. If using, thinly slice the banana lengthways into 4 long slices. Cut the slices down their length into pencil-like strips and lay across the width of the cake at even intervals. This might seem a stingy amount, but over-filling will make the cake difficult to roll. Pick up the paper under the near short edge of the cake and use it to lift and roll into a neat cylinder. Wrap the roll snugly in both pieces of paper and chill in the fridge for 30 minutes.

11. After 15 minutes, start the ganache glaze so it's ready to pour when the cake is chilled. Chop the chocolate into small chunks and add to a bowl. Heat the cream to almost boiling point in the microwave or a pan and pour over the chocolate. Leave it in peace for 3 minutes, then stir to blend the cream and chocolate together. Leave to cool to 35°C (95°F).

12. Unwrap the chilled, rolled cake and sit it on your serving plate. Start by spooning a little of the ganache onto the cake and spread it thinly all over the top and sides, leaving the ends. The chilled cake should stop the ganache running off too quickly. Pour or spoon larger amounts of ganache over the cake to thickly cover it – use a palette knife to guide it to where it needs to be. Don't worry about any run-off onto the serving plate. Cover the cake then use a knife or spatula to scrape away any dribbles or pools of ganache and wipe the plate clean with kitchen paper.

13. Trim each end with a very sharp knife to neaten up the roll and sprinkle the reserved biscuit crumbs over the glaze. Serve straight away or within 12 hours. The gluten-free version is best eaten within 4 hours.

BUNOFFEE

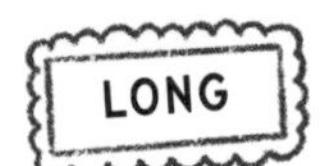

Hands on **45 minutes**
Ready in **4 hours 30 minutes**

MAKES
12 buns

EQUIPMENT
20 x 30-cm (8 x 12-inch) brownie tin

Made with a mashed banana dough, these banoffee-flavoured buns are literal banana bread. Spirals of light, bouncy banana bread are rolled up with salted caramel sauce, fresh banana and topped with a digestive crumble. This dough is perfect for using up frozen bananas, the fruit collapsing to a ready-mashed pulp as it thaws. And despite using the ripest, fizziest, most banana-ry bananas you can muster, these buns have convinced more than one banana hater to relent.

DOUGH

280g (10 oz) mashed banana (from approximately 3 very ripe, black-spotted bananas)

2¼ tsp fast-action dried yeast

10g (⅓ oz) granulated sugar

370g (13 oz) strong white bread flour

½ tsp salt

45g (1½ oz) sunflower oil or any other flavourless oil

1 tsp flavourless oil, if using the pull-and-fold kneading method

DIGESTIVE CRUMBLE TOPPING

75g (2⅔ oz) strong wholemeal flour

25g (1 oz) light brown soft sugar

Pinch of salt

55g (2 oz) salted butter, slightly softened

CARAMEL FILLING

150g (5¼ oz) Salted Caramel Sauce (dairy or plant-based, page 230) OR ready-made

1 very large or 2 small yellow bananas

MAKE THE DOUGH

1. To make the dough, mash the very ripe or defrosted bananas to a runny, lump-free pulp. Sprinkle in the yeast and sugar, then mix briefly. Add the flour, salt and oil and use a table knife to mix to a ragged dough. Pull the dough into a ball with your hands.
2. This is a sticky dough so I recommend using the pull-and-fold kneading method (page 212) or a stand mixer. If using pull and fold, it's more a case of folding than pulling as the dough isn't very elastic until after its first proof. For pull and fold, pour 1 teaspoon of oil into the bowl, roll the dough around in the oil, then follow the instructions on page 212. For a stand mixer, use a dough hook on medium and knead for 10 minutes.
3. This dough needs a long first proof. To help it along, switch your oven on for 30 seconds to bring the temperature up to 25–30°C (75–85°F), then switch it off. You can put a digital thermometer into the oven for an accurate temperature reading – don't worry, it won't melt at 30°C (85°F). Cover the bowl with a plastic shower cap or cling film (plastic wrap) and leave in the oven for about 2 hours or until doubled in size. Once or twice throughout the proof, you can switch the oven on for 30 seconds at a time to keep the temperature up. Just don't forget to switch it off!

MAKE THE DIGESTIVE CRUMBLE TOPPING

4. While the dough proofs, make the digestive crumble topping. To a medium bowl, combine the wholemeal flour, sugar and salt. Add the butter in small chunks and rub into the dry ingredients with your fingertips. Once you have an even texture of fine crumbs, take handfuls and squash them into larger clumps. Chill the crumble clumps in the fridge until needed.
5. When the dough is ready, tip it onto your floured work surface and pat into a vague oblong with the longest side running from your left to your right. Roll to a 40 x 25-cm (16 x 10-inch) rectangle.

6. Leaving a clear 1-cm (1/3-inch) border along the long edge furthest from you, cover the rest of the rolled-out dough with the salted caramel sauce – you may have to warm it slightly to make it easily spreadable. Peel a firm yellow banana and chop it into chunks no bigger than 1cm (1/3 inch), then scatter them evenly over the caramel. Moisten the filling-free border with water, then roll up the dough from the near long side into a 40-cm (16-inch) cylinder. Gently press the long edge of the dough into the roll to seal the join. Measure and mark the cylinder into 12 equal portions, then cut it into rounds using a sharp knife or length of thread. Line the brownie tin with baking paper, then arrange the rounds 4 x 3 in the tin.

7. The rolls need only a short second proof, approximately 15 minutes, so now is the moment to preheat the oven to 185°C fan (400°F/gas 6). When ready (see the pull-and-fold kneading method on page 212 for how to tell), cover each roll with a tablespoonful of crumble topping and scatter over any remaining mixture. Bake in the middle of the oven for 25 minutes; the buns should be puffed and the crumble topping toasted and golden brown. Use a probe thermometer to check the internal temperature; to be fully baked, it must reach at least 90°C (195°F).

8. Leave the buns to cool for at least 30 minutes before eating. Store any leftover buns in an airtight tub. The mashed banana in the dough will keep them soft for several days. You can also freeze any that escape being eaten; just defrost and warm slightly in the oven when needed.

BATTENBERG

IS THAT JUST
THE TIP OF THE
BATTENBERG?

I fell down a pink and yellow rabbit hole researching the Battenberg's origins, emerging days later, sticky with marzipan, knowing it's probably got nothing to do with Queen Victoria's granddaughter marrying a German aristocrat. The first recorded cakes consisting of chequerboard sponges appear 12 years after Princess Victoria married Prince Louis of Battenberg, which is a bit late for a cake named in their honour. Exactly how a nine-panelled 'Domino Cake' or a four-panelled 'Neapolitan Roll' evolved into what we now know as Battenberg is lost to baking lore, but at least we still have the cake. In this chapter I've been relatively respectful to its principles: pink and yellow almond-flavoured sponge, admittedly with a hint of lemon, stuck together with apricot jam and covered in marzipan. Although I've thrown in a marzipan buttercream in case you think I've gone soft. Ultimately, when a bake is as delicious as Battenberg, it's not important which cakes begat it. With so much shared DNA, they're clearly all part of one big happy family. Funnily enough, that was also Queen Victoria's excuse for marrying her first cousin and her granddaughter's for marrying her father's first cousin.

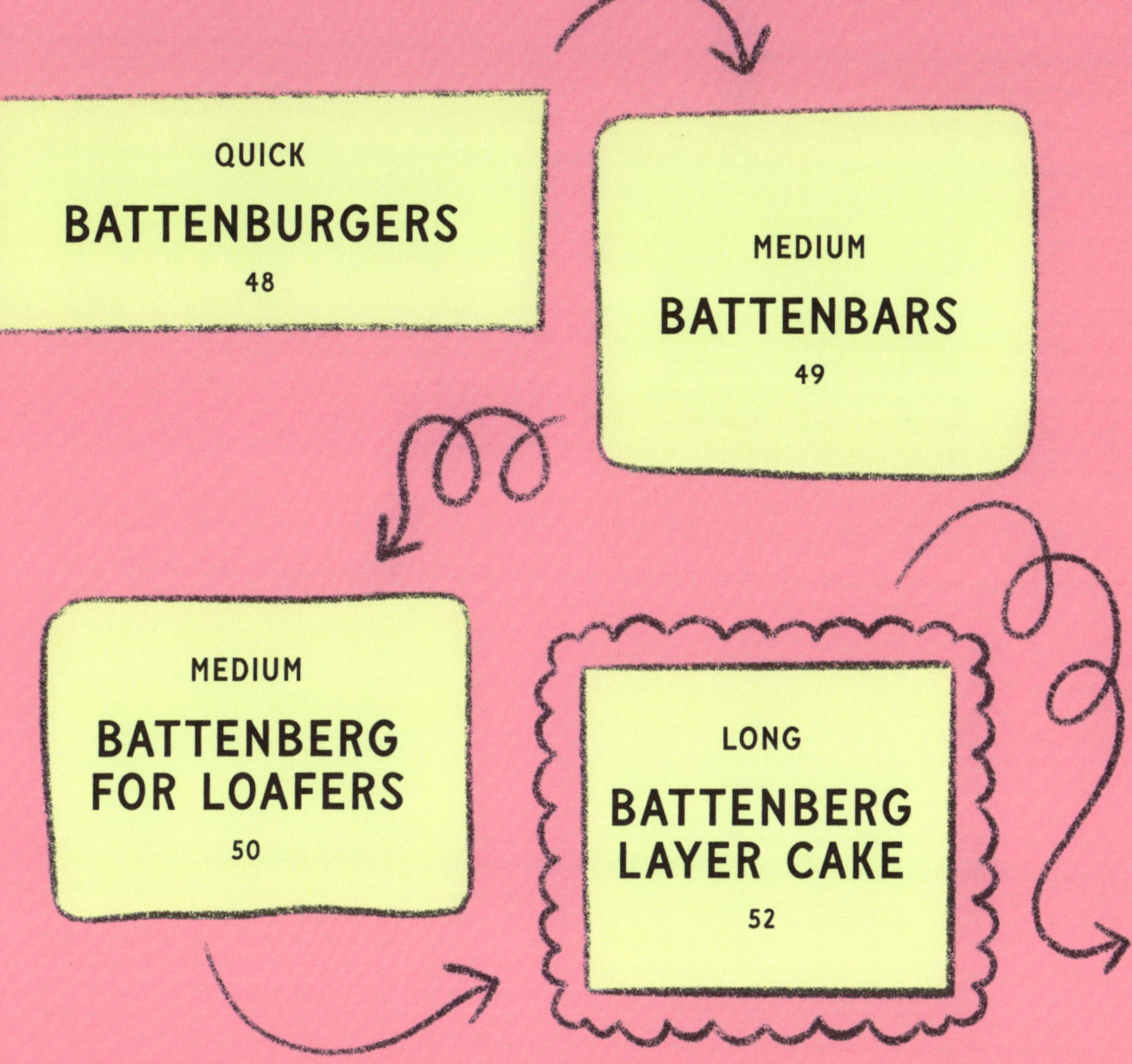

BATTENBURGERS

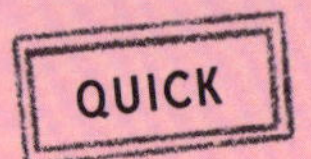

Hands on **15 minutes**
Ready in **50 minutes**

MAKES
6 'burgers'

EQUIPMENT
Non-stick 12-cup muffin tin (pan)

This may be the strongest evocation yet of my 'buns plus puns' mission statement. Little buns of moist, almond-flavoured sponge sandwiching a patty of marzipan with jam relish. They're like burgers, see? Battenburgers. BattenBURGERS. Oh, never mind. This is a really quick and simple egg-free cake batter that works perfectly with plant-based butter and milk for a vegan-friendly bake. However, if you want to use an egg-based batter, use one batch of the Battenbars recipe opposite. Use 25g (3/4 oz) of batter per bun and bake for 13 minutes or until a metal skewer comes out clean.

125g (4 1/2 oz) plain (all-purpose) flour or 135g (4 3/4 oz) gluten-free self-raising mix + small pinch of xanthan gum

1 1/2 tsp baking powder (omit if using gluten-free flour)

90g (3 1/4 oz) granulated sugar

Pinch of salt

60g (2 oz) salted butter (dairy or plant-based), melted

100g (3 1/2 oz) milk (full-fat dairy or any plant-based)

1 tsp lemon juice, white wine vinegar or cider vinegar

1/4 tsp almond extract

Pink gel food colouring

100g (3 1/2 oz) yellow marzipan

60g (2 oz) apricot jam (preserve)

1. Set the oven to 160°C fan (350°F/gas 4). If your muffin tray is not non-stick, oil or use cake release in the cups – it's essential the buns come out pristine with no raggedy bits.
2. To a medium bowl, add the dry ingredients and mix well.
3. To a jug (pitcher), add the wet ingredients and colouring, then mix well.
4. Add the wet ingredients to the dry, whisking as you pour. Stop whisking as soon as the batter is smooth. Spoon the batter equally into all 12 cups, approximately 30g (1 oz) in each.
5. Bake in the middle of the oven for 16 minutes. A metal skewer will come out clean when the buns are ready.
6. Leave the buns in the muffin tray for 15 minutes to firm up, then turn out to cool completely.
7. Roll out the marzipan to a thickness of 5mm (1/4 inch) and cut six 6-cm (2 1/3-inch) squares from it.
8. Spread the wide tops of the buns with a slick of jam, sit a square of marzipan on six of them, then top with the remaining upended buns.

BATTENBARS

Hands on **30 minutes**
Ready in **1 hour 20 minutes**

MAKES
12–14 cake bars

EQUIPMENT
20 x 30-cm (8 x 12-inch) brownie tin (pan)

If you've been looking for a socially acceptable way to devour a whole Battenberg in three bites, may I introduce you to my Battenbars. Almond-flavoured sponge is alternated with lemon-flavoured sponge, baked as a sheet and topped and bottomed with jam and marzipan. Neat miniatures with all the flavour and harlequin aesthetic of the original, but without any precision measuring and cutting required.

CAKE

You need two batches of this, one coloured yellow, one pink.

1 large (US extra-large) egg

60g (2 oz) granulated or caster (superfine) sugar

1 tbsp milk (any)

Grated zest of 1 lemon or ¼ tsp almond extract

Yellow or pink gel food colouring

70g (2½ oz) salted butter, softened

30g (1 oz) ground almonds (almond meal)

75g (2⅔ oz) plain (all-purpose) flour or gluten-free plain (all-purpose) flour + ¼ tsp xanthan gum

1 tsp baking powder

TO DECORATE

150g (5¼ oz) apricot jam (preserve)

2–3 tbsp icing (confectioners') sugar

400g (14 oz) yellow marzipan

1. Set the oven to 160°C fan (350°F/gas 4) and line the brownie tin with baking paper, leaving an overhang to help lift the cake from the tin later.
2. In separate bowls, make two batches of cake batter. Add the ingredients to the bowl in the order they are listed. Add yellow colouring and lemon zest to one bowl, and pink colouring and almond extract to the other.
3. Starting with the yellow bowl, beat all the ingredients together until you have a smooth, evenly combined batter. Next, make the pink batter in the same way. There is no need to clean the beaters. Scrape each batter into its own piping (pastry) bag fitted with a 2-cm (¾-inch) nozzle.
4. Pipe alternating lines of yellow and pink batter along the length of the tin, five in each colour. If any batter is left in the bags, go over the lines again.
5. Bake in the middle of the oven for 18–19 minutes or until a metal skewer comes out clean.
6. Leave the cake to cool in the tin for 10 minutes. Using the paper, lift the cake onto a flat baking sheet to cool completely. You can put it on a wire rack, although the indentations left spoil the finished cake's appearance.
7. Once cool, spread half the jam over the cake's top.
8. Dust your work surface with icing sugar, then roll out half of the marzipan until it's large enough to cover the top of the cake. Drape the marzipan over the cake and pat it onto the jam to stick it in place. Cover the top of the cake with baking paper and a flat baking sheet, then flip it upside down.
9. Peel off the paper from the base of the cake. Spread it with the remaining jam. Roll out the remaining marzipan, drape and pat it onto the cake.
10. Trim just enough off each edge so the cake has sharp sides. Cut once lengthways down the middle then make 5 or 6 cuts widthways into 12 or 14 bars. Store any leftovers in an airtight container at room temperature.

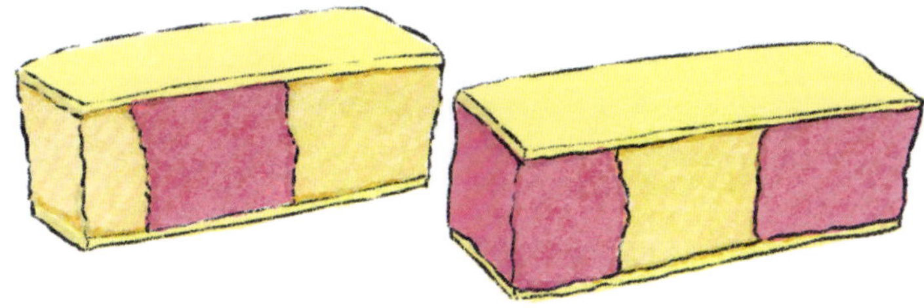

BATTENBERG FOR LOAFERS

Hands on **45 minutes**
Ready in **1 hour 50 minutes**

MAKES
One 8 x 18-cm (3 x 7-inch) loaf cake

EQUIPMENT
1-kg (2-lb) loaf tin (pan), measuring 8 x 21cm (3 x 8 inches)*

CAKE

2 large (US extra-large) eggs

120g (4¼ oz) granulated or caster (superfine) sugar

2 tsp milk (any)

1 tsp vanilla extract

¼ tsp almond extract

Grated zest of 1 lemon

Yellow gel food colouring**

120g (4¼ oz) salted butter, softened

30g (1oz) ground almonds (almond meal)

170g (6oz) plain (all-purpose) flour or 180g (6⅓ oz) gluten-free plain (all-purpose) flour + ½ tsp xanthan gum

1¾ tsp baking powder

TO DECORATE

2–3 tbsp icing (confectioners') sugar

220g (7¾ oz) white marzipan

Pink paste food colouring**

75g (2⅔ oz) sieved or seedless raspberry or cherry jam (preserve)

50g (1¾ oz) lemon curd

Making a traditional Battenberg is all about cutting corners in a cake trimming sense; making this slightly lazy version is all about cutting corners in a time and effort saving sense. Here yellow almond batter is baked as a loaf cake, trimmed, quartered, stuck back together with a pink jam and wrapped in pink marzipan. Giving you all the right pink and yellow Battenberg notes, just not necessarily in the right order.

1. Set the oven to 160°C fan (350°F/gas 4) and line the base and long sides of the loaf tin with a single piece of baking paper. Leave an overhang of 6cm (2⅓ inches) on each side to lift the cake out of the tin after baking.
2. Make the cake batter. Add the ingredients to a large bowl in the order they are listed. Use an electric hand mixer to beat everything together. Stop as soon as you have a smooth, evenly combined batter.
3. Scrape the cake batter into the lined tin. If using gluten-free flour, carefully level the top of the batter in the tin – the added xanthan gum means this cake won't completely self-level in the oven. Bake in the middle of the oven for 38 minutes or until a metal skewer comes out clean. Don't open the oven before 35 minutes or the cake may collapse.
4. Leave the cake to cool in its tin for 5 minutes, then transfer to a wire rack and peel off the paper to cool completely.
5. While the cake cools, colour the marzipan. Dust the work surface with icing sugar and lightly knead the marzipan to soften it up. Add a generous dab of colouring paste to the centre of the marzipan and fold up the sides to enclose it. Knead the colouring paste through the marzipan until it's an even pink. Add as much paste as you need to get the intensity of colour you like. Wrap up the marzipan and set aside until needed.
6. When the cake is completely cool, very slightly trim away the flare of the sides created by the loaf tin. This is optional, but it does give the cake those traditional Battenberg right angles. Cut the whole cake lengthways down the centre. Spread one cut side generously with the jam and stick the halves back together. Turn the cake on its side through 90 degrees and cut again down the centre. Spread generously with jam as before and press the halves back together. You should now have four lengths of cake stuck together with jam.

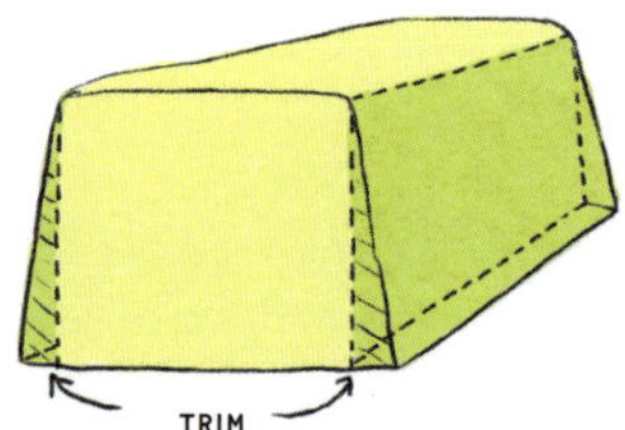

7. Take a length of thread and wrap it around the cake to take its 'waist' measurement – this is a guide for rolling out the marzipan. Dust the work surface with icing sugar. Roll out the marzipan to the length of your guide measurement (plus a bit extra for an overlap) and slightly wider than the cake. Spread the marzipan with the lemon curd.
8. Sit the cake on the edge of the marzipan closest to you and trim the marzipan along the edge of the cake. Holding the marzipan against the cake, roll the cake onto its next side. Pat the marzipan onto the cake so it's firmly stuck, then roll again. Repeat until fully wrapped. Trim the marzipan so the join overlaps in the middle of one side (there will be a section that has a double layer). Gently press the seam flat with the back of a teaspoon. Turn the cake so it sits on the overlapping join.
9. Using a very sharp knife, trim the ends of the cake and the overhanging marzipan so they are neat and straight.

***LOAF TINS:** Despite having the same capacity, 1-kg (2-lb) loaf tins can have quite different dimensions. Use a tin that's between 8 and 9cm (3 and 3½ inches) wide at the base, as anything wider will give you a much shallower cake that won't look quite so much like a traditional Battenberg.

****FOOD COLOURING:** To colour the cake batter, use concentrated gel food colouring. Gels deliver an intense colour and disperse easily in a batter so you don't risk overbeating and making the cake tough. To colour marzipan, use a colouring paste which is much thicker and won't affect the consistency by adding too much moisture.

BATTENBERG LAYER CAKE

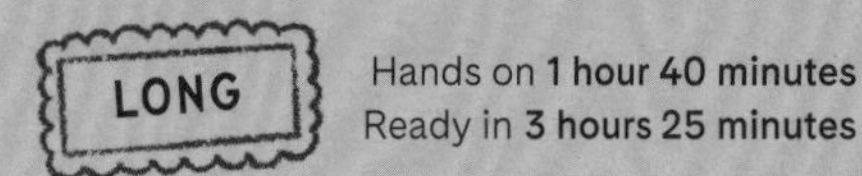

Hands on **1 hour 40 minutes**
Ready in **3 hours 25 minutes**

SERVES 12+
Makes one 18-cm (7-inch) four-layer cake

EQUIPMENT
Two 18-cm (7-inch) round cake tins (pans)

9-cm (3½-inch) round cookie cutter

This chequerboard interpretation of Battenberg flavours and colours deploys a slightly cheaty method to achieve its harlequin pattern. Bake two cakes, one pink and almond flavoured, one yellow and lemon flavoured, split each into two layers, cut those layers into rings, reassemble alternate colours with apricot curd, then cover the whole thing in a luscious marzipan buttercream. As this is the chapter's long recipe, maybe it's a bit naughty to deploy a shortcut, but if the resulting cake looks like it takes days to achieve, hopefully you'll forgive me.

CAKE

You need two batches of this, one coloured yellow, one pink.

JUG (PITCHER)

2 large (US extra-large) eggs

30g (1 oz) sunflower oil or vegetable oil

30g (1 oz) / 2 tbsp water

Yellow or pink gel food colouring

Grated zest of 2 lemons or ½ tsp almond extract

MIXER

120g (4¼ oz) granulated or caster (superfine) sugar

140g (5 oz) plain (all-purpose) flour or gluten-free plain (all-purpose) flour + ½ tsp xanthan gum

25g (¾ oz) ground almonds (almond meal)

½ tbsp baking powder

90g (3¼ oz) salted butter, softened

Ingredients continued overleaf

MAKE THE CAKES

1. Set the oven to 160°C fan (350°F/gas 4) and line the base of each cake tin with a disc of baking paper.
2. Start with the yellow batter. To a jug (pitcher), add the eggs, oil, water, yellow gel food colouring and lemon zest. Roughly blend with a fork.
3. To a stand mixer fitted with a whisk attachment or a large bowl, add the sugar, flour (and xanthan gum if using gluten-free flour), ground almonds and baking powder. Mix briefly then add the very soft butter. Start the mixer on slow to combine everything to a damp, breadcrumb-like mix.
4. Increase the speed to fast and slowly pour in half the egg mix from the jug. Beat for 30–60 seconds or until the batter becomes thick, fluffy and lump free. Stop the beaters and scrape down the sides of the bowl.
5. Start the mixer again on fast and trickle in the remaining egg mix. Once it has all been added, beat for a further 30 seconds or until the batter looks smooth. Scrape the batter into one of the lined tins and set aside while you make the pink batter. If using gluten-free flour, carefully level the top of the batter in the tin – the added xanthan gum means this cake won't completely self-level in the oven.
6. Repeat the above steps for the pink batter, using pink gel food colouring and almond extract. There's no need to clean the bowl or beaters as any yellow batter remaining on them will be overpowered by the pink. Scrape the pink batter into the second cake tin.

Continued overleaf

APRICOT CURD

225g (8 oz) apricot jam (preserve), sieved

15g (1/2 oz) cornflour (cornstarch)

65g (2 1/3 oz) water

1 large (US extra-large) egg

105g (3 3/4 oz) unsalted butter

Micro pinch of salt

MARZIPAN BUTTERCREAM

315g (11 oz) yellow marzipan

3 1/2 tbsp boiling water

250g (9 oz) salted butter, softened

60g (2 oz) icing (confectioners') sugar

Yellow gel food colouring (optional)

7. Bake both the yellow and pink cakes at the same time in the middle of the oven for 37–38 minutes or until a metal skewer comes out clean. Leave the cakes to cool in their tins for 10 minutes, then turn out onto a wire rack to cool completely.

MAKE THE APRICOT CURD

8. While the cakes are baking, using the quantities given here, make the apricot curd following the instructions on page 233. Scrape into a piping (pastry) bag fitted with a 1-cm (1/3-inch) nozzle and leave the curd to cool in the fridge.

MAKE THE MARZIPAN BUTTERCREAM

9. Roughly grate the marzipan into a food processor and add the boiling water, then blitz. Keep going until it becomes a soft, smooth paste – there will be texture from the nuts, but process until there are no lumps of marzipan. Cut the butter into chunks and add to the processor with the sugar and colouring (if using). Blitz until everything is smoothly blended into a buttercream. Scrape the buttercream into a bowl and chill it to firm up slightly, but don't let it set hard.

ASSEMBLE THE CAKE

10. Cut the top 2–3mm (1/8–1/16 inch) off each cake to level their tops. Save the offcuts, setting them aside separately for decoration. Split each cake (page 9) so you have two pink layers and two yellow layers, but don't separate them yet. Take a 9-cm (3 1/2-inch) round cookie cutter, centre it on the yellow cake and press down through both layers. Do the same to the pink cake, so each layer is cut into a large ring and a medium circle. Carefully separate the pieces.

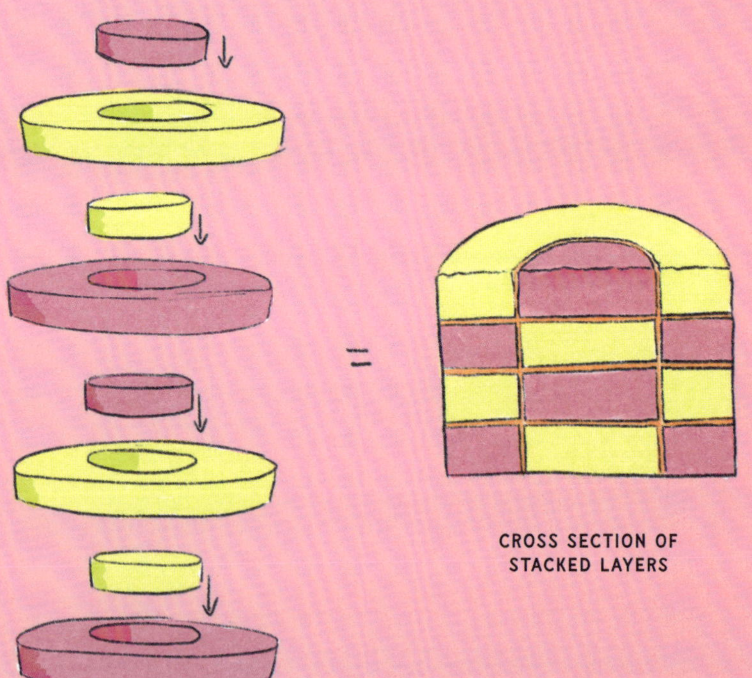

CROSS SECTION OF STACKED LAYERS

11. To assemble the cake, place one ring of cake on your serving plate, pipe a little apricot curd around its inside cut edge and spread it out with a palette knife. Hold the small circle of cake in the contrasting colour between your thumb and index (pointer) finger, pipe apricot curd all around its outside cut edge and spread it out with the palette knife. Press it into the empty centre of the cake ring on the plate. Some curd will be forced out, but pipe on more curd to make a 5mm (1⁄4 inch) covering when spread over the cake layer. Repeat the process with the remaining three cake layers and curd, alternating the colours to build up the chequerboard effect, but don't cover the top of the final layer with curd.
12. Using a large palette knife, cover the assembled cake with a thin coating of marzipan buttercream to trap the crumbs. Chill the cake for 30 minutes to firm the crumb coat.
13. Scrape 120g (4 1⁄4 oz) of the buttercream into a piping (pastry) bag fitted with a 1-cm (1⁄3-inch) nozzle (either plain or star) and set aside for the final decoration. Use the rest of the marzipan buttercream to thickly cover the cake. Spread it over the top and sides with a large palette knife and smooth it as much as you can be bothered. I prefer a slightly relaxed finish where you can see the swipes of the palette knife, but if you want it super smooth use a tall cake scraper and a turntable.
14. Crumble the pink cake offcuts into fine crumbs. Tip 1 tablespoon of pink crumbs at the base of the cake and use a table knife to lift and gently pat them up onto the buttercream. Tip on more pink crumbs as you need them and work around the whole cake. Vary the top line of crumbs between 3–6cm (1–2 1⁄3 inches) high, so it looks like a wave around the base of the cake. Scatter some more pink crumbs over the top of the cake but leave the edge free of them. Pipe small kisses of buttercream around the top, crumb-free edge of the cake. (Eat the yellow offcuts as a reward.)
15. Serve the cake at room temperature. Leftovers will keep well in an airtight container for 2 or 3 days.

BLACK FOREST GATEAU

BLACK FOREST CHAPEAU

The Black Forest gateau's melange of chocolate, cherries, cream and booze is, as far as I'm concerned, the only, *the only*, acceptable pairing of brown chocolate with fruit. White chocolate is a different story, that goes with anything. However, putting a sharp, wet, juicy berry, like a raspberry or a strawberry, with luscious, creamy, melty brown chocolate, no. It's all wrong. However, in the context of a BFG (big friendly gateau?), cherries rub alongside chocolate in a much more harmonious way. I can't completely put my tongue on why, but maybe the cake, cream and booze act as delicious buffers between the two so they complement rather than clash. In these recipes, chocolate takes the form of cake, cookie dough and even breadcrumbs. Cherries are present in almost all forms except glacé: fresh, frozen, jammed, steeped in booze. And booze makes a surprise appearance in the form of red wine, not just in its traditional guises of kirsch or cherry brandy. Maybe that's why I don't mind the fruit and chocolate holding hands? I'm too squiffy to care.

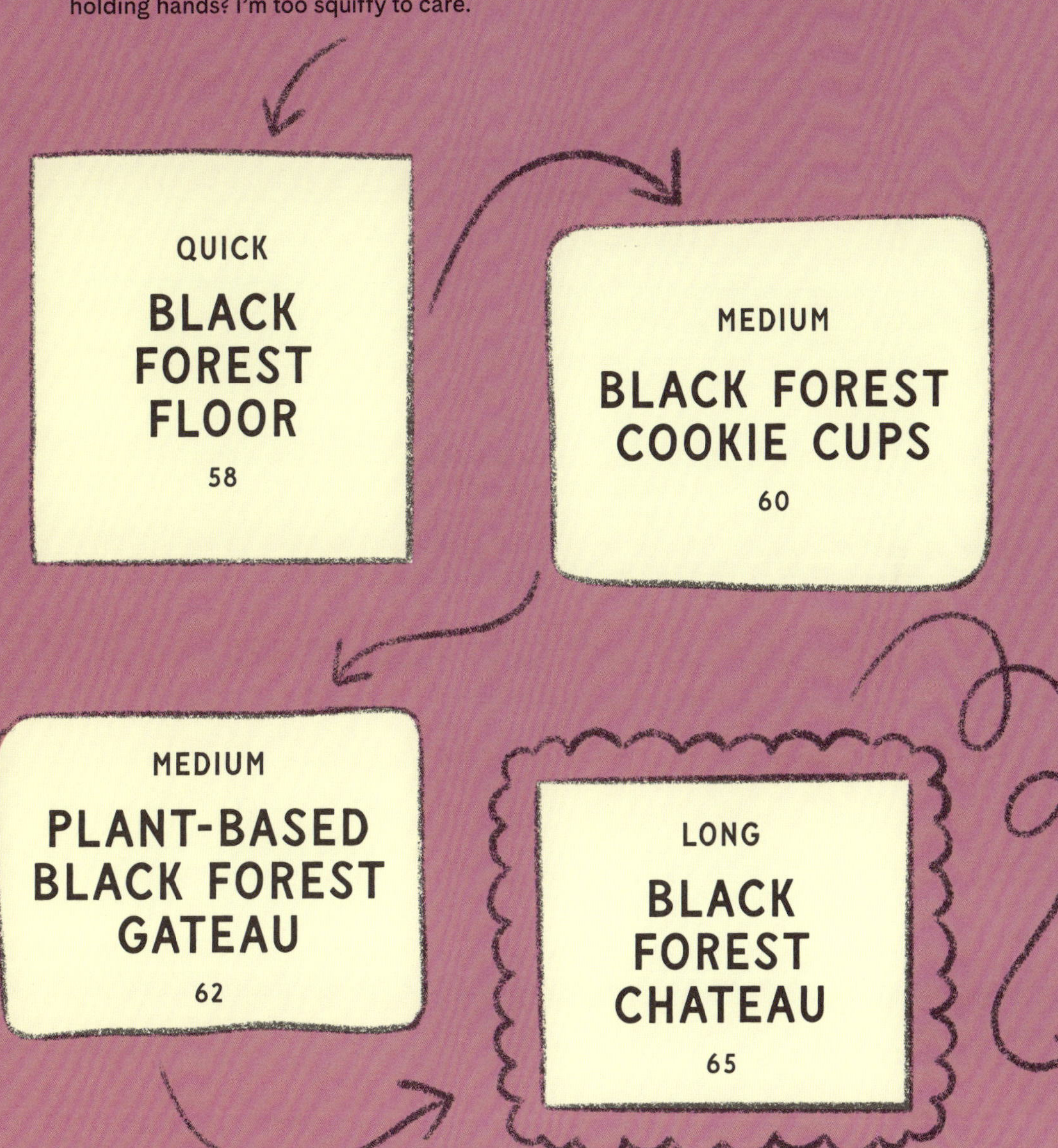

BLACK FOREST FLOOR

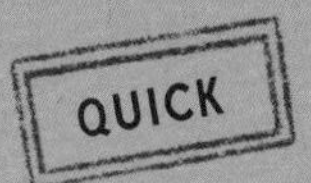

Hands on **20 minutes**
plus 20 minutes for decorations
Ready in **20 (or 40) minutes**

SERVES 6–8

EQUIPMENT
20-cm (8-inch) square serving dish

This dish is based on a dessert that was a staple at my dearest friend Lal's family parties. It was simply whipped cream layered in a trifle bowl with chocolate and coffee-flavoured brown breadcrumbs. It tasted divine, but it looked like dirt – presumably how it earned its name of Peat Pudding. I'm telling you this to give rightful credit for the inspiration, but mostly to point out that I wasn't the pervert who originally had the idea of turning worthy brown bread into a filthy chocolate dessert. What's more, my version, as you'd expect in a Black Forest chapter, heavily features cherries (layered with cream and chocolate breadcrumbs). Fruit, see, I am a saint.

CHERRIES

600g (21 oz) frozen cherries (sour, if possible, defrosted)

3 tbsp cherry brandy, kirsch or Amaretto (optional)

2 tbsp cherry syrup (optional)

40g (1⅓ oz) cherry jam (preserve), if needed

CHOCOLATE SOIL

240g (8½ oz) brown bread (about 4 slices, crusts are fine)

35g (1¼ oz) unsweetened cocoa powder

45g (1½ oz) icing (confectioners') sugar

25g (¾ oz) dark (bittersweet) chocolate (40–70% cocoa)

CREAM

580g (20½ oz) double (heavy) or whipping cream

20g (¾ oz) granulated sugar

2 tsp vanilla extract

TO DECORATE (OPTIONAL)

75g (2⅔ oz) dark (bittersweet) chocolate (40–70% cocoa)

1. To a medium bowl, add the defrosted cherries. If any fruit is whole, snip it in half. If using, stir in the alcohol and syrup. If the fruit tastes too sour, add enough cherry jam to sweeten it (you might not need any at all).
2. To a food processor, add the brown bread, torn into chunks, the cocoa powder and icing sugar. Finely grate in the chocolate. You can use the food processor with an attachment to grate the chocolate beforehand, but it's such a small amount that it's not really worth the washing-up, so I just do it by hand.
3. Blitz everything in the food processor until you have fine, dark brown breadcrumbs that look uncannily like soil.
4. To a large bowl, add the cream, sugar and vanilla. Whip until airy but not thick enough to hold any sort of peak; it needs to be pourable and almost self-levelling when used. Cream will thicken slightly after you've stopped beating it, so stop a little before you think it's ready.
5. Spoon half the fruit into the base of the dish, leaving most of the juice with the remaining fruit.
6. Pour half the airy cream over the cherries and level, if the cream hasn't already done that itself.
7. Scatter half the chocolate 'soil' over the cream to make an even layer.
8. Spoon the remaining cherries over the 'soil', reserving most of the juice for finishing the dessert.
9. Pour the remaining cream over the fruit and level as before.
10. Scatter the remaining 'soil' over the top and drizzle the cherry juice over that.
11. Chill in the fridge while you make the decoration or eat straight away.

TO DECORATE (OPTIONAL)

12. Scrunch up a large piece of non-stick baking paper and then partially re-flatten it.
13. Temper the chocolate (page 226).
14. Dollop teaspoons of melted chocolate onto the baking paper. Using the back of the spoon, form it into vague leaf shapes of different sizes. You can also drag lengths of chocolate along the paper for bark. Sit the baking paper in a large bowl so the chocolate leaves set curled rather than flat.
15. When solid, peel the 'leaves' and 'bark' off the paper and use them to decorate the top of the dessert.

BLACK FOREST COOKIE CUPS

Hands on **45 minutes**
Ready in **1 hour 15 minutes**

MAKES
12 cookie cups

EQUIPMENT
12-cup muffin tin (pan)

I've called these cookie cups because their base is a cookie dough, but I think of them as mini pies. But as Black Forest pies sound like they should contain rabbit, and they don't, I went with cookie cups. The double chocolate cookie dough holds a boozy whipped chocolate ganache and a cherry, which is topped with a generous dollop of mascarpone cream and an extra cherry. Sorry to disappoint if you were hoping for rabbit.

COOKIE CUP DOUGH

150g (5¼ oz) salted butter, softened

150g (5¼ oz) granulated sugar

60g (2 oz) unsweetened cocoa powder

200g (7 oz) plain (all-purpose) flour or 240g (8½ oz) gluten-free plain (all-purpose) flour + ½ tsp xanthan gum

4 tsp baking powder

Pinch of salt

80g (2¾ oz) white chocolate, chopped into small chunks

2 tsp vanilla extract

60g (2 oz) / 4 tbsp water

CHOCOLATE FILLING

150g (5¼ oz) milk chocolate, chopped into small chunks

3 tbsp cherry brandy, syrup or kirsch from a jar of cherries

110g (3¾ oz) double (heavy) cream

12 pitted fresh cherries, frozen cherries or cherries in kirsch

MASCARPONE CREAM

100g (3½ oz) mascarpone

200g (7 oz) double (heavy) cream

20g (¾ oz) granulated sugar

2 tsp vanilla extract

TO DECORATE

20g (⅔ oz) milk chocolate

12 pitted fresh cherries, frozen cherries or cherries in kirsch

1. Set the oven to 175°C fan (375°F/gas 5). Lightly oil the cups of the muffin tin. Cut 2-cm (¾-inch) wide strips of baking paper, 15cm (6 inches) long. Lay one strip in each cup to hoist the cookie cups out after baking.
2. Start with the cookie cup dough. To a large bowl, add the soft butter, sugar, cocoa powder, flour (and xanthan gum, if using gluten-free flour), baking powder and salt. Mix briefly with a hand mixer to a sandy texture.
3. Add the white chocolate, vanilla and water. Mix briefly until clumps of dough just start to form, then pull into a large ball, but don't overwork it.
4. Scoop up 60g (2 oz) of the dough, roll it into a ball and drop it in a muffin cup. Using the end of an oiled rolling pin or a shot glass, push it into the centre of the ball, forcing the dough up around the sides to form a cup. Repeat until all 12 cups of the tin are filled with cookie dough.
5. Bake in the middle of the oven for 15 minutes or until the dough puffs and starts to lose its cup shape.
6. While the cookie cups are baking, make the chocolate filling. To a microwave-safe bowl, add the milk chocolate, cherry brandy and double cream. Microwave in 15-second bursts to slowly melt everything together, then mix until blended. If you don't have a microwave, sit a heatproof bowl over a pan of hot water to melt. Chill in the fridge.
7. Remove the cookie cups from the oven and press the oiled rolling pin or shot glass into the puffy dough to re-form the cookie cup. Leave the cups in the tin to set for at least 20 minutes before removing with the paper strips to cool completely on a rack.
8. When the chocolate filling has set firm, beat until it goes lighter in colour and mousse-like in consistency. Spoon 25g (¾ oz) of ganache into each cooled cookie cup then press a cherry into the centre of the filling.
9. In a large bowl, break up the mascarpone with a spoon. Add the cream a little at a time, mixing the two to smooth out any lumps of mascarpone. Add the sugar and vanilla, then beat until the cream thickens.
10. Pipe or spoon the mascarpone cream over the chocolate filling. Create curls by drawing a vegetable peeler along the side of the chocolate block. Tumble the curls over the cream, then finish with another cherry.

PLANT-BASED BLACK FOREST GATEAU

Hands on **40 minutes**
Ready in **1 hour 40 minutes**

SERVES 10–12

EQUIPMENT
2 x 18-cm (7-inch) round cake tins (pans)

It seems entirely apt that I should include a plant-based version of a Black Forest gateau, seeing as the cake is named after a massive collection of big plants. This is a really simple, two-bowl chocolate cake, which you can whisk together by hand in minutes, filled with cherry jam and cream, then covered in your choice of chocolate coating. It also uses mostly store cupboard ingredients, the exceptions being the plant-based cream and butter alternatives, but you'll find most baking spreads are dairy-free anyway.

WET INGREDIENTS

60g (2 oz) cocoa powder

1 tsp instant coffee

270g (9½ oz) boiling water

140g (5 oz) mild olive oil, sunflower oil or any other flavourless oil

1 tbsp white wine vinegar or cider vinegar

1 tbsp vanilla extract

DRY INGREDIENTS

320g (11¼ oz) plain (all-purpose) flour

130g (4½ oz) dark brown soft sugar

130g (4½ oz) granulated sugar

2 tsp baking powder

½ tsp bicarbonate of soda (baking soda)

¼ tsp salt

CHOCOLATE FROSTING

Full quantity of Easy Chocolate Buttercream (page 64) or Plant-Based Ganache (page 224)

CHERRY FILLING

220g (7¾ oz) whippable plant-based cream

1 tbsp kirsch (optional)

200g (7 oz) cherry jam (preserve)

1. Set the oven to 165°C fan (350°F/gas 4). Line the bases of the two cake tins with a disc of baking paper.
2. To a medium bowl, add the cocoa and coffee. Weigh the boiling water over and whisk together until lump free.
3. To a large bowl, add all the dry ingredients and mix well to evenly combine.
4. To the cocoa / water bowl, add the oil, vinegar and vanilla. Whisk briefly – the mix won't emulsify.
5. Pour the wet ingredients onto the dry and mix by hand with a balloon whisk to a smooth batter. Keep whisking for 30 seconds to activate the gluten, which will help with the cake's structure.
6. Divide the batter between the two cake tins and bake in the middle of the oven for 25–26 minutes. A metal skewer will come out clean when the cakes are ready.
7. Leave the cakes in their tins for 10 minutes before transferring to a wire rack to cool completely. Sit the cakes on their flat bottoms to avoid any potential cracking.
8. While the cakes are baking and cooling, make either the Easy Chocolate Buttercream (overleaf) or Plant-Based Ganache (page 224). Scrape into a piping (pastry) bag fitted with a 1.5-cm (½-inch) nozzle.
9. When the cakes are cool, slice the top 5mm (¼ inch) off each one to level their tops. Crumble any offcuts into a bowl and set aside for later.
10. To a large bowl, add the plant-based cream and whip.
11. Mix the kirsch (if using) into the cherry jam.
12. Put the first cake on your serving plate, flat bottom down, and pipe a wall of chocolate buttercream or ganache around its top edge. Spoon half the jam into the centre and spread up to the buttercream or ganache wall. Pipe or spoon over half the cream.

Continued overleaf

13. Gently top with the second cake, placing it upside down so its flat bottom is facing up. Pipe a wall of buttercream / ganache around the edge of the top cake, leaving the rest of the top uncovered.
14. Generously coat the sides of the assembled cake with more buttercream or ganache. When you have smoothed the cake's sides, spoon the remaining jam onto the top and spread up to the buttercream or ganache wall. Pipe or spoon the remaining cream over the jam. Sprinkle the reserved cake crumbs over the cream and serve.

EASY CHOCOLATE BUTTERCREAM

As this is an easy buttercream, it's perfect for an easy Black Forest Gateau, but you can use it for any cake that needs a deliciously no-nonsense chocolate covering. It's made with dark (bittersweet) chocolate with 70% cocoa, but don't worry if you prefer dark intensity in your vampire novels and not your chocolate – when it's beaten with all that luscious butter and sugar you don't get any astringent bitterness, just the best cocoa flavour.

125g (4½ oz) dark (bittersweet) chocolate (70% cocoa) – check the packet for any dairy

250g (9 oz) icing (confectioners') sugar

250g (9 oz) plant-based salted butter, softened

1. Chop up the chocolate and melt in the microwave or in a bowl over a pan of hot water and set aside to cool.
2. Into a large mixing bowl, sift the icing sugar and add the butter – it should be soft enough that you can give the two an initial mix together by hand.
3. Beat with an electric mixer for a minute until the butter is pale.
4. Check the temperature of the melted chocolate. It should be under 30°C (85°F) when you add it to the buttercream; any hotter and it risks melting the butter and turning the buttercream runny.
5. With the beaters going, pour in the melted chocolate, stopping as soon as it's evenly mixed through the buttercream.
6. Leave at room temperature until needed, then use as the recipe requires.

BLACK FOREST CHATEAU

Hands on **1 hour 25 minutes**
Ready in **2 hours 30 minutes**

SERVES 12+

EQUIPMENT
2 x 18-cm (7-inch) round cake tins (pans)

This airy, red wine-infused chocolate cake, layered with cherries and whipped ganache, is absolutely delicious, but it's absolutely not suitable for anyone who can't – or doesn't want to – consume alcohol. The cake batter contains almost one-third of a bottle of wine and it's not in the oven long enough for much of the alcohol to evaporate. Don't worry about the calibre of the wine, use whatever you like. It's there to bring out the flavour of the cherries, give the chocolate a bit of extra depth and add a delicious warmth to the whole thing. At least, I think it does. I don't really know what I'm saying, I think I'm a... a bit pissed. Cheersh.

CHOCOLATE CAKE

100g (3½ oz) unsweetened cocoa powder

¼ tsp salt

225g (8 oz) red wine (any type)

75g (2⅔ oz) salted butter

5 large (US extra-large) eggs

250g (9 oz) granulated sugar

100g (3½ oz) mild olive oil, sunflower oil or any other flavourless oil

125g (4½ oz) plain (all-purpose) flour or gluten-free plain (all-purpose) flour + ½ tsp xanthan gum

5 tsp baking powder

CHERRY FILLING

20g (¾ oz) cornflour (cornstarch)

40g (1⅓ oz) cherry syrup

50g (1¾ oz) cherry jam (preserve)

200g (7 oz) frozen cherries

MILK CHOCOLATE WHIPPED GANACHE

300g (10½ oz) milk chocolate

225g (8 oz) double (heavy) cream

WHITE CHOCOLATE WHIPPED GANACHE

385g (13½ oz) white chocolate

290g (10¼ oz) double (heavy) cream

'WINE' DRIP

35g (1¼ oz) white chocolate, finely chopped

15g (½ oz) unsalted butter

10g (⅓ oz) glucose syrup

2 tsp boiling water

Red and purple paste food colouring

20g (¾ oz) dark (bittersweet) chocolate (70% cocoa), finely chopped

Continued overleaf

MAKE THE CAKE

1. Set the oven to 160°C fan (350°F/gas 4). Line the base of each cake tin with a disc of baking paper.
2. To a large bowl, add the cocoa powder and salt. Into a microwave-safe jug (pitcher), weigh the wine and butter and heat until the butter has just melted. If you don't have a microwave, warm the wine and butter in a pan on a medium-low heat. Pour the warm wine and melted butter over the cocoa powder and mix with a balloon whisk until smooth. Leave for 5 minutes for the cocoa to bloom.
3. Add the eggs, sugar and oil, then whisk until combined.
4. Add the flour and baking powder, then whisk in until no dry pockets of flour remain and the batter is smooth. If using gluten-free flour, combine the flour, xanthan gum and baking powder before adding.
5. Divide the batter between the two cake tins and bake in the middle of the oven for 37 minutes or until a metal skewer comes out clean. (Use a metal skewer, rather than a wooden one, as the batter sticks to wood and gives a false impression of being underdone.) While the cakes bake, start the cherry filling and ganache.
6. Leave the cakes in their tins for 10 minutes, then turn out onto a wire rack to cool completely.

MAKE THE CHERRY FILLING

7. To a pan, add the cornflour and cherry syrup and mix until there are no lumps. Add the jam and cherries and put on a medium heat. As the cherries defrost in the pan, use scissors to snip the fruit into smaller pieces, roughly into quarters. Keep stirring; when the fruit comes up to the boil it will thicken. Remove from the heat and scrape into a bowl to cool.

MAKE THE GANACHE

8. Roughly chop the milk chocolate into 1-cm (1⁄3-inch) chunks and add to a medium bowl. Heat the cream to almost boiling point in a jug (pitcher) in the microwave or in a pan on the hob. Pour over the chocolate, leave for 2 minutes, then stir the cream and chocolate together until blended. Put the bowl in the fridge to chill.
9. Repeat the above step with the white chocolate and cream.

WHIP THE GANACHE

10. When both the ganaches have chilled and firmed to a peanut butter consistency, beat until mousse-like and lighter in colour. Scrape the milk chocolate ganache into a piping (pastry) bag fitted with a 1-cm (1/3-inch) nozzle.

ASSEMBLE THE CAKE

11. Split each cake in two so you have four layers (page 9). Set the first layer of cake on your serving plate. Pipe on enough milk chocolate ganache to spread a 5-mm (1/4-inch) layer over the cake then pipe a wall of ganache around the top edge. Spoon on one-third of the cooled cherry filling and spread out to the wall of ganache. Repeat with the next two layers, using up the cherry filling, and top with the fourth layer of cake, placing it cut side down so the top is perfectly flat.
12. Cover the whole cake in a thin layer of white chocolate ganache and chill for 30 minutes. This crumb coat will stop any dark cake crumbs showing on the final white chocolate ganache layer.
13. When the crumb coat is firm, use the remaining white chocolate ganache to cover the top and sides so no dark cake is visible. Return the cake to the fridge to chill.

ADD THE 'WINE' DRIP

14. To a small bowl, add the finely chopped white chocolate, butter and glucose syrup. Half fill a slightly bigger bowl with boiling water and sit the chocolate bowl over it so the gentle heat melts the contents. Don't use a microwave as this needs a slow, even melt. As you stir slowly to melt and mix, you'll see the mixture starting to separate and look split. Don't worry, just add the boiled water and keep stirring – it will come back together. When the mix is smooth and emulsified, start to add the food colouring. The darkness of the red wine colour will come from the dark chocolate later, so for now, concentrate on getting a really deep red with a little purple. When you're happy with the red, add half the dark chocolate and melt in. Add more or all of the dark chocolate to get a deep, rich red wine colour.
15. Use the drip as soon as it has cooled to a slow, syrupy consistency. If the drip sets before you're ready to use it, just re-warm it over more hot water. If it separates, stir in more boiling water, 1/4 teaspoon at a time, until it emulsifies again.
16. Remove the cake from the fridge, spoon the drip onto the top of the cake and encourage it to trickle down the sides – it will firm up quickly once it's in contact with the chilled cake. Upend a small wine glass on top of the cake and push its rim into the ganache and cake to firmly anchor it so that it looks like the drip has flooded from the glass.
17. Leave the cake to come up to room temperature before serving. Any leftover cake stored in an airtight container will keep for up to 3 days.

CARROT CAKE

I always think of carrot cake as the mixed recycling skip at the municipal dump; everyone just chucks stuff in and hopes for the best. Nuts, seeds, coconut, raisins, cinnamon, cardamom, ginger, beetroot, I've seen it all go in and still claim the title of a carrot cake. So beyond the inclusion of some carrot, the brief for what constitutes a carrot cake seems to be pretty loosey goosey. That's certainly how I've approached the concept for this chapter. With a huge range of ingredients that can claim to be legitimate inclusions, I've added whatever I like with a clear conscience. As you would hope, carrot is mandatory, as is the inclusion of some deliciously warming spices. Nuts and coconut are represented, although not in cake form. I prefer that my moist mouthful of cake is uninterrupted by the need to chew something too vigorously. Finally, to top it all, literally, there must be a creamy frosting or topping, just to challenge any claims carrot cake may try to make about being a health food.

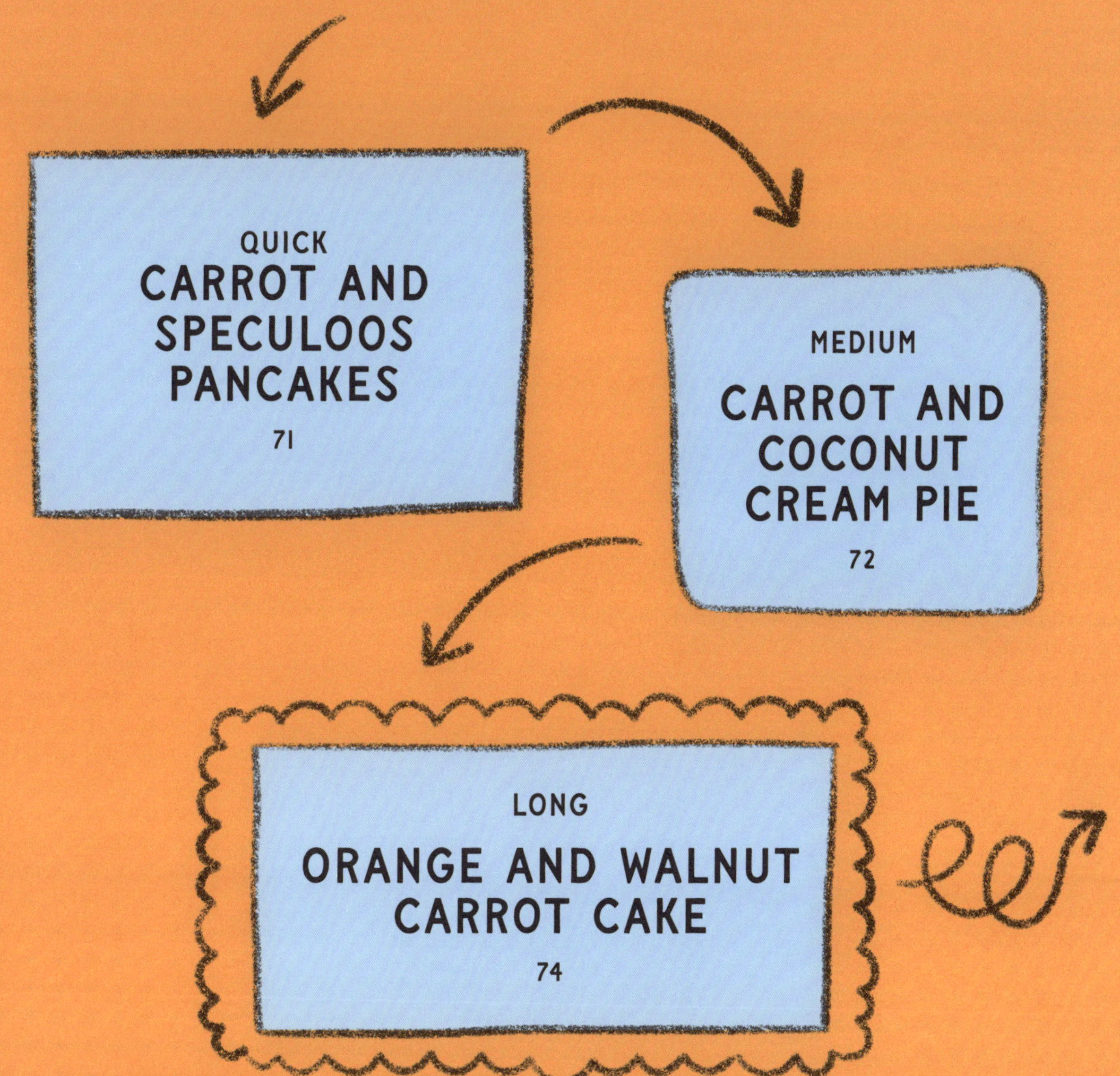

CARROT AND SPECULOOS PANCAKES

Hands on **25 minutes**
Ready in **25 minutes**

MAKES
8 snack-sized pancakes

EQUIPMENT
Frying pan (skillet) with a lid

I've never been a massive fan of speculoos biscuits. I will always think of them as that saucer-balanced, plastic-wrapped consolation prize for not ordering a slice of cake with your coffee. The spread, however, I can eat jars of. Mixing speculoos spread with grated carrot doesn't make sense either, until you try it and realise the mildly spiced caramel spread gives you instant carrot cake flavour when the two are combined. As they are in these deliciously quick and simple pancakes topped with sweetened cream cheese and a speculoos drizzle.

PANCAKES

120g (4¼oz) peeled and trimmed carrots

100g (3½oz) speculoos spread (I use Biscoff)

2 tsp lemon juice

40g (1⅓oz) milk (dairy or plant-based)

60g (2 oz) plain (all-purpose) flour

2 tsp baking powder

SPECULOOS TOPPING

10g (⅓oz) icing (confectioners') sugar

1 tbsp orange juice

100g (3½oz) cream cheese

50g (1¾oz) speculoos spread, melted

1. Into a medium bowl, coarsely grate the peeled, topped and tailed carrots. Add the speculoos spread, lemon juice and milk, then mix together until evenly mixed through the carrot.
2. Put the dry frying pan (skillet) on a medium heat.
3. Add the flour and baking powder to the bowl with the carrot and mix well until there are no patches of dry.
4. Add a small amount of butter, approximately ¼ teaspoon, to the pan and use a spatula to spread it around. When the butter starts to just bubble, spoon 40g (1⅓oz) of the batter into the pan for each pancake. Spread each dollop out lightly with the back of a spoon to 7cm (2¾ inches) in diameter – you may only fit four pancakes in the pan at one time. Put the lid on and cook for 4 minutes or until bubbles break the surface of the pancake and the batter is starting to look more set than wet.
5. Using a fish slice or turning spatula, flip over each pancake, put the lid back on and cook for a further 4 minutes. Turn the heat down if the pancakes are cooking too much.
6. Slide the cooked pancakes onto a wire rack and keep warm in the oven while you cook the rest.
7. Mix up the topping. To a small bowl, add the icing sugar and orange juice and mix until smooth, then fold in the cream cheese.
8. Serve the pancakes with a dollop of cream cheese on each one and a drizzle of warmed-up speculoos spread.

CARROT AND COCONUT CREAM PIE

Hands on **1 hour**
Ready in **2 hours 15 minutes**

SERVES 8–10

EQUIPMENT
21-cm (8½-inch) loose-bottomed tart tin (pan)

My starting point for this luscious cream pie is the Indian and Pakistani dessert gajar ka halwa. An ambrosial combination of carrots, cardamom and ghee cooked down in sweetened dairy milk, it tastes like a pudding version of the best carrot cake you've ever eaten. I have veered from that delicious starting point, swapping the dairy milk for coconut milk, mainly because cardamom plus coconut is my catnip, but also making it easier to veganise. Look for coconut milk with the highest percentage of coconut extract (at least 60%) to get the best flavour. The fragrant, fudgy filling sits on a base of buttery, caramelised nuts and is topped with sour cream. Sounds indulgent but it's basically just grated carrots. Think of it as coleslaw.

FILLING

850g (30 oz) peeled carrots

6 cardamom pods

400g (14 oz) can coconut milk (at least 60% coconut extract)

50g (1¾ oz) granulated sugar

50g (1¾ oz) block creamed coconut

BASE

100g (3½ oz) walnut pieces

100g (3½ oz) cashew nuts

100g (3½ oz) light brown soft sugar

2 tbsp water

100g (3½ oz) salted butter (dairy or plant-based)

TOPPING

2 cardamom pods

1 tbsp sunflower oil or any other flavourless oil

25g (1 oz) walnuts and cashews

Tiniest pinch of ground turmeric

Pinch of salt

1 tsp icing (confectioners') sugar

300g (10½ oz) sour cream (dairy or plant-based – if you can't find plant-based sour cream, use plant-based crème fraîche or a mixture of plant-based cream cheese and yogurt)

1. Line the base of the tart tin with a disc of baking paper.
2. Coarsely grate the carrots. Use a food processor for this, if you have one; even though it's a pain to hunt out the grating disc, it's more of a pain to grate almost a kilo of carrots by hand.
3. To a mortar, add the cardamom pods and lightly crush with the pestle to open them up. Remove the pod cases and finely grind the seeds.
4. To a large pan with a lid, add the coconut milk, cardamom and sugar, put on a medium heat and stir briefly. Stir the grated carrot through the liquid. Add the creamed coconut as a lump; it will melt during cooking.
5. Put the lid on and cook for 15 minutes at a gentle boil, stirring occasionally.
6. Remove the lid and cook for a further hour. In the first 30 minutes, there will be a lot of liquid that needs evaporating and so you can leave it to cook with just the occasional stir. In the last 30 minutes, it will need more attention. As the mix gets thicker and stickier, stir it regularly so nothing burns and lower the heat if it is catching on the bottom of the pan.
7. While the carrot doesn't need too much attention, make the base. In a food processor, blitz the nuts to a gravelly / rice grain texture, but don't make them too fine. Add the nuts to a dry frying pan (skillet) on a medium heat and stir regularly so they toast evenly. When the nuts are lightly golden and smell nicely nutty, scrape them out of the pan into a bowl. Wipe out the pan.
8. Add the sugar and water to the frying pan, put back on a low heat and stir. When the sugar has dissolved, add the butter and mix in. When the butter has emulsified with the sugar, turn the heat up to medium and gently bubble for 2½ minutes, but don't stir it. Remove from the heat and stir in the toasted nuts. As soon as everything is evenly mixed, tip into the lined tart tin. Working swiftly so the mixture stays warm and workable, use the back of a spoon to press the nuts evenly over the base and up the sides of the tin to make the pie case. Chill in the fridge until needed.

9. When the carrots have cooked for 1 hour 15 minutes or are thick, sticky and deep orange in colour, rather than opaque and creamy, remove from the heat. Leave to cool for 5 minutes, then spread the filling onto the pie case and level the top. Chill in the fridge for 30 minutes.
10. While the pie filling cools, make the topping. Crush the cardamom pods in a mortar and pestle, remove the cases and grind the seeds to a powder. To a frying pan, add the oil and nuts and put on a medium-low heat. Use the handle of a teaspoon to add the tiniest amount of turmeric to the pan and stir it in. (The turmeric is only there to tint the oil yellow, rather than flavour it.) When the nuts are golden brown, switch off the heat, stir in the cardamom, salt and icing sugar and leave to cool.
11. Once the pie filling has chilled, cover with the sour cream, then spoon on the toasted nuts and drizzle over the sweet, fragrant oil from the pan.
12. This pie can be made the day before serving and keeps perfectly in the fridge.

ORANGE AND WALNUT CARROT CAKE

Hands on **1 hour 50 minutes**
Ready in **2 hours 15 minutes**
if using Cream Cheese Frosting
or **26 hours 15 minutes**
if using Yogurt Frosting

SERVES 10–12

EQUIPMENT
Two 18-cm (7-inch) cake tins (pans)

If you wake up one day and really fancy crafting with carrots, this is the recipe for you. If you wake up and just fancy making a carrot cake, this is also the recipe for you. Decorating this orange-infused, lightly spiced, walnut-tinged cake with woven candied carrots is entirely optional. You also have a choice of frostings to coat the moist cake layers: classic cream cheese or a slightly sharper yogurt frosting for a little more bite. If you're going for the yogurt option, don't forget to start draining it the night before; after that you can go to bed and dream of tomorrow's carrot weaving fun.

WALNUT BUTTER

175g (6¼ oz) walnut pieces

2 tsp sunflower oil or any other flavourless oil

Pinch of salt

OR

150g (5¼ oz) ready-made nut butter, such as walnut, hazelnut, almond or cashew

CAKE

300g (10½ oz) carrot (4 medium carrots)

Grated zest of 1 large orange

3 large (US extra-large) eggs

1½ tsp ground cinnamon

2 tsp vanilla extract

½ tsp salt

270g (9½ oz) light brown soft sugar

60g (2 oz) sunflower oil or any other flavourless oil

150g (5¼ oz) walnut butter (see above)

240g (8½ oz) plain (all-purpose) flour or 260g (9¼ oz) gluten-free self-raising mix

3½ tsp baking powder (omit if using gluten-free flour)

Ingredients continued overleaf

START THE YOGURT FROSTING

1. If using Yogurt Frosting, start draining the yogurt 24 hours before making the frosting (page 222). Alternatively, use the given quantities to make Cream Cheese Frosting on the same day as the cake (see overleaf).

MAKE THE CAKES

2. If making your own, prepare the walnut butter. Break the walnuts into smaller pieces and add them to a dry frying pan (skillet) on a medium-low heat. Stir the nuts so they toast evenly. Once they smell toasty and nutty, scrape them into a food processor or blender and add 1 teaspoon of oil and a pinch of salt. Blitz to break them down to smooth nut butter. If it takes a long time for the nuts to turn to butter, add an extra 1 teaspoon of oil. You will need 150g (5¼ oz) nut butter for the cake; the extra 25g (1 oz) of walnuts is to account for the nut butter left behind in the processor or eaten in the name of testing.
3. Set the oven to 175°C fan (375°F/gas 5). Line the bases of the cake tins with discs of baking paper.
4. Peel and coarsely grate the carrots either by hand or in a food processor. Set aside.
5. To a large bowl, add the orange zest, eggs, cinnamon, vanilla, salt, sugar, oil and nut butter, then mix by hand with a balloon whisk. When everything is blended, stir through the grated carrot. Add the flour and baking powder (if using wheat flour), then mix thoroughly so there are no dry pockets of unmixed flour.
6. Divide the cake batter between the two tins and bake straight away in the middle of the oven for 36 minutes or until a metal skewer comes out clean.
7. Leave the cakes to cool in their tins for 10 minutes, then turn out onto a wire rack to cool completely.

Continued overleaf

YOGURT FROSTING

1kg (2lb 3 oz) full-fat plain yogurt, strained overnight to approximately 500g (17½ oz) – use 400g (14 oz) for the recipe

200g (7 oz) salted butter

200g (7 oz) icing (confectioners') sugar

OR

CREAM CHEESE FROSTING

280g (10 oz) salted butter or unsalted with a small pinch of salt

150g (5¼ oz) icing (confectioners') sugar

2 tsp vanilla extract

350g (12⅓ oz) full-fat cream cheese

TO DECORATE (OPTIONAL)

3 long large carrots

Juice of 1 large orange (from the orange zested for the cakes)

45g (1½ oz) caster (superfine) sugar

Boiling water, to cover

MAKE THE FROSTING

8. Using the quantities given here, make either the Yogurt Frosting with the 24-hour drained yogurt or the Cream Cheese Frosting (page 222).

ASSEMBLE THE CAKE

9. Split each cake in two so you have four layers (page 9). Sandwich the layers together with the frosting and use the remainder to cover the top and sides of the cake. I prefer the relaxed finish you get from using a palette knife to smooth out the frosting. If you want a sharper look, use a cake scraper and a turntable. Chill the cake for 30 minutes to firm the frosting.

CANDY THE CARROTS

10. Top, tail and peel the carrots. Use the peeler to make long ribbons of carrot.
11. Into a medium pan, squeeze the juice of the orange and add the sugar. Lay the carrot ribbons in the pan, being careful not to snap their length. Add enough boiling water to cover all the ribbons and put the pan on a medium heat.
12. Gently boil for 4–5 minutes or until the carrot ribbons have softened just enough for a sharp knife to effortlessly cut through them. Carefully lift out the ribbons, making sure they don't break, and lay them out flat on some baking paper.
13. When the ribbons are cool, stack five on top of each other and trim down both sides of their length so the ribbons are all the same width. Do this for all the ribbons you have. (Listen, no one ever said this was the quick recipe.) Arrange enough ribbons vertically, side by side, to make a square. Fold back alternate ribbons, leaving the top 1cm (⅓ inch) of carrot stuck to the paper. From the rest of the carrot ribbons, lay one horizontally across the carrots that are lying flat, tight up to the folded-back verticals. Fold the vertical carrots back down, over the horizontal one. Now fold back the set of alternate vertical carrots that are under the horizontal ribbon. As before, lay a second horizontal ribbon over the flat carrots and fold back down the folded-back verticals. Repeat until you have a square of latticed carrot, then freeze the lattice flat on its paper. Congratulations, you have just woven carrots. Make as many sheets of latticed carrot as you have carrot for, or can be bothered to.
14. When the carrot is frozen, use circular cookie cutters to punch out circles from the latticed carrot sheets – a choice of differing sizes looks great. Gently press the discs of woven carrot onto the sides and top of the cake to decorate.
15. Serve the cake at room temperature.

For a low-key decoration option, cut a large, peeled carrot in half lengthways and thinly slice into 2-mm (1/16-inch) half moons. Gently boil in the candying liquid for 10 minutes, drain and cool. Decorate the top of the cake with candied carrot pieces.

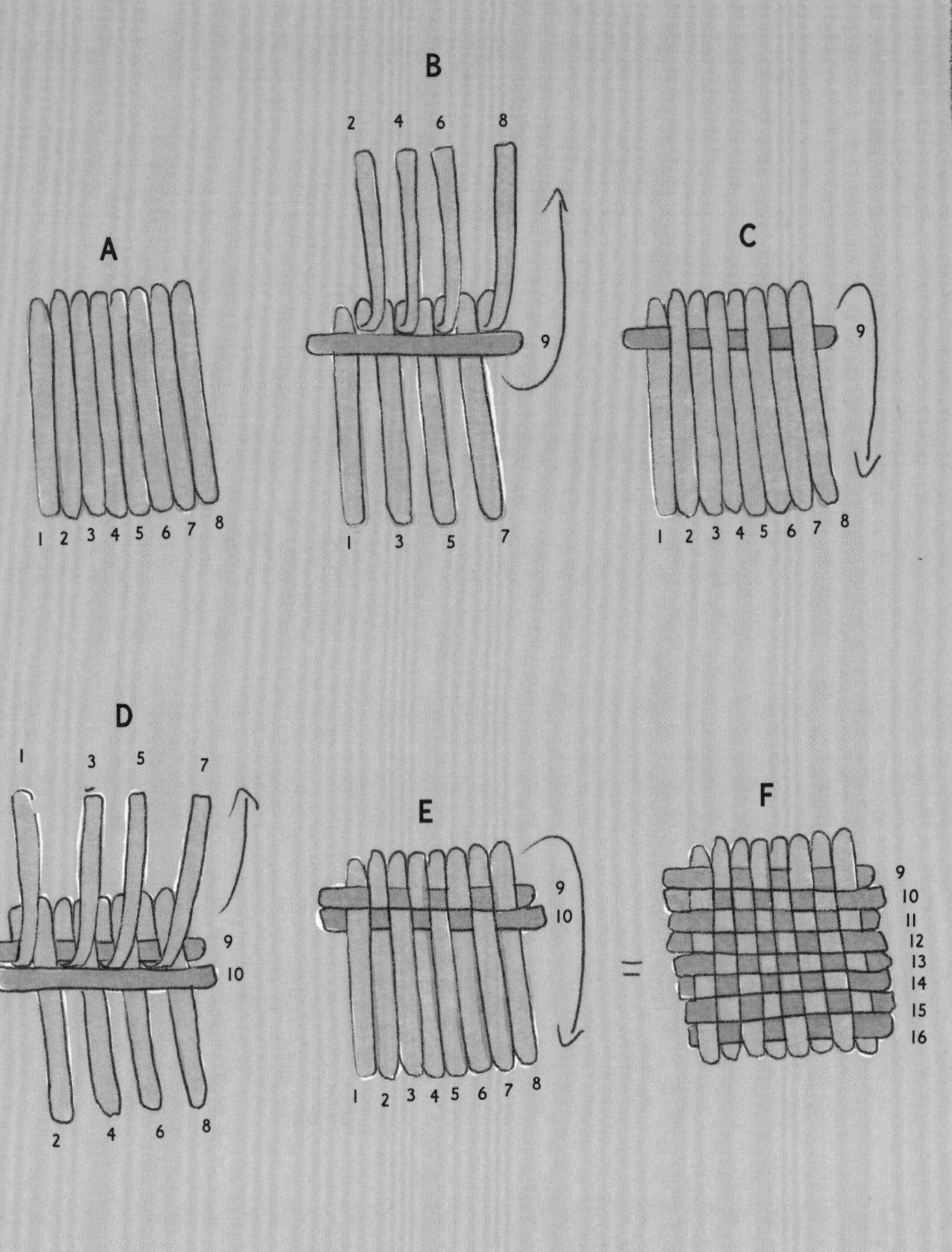
WEAVING CARROTS
A
1 2 3 4 5 6 7 8
B
2 4 6 8
9
1 3 5 7
C
9
1 2 3 4 5 6 7 8
D
1 3 5 7
9
10
2 4 6 8
E
9
10
1 2 3 4 5 6 7 8
=
F
9
10
11
12
13
14
15
16

CHEESECAKE

As a genre, cheesecake is a broad church and, as a heathen, it's pretty much the only one I'm prepared to worship in. Provided I can worship it with a spoon. A no-bake cheesecake with a simple, soft-set filling and a slow-baked, water-bathed cheesecake may be at different ends of the textural spectrum but they do share three common factors. Firstly, whether it's baked or chilled to set it, cream cheese brings its creamy, mild tang to all the recipes in this chapter. Second, a biscuit base appears across the board here. Sure, you can sit a cheesecake on a pastry base or even a cake, but I'll always go for the biscuit option. Not because it's a shortcut, thank you very much, particularly if you're making your own, but because its buttery crunch offers the most moreish contrast. The third component of the holy cheesecake trinity is the topping or flavour; citrus fruit features heavily, but then so does salted caramel, just so we don't get too pious about it all.

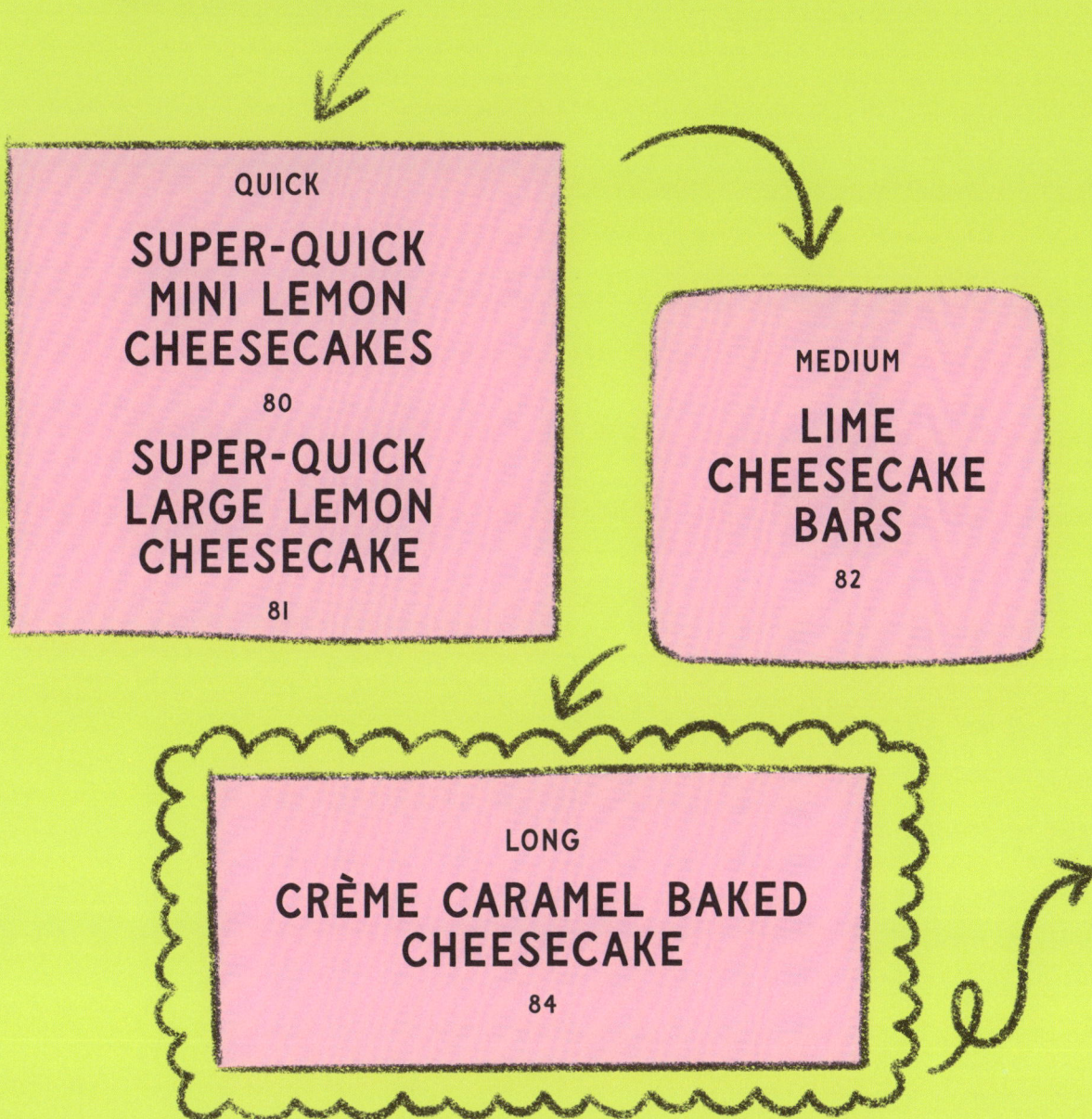

SUPER-QUICK MINI LEMON CHEESECAKES

Hands on **15 minutes**
Ready in **45 minutes**

MAKES
12 mini cheesecakes

EQUIPMENT
12-cup muffin tin (pan)

This is such a lazy pudding I can barely summon the energy to encourage you to make it. But I'm a trooper, so here goes... These incredibly quick mini cheesecakes rely on the citric acid in the lemon juice coagulating (yum!) the proteins in the condensed milk, instantly thickening the filling to the perfect no-bake cheesecake consistency. And to top it all, although in truth, to bottom it all, that lovely, light, zesty lemon cheesecake sits on a literal biscuit base. Yep, just put a biscuit in the base of a muffin case and then spoon filling on. Now excuse me, I need a lie down.

12 ginger nut (ginger snap) biscuits (or similar sized biscuits to fit in your muffin tin)

400g (14 oz) full-fat cream cheese

1½ lemons

260g (9¼ oz) sweetened condensed milk

180g (6⅓ oz) lemon curd

1. Put a paper muffin case in each cup of the muffin tin. Place a ginger nut biscuit in the base of each case.
2. To a large bowl, add the cream cheese and gently break it up with a spoon to loosen it slightly. Zest a lemon over the cream cheese, then juice it. Use a second lemon, if needed, to extract 80g (2¾ oz) of juice. Set the juice aside.
3. Add the sweetened condensed milk to the cheese in three goes, folding each addition in fully before adding the next. Overbeating cream cheese can cause it to release its liquid and make the mix so runny that it won't set; stop folding as soon as the condensed milk is evenly incorporated.
4. Gently fold the lemon juice into the cream cheese mix. The juice will thicken the mixture almost instantly, so stop folding as soon as it is fully incorporated.
5. Divide the cream cheese between the muffin cases, spooning it on top of the biscuit bases. Level the tops. Next, stir the lemon curd to loosen it if needed and spoon a rounded teaspoon over each of the cheesecakes.
6. Put the cheesecakes in the fridge to chill; it only takes 30 minutes for the cheesecakes to set firm, after which point you can eat them. They can be left longer, but after 1–2 hours the base will start to soften slightly, which I actually prefer.

SUPER-QUICK LARGE LEMON CHEESECAKE

Hands on **20 minutes**
Ready in **1 hour 20 minutes**

SERVES 12

EQUIPMENT
21-cm (8½-inch) loose-bottomed flan tin (pan), ideally with high sides

250g (9 oz) digestive biscuits (graham crackers, or any other biscuit of your choice, such as ginger, oat, shortbread, etc)

125g (4½ oz) salted butter, melted

600g (21 oz) full-fat cream cheese

Grated zest of 1 lemon

397-g (14-oz) can sweetened condensed milk

120g (4¼ oz) lemon juice (approximately 3 lemons)

120g (4¼ oz) lemon curd, plus 1–2 tsp lemon juice

The only extra effort involved in making a single large cheesecake is to crush some biscuits and melt some butter. It hardly seems decent that such a delicious pudding should take so little time and effort; proof, as if it were needed, that life just isn't fair.

1. Finely crush the biscuits to sandy crumbs. You can either use a food processor, put them in a large bowl and crush them with the base of a heavy glass or seal them in a strong plastic food bag and roll a rolling pin over them.
2. However you crush the biscuits, tip the fine crumbs into a large bowl and stir in the melted butter. Tip the buttery crumbs into the loose-bottomed tin, then use the back of a spoon to press them firmly into the base and up the sides so they are well compacted and not crumbly. Freeze the biscuit base for 20 minutes.
3. Once the base has chilled and set, make the cheesecake filling as for the mini cheesecakes opposite, using the quantities given here. Spoon over the biscuit base and level the top.
4. If the lemon curd is very firm, stir it or warm it slightly to loosen it. If your shop-bought curd isn't very lemony, add the extra lemon juice to taste. To decorate, use a teaspoon to drizzle the curd over the cheesecake or fill a piping (pastry) bag with a 2-mm (1/16-inch) nozzle and zigzag it over.
5. Chill the cheesecake for at least 40 minutes before serving.

LIME CHEESECAKE BARS

Hands on **45 minutes**
Ready in **1 hour 50 minutes**

MAKES
21 bars

EQUIPMENT
20 x 30-cm (8 x 12-inch) brownie tin (pan)

Man walks into a bar... it was a cheesecake bar. He said it was delicious. (Tumbleweed...) With an oaty biscuit base, a baked cheesecake filling and a zesty lime glaze, these baked lime cheesecake bars are really good, no joke. The cheesecake filling doesn't use eggs, just the power of flour, so if you want to make these vegan friendly just swap the butter and cream cheese for plant-based alternatives. If you want to be vegan unfriendly, well just don't, there's no need for that sort of energy here.

BISCUIT BASE

75g (2⅔ oz) light brown soft sugar

135g (4¾ oz) plain (all-purpose) flour or 140g (5 oz) gluten-free self-raising mix

1½ tsp baking powder (omit if using gluten-free flour)

90g (3¼ oz) rolled oats

120g (4¼ oz) salted butter, softened

CHEESECAKE FILLING

2 limes

135g (4¾ oz) salted butter, softened

240g (8½ oz) icing (confectioners') sugar

85g (3 oz) plain (all-purpose) flour or gluten-free plain (all-purpose) flour

210g (7½ oz) full-fat cream cheese

WHITE CHOCOLATE GLAZE

100g (3½ oz) white chocolate, broken into pieces

40g (1⅓ oz) salted or unsalted butter

30g (1 oz) / 2 tbsp lime juice

Lime green food colouring (optional)

1. Set the oven to 175°C fan (375°F/gas 5) and line the brownie tin with a single sheet of baking paper.
2. To a medium bowl, add the dry ingredients for the base and mix well. Add the softened butter; it should be soft enough that it can be easily mixed in by pushing it into the flour with the back of a spoon.
3. When the butter is well mixed in and you have a rough, crumble-like texture, tip the dough into the lined brownie tin and level it out so it evenly covers the base of the tin with no gaps. Very lightly press the crumbled dough down with a flat hand, but don't compact it.
4. Bake in the middle of the oven for 20 minutes.
5. Next, make the filling. Zest the limes into a large bowl, then juice the fruit into a separate jug (pitcher) or bowl until you have 60g (2 oz) – enough for the filling and the glaze. To the zest in the large bowl, add the softened butter, icing sugar and half the lime juice, then beat with an electric mixer until smooth, pale and fluffy.
6. Add the flour and beat in briefly, stopping as soon as no dry patches are visible.
7. Add the cream cheese, breaking it up with a spoon to loosen it a little, then beat it in just long enough to evenly combine. (Overbeating will cause the cream cheese to release its water and make the filling too runny.)
8. Remove the brownie tin from the oven, spread the cheesecake filling over the hot base and return to bake for a further 17–18 minutes. The filling will be ready when the whole surface has lost its wet gloss, is set enough that it can be lightly touched and not leave a mark but still has a little wobble when the tin is gently shaken.
9. Leave the cheesecake slab in the brownie tin for 5 minutes after baking. Using the paper, carefully lift the cheesecake onto a wire rack to cool.
10. Chill the slab in the fridge for an hour or the freezer for 30 minutes.

11. While the slab is chilling, make the glaze. Add the chocolate, butter and remaining lime juice. Microwave in short bursts until just warm enough to melt the chocolate and butter, then gently mix until blended. If you don't have a microwave, put the bowl over a pan of hot water. Once the glaze is smooth, add the food colouring, if using.
12. When the slab has chilled, pour the glaze over the filling and chill again until the glaze has set.
13. When ready to serve, cut the slab into 21 bars – I slice it into three widthways, then into seven lengthways. These bars can be eaten at room temperature but taste best when chilled.

CRÈME CARAMEL BAKED CHEESECAKE

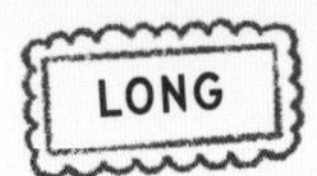

Hands on **45 minutes**
Ready in **4 hours 15 minutes**

SERVES 10–12
Makes one 20-cm (8-inch) cheesecake

EQUIPMENT
20-cm (8-inch) springform cake tin (pan)

Roasting tray (sheet pan)

3 cuboid chopsticks

CARAMEL

200g (7 oz) granulated sugar

4 tbsp boiling water

BISCUIT BASE

75g (2⅔ oz) shop-bought digestive biscuits (graham crackers) OR gluten-free digestive biscuits OR make your own (page 215)

30g (1 oz) wholemeal bread flour or gluten-free brown flour or gluten-free oat flour

50g (1¾ oz) plain (all-purpose) flour or gluten-free plain (all-purpose) flour

50g (1¾ oz) light brown soft sugar

60g (2 oz) cold salted butter

CHEESECAKE FILLING

20g (¾ oz) cornflour (cornstarch)

115g (4 oz) icing (confectioners') sugar

1 tbsp vanilla extract

50g (1¾ oz) salted butter, softened

2 large (US extra-large) eggs

500g (17½ oz) cream cheese

200g (7 oz) full-fat Greek yogurt (7–10% fat)

TO SERVE

300g (10½ oz) sour cream

Any adrenaline surges you may experience making this pudding will be more than balanced out by the soothing comfort provided by eating a slice. This is a smooth, creamy vanilla cheesecake baked on a biscuit base that, like its namesake the crème caramel, sits in a moat of caramel syrup of its own making. While presiding over a pan of molten caramel, and holding your breath as you upend the cheesecake, hoping to reveal a bottom as perfect as yours, might be slightly stressful, it will be worth it. Although your bottom might not thank you for it.

1. Line the springform cake tin with a single piece of baking paper. Scrunch it first so it's easier to press into the corners and will stay there. Wrap the outside of the tin with a single piece of thick foil so it's watertight in its water bath.

MAKE THE CARAMEL

2. To a heavy-bottomed pan, add the granulated sugar and make a dry caramel (page 227). When all the sugar has caramelised, switch off the heat and add 2 tablespoons of boiling water. Swirl the water around the pan with the caramel to make a thick syrup. Sit your lined springform tin on the scales and pour in 140g (5 oz) of caramel, rolling the tin around so the base is evenly covered.

3. Add another 2 tablespoons of boiling water to the caramel left in the pan, put on a low heat and stir to encourage all the remaining caramel to dissolve into the liquid. Save this extra sauce for serving the cheesecake.

MAKE THE BISCUIT BASE

4. Break the digestive biscuits into 5-mm (¼-inch) pieces; use your fingers to snap them rather than crush them with a rolling pin; you don't want them finely crumbed. Set aside for later.

5. To a medium bowl, add the flours and sugar and mix. Coarsely grate the butter over and work it into the flour with your fingertips until you have a fine breadcrumb-like consistency. Set aside for later.

MAKE THE CHEESECAKE FILLING

6. To a medium bowl, add the cornflour, sift in the icing sugar and mix together. Add the vanilla and butter, which should be very soft with the consistency of yogurt, and mix together until lump free. Add the eggs and gently whisk in by hand with a balloon whisk, stopping as soon as they are evenly combined.

7. To a large bowl, add the cream cheese and break up with a spoon so it relaxes and there are no lumps. Add the Greek yogurt, large spoonfuls at a time, and fold in until well combined.

Continued overleaf

8. Add the egg mixture, a little at a time, to the cream cheese bowl, stirring to evenly mix the two until smoothly combined. When mixing all these ingredients, aim to stir them together rather than whip; for the best finished consistency, avoid adding air to this mixture.

ASSEMBLE THE CHEESECAKE

9. Pour the cheesecake filling into the tin over the caramel base. Give the tin a few bangs down on the work surface to release any air pockets in the mixture, then smooth the top.
10. Sprinkle the top of the cheesecake with the broken digestive biscuits so there's no white showing. Scatter the base mixture over the top of the digestives, gently level and lightly tamp down the fine crumble, but don't press hard enough to disturb the cheese filling underneath. If the crumble base goes directly on the cheesecake filling, it stays too damp to properly bake; the digestives act as a barrier between the two, giving the crumble time to form a deliciously crisp, biscuity base.
11. Set the oven to 130°C fan (300°F/gas 2).
12. Boil a full kettle for the water bath. Set three chopsticks in the roasting tray and sit the cake tin on them. (This is so the base of the cheesecake sits in water and doesn't directly touch the bottom of the roasting tray and overheat.) When the kettle has boiled, put the roasting tray and cheesecake in the oven, on the middle shelf, and pour the hot water into the tray so it comes 3cm (1 inch) up the sides of the cake tin but no higher than the watertight foil.
13. Bake for 1 hour 30 minutes then switch off the oven. Prop the oven door open but leave the cheesecake in there for a further 30 minutes.
14. Remove the cheesecake from the oven and leave to cool to room temperature. Once cool, chill for at least 2 hours or overnight.
15. When ready to serve, sit a serving plate with a lip (to catch the syrup) upside down over the top of the springform tin. Hold the plate and the tin firmly together and invert. Release and remove the springform sides and the base and peel away the baking paper. Slices can be served chilled or room temperature with sour cream on the side and extra caramel sauce. Store any leftovers in an airtight container in the fridge.

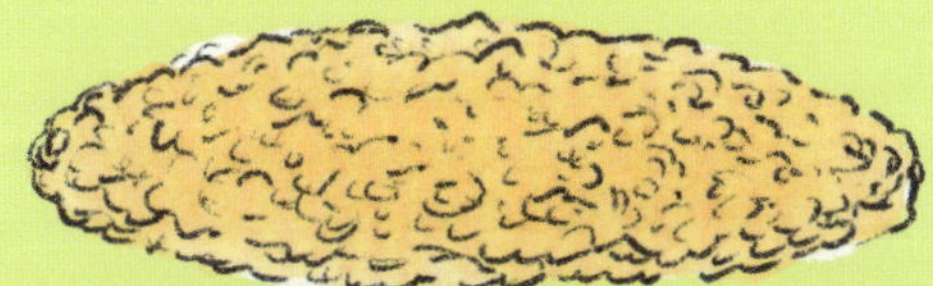

BISCUIT BASE

BROKEN DIGESTIVES

CHEESECAKE FILLING

CARAMEL

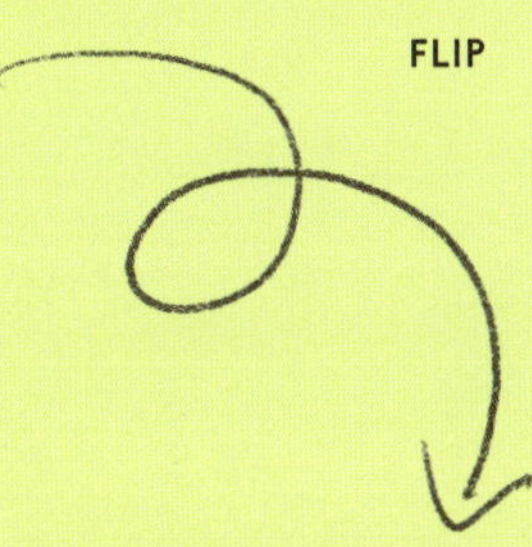

FLIP

CINNAMON ROLLS

Cinnamon rolls, with their light, fluffy dough spiralled with sweet cinnamon butter, speak of pure comfort to me. In fact more than that, they whisper it soothingly in my ear, having tucked me up with a teddy and left the landing light on. Cinnamon, as you'd hope for a cinnamon roll chapter, is common throughout the recipes, although you can swap it for another spice or a blend of your favourites. Ground cardamom, ginger, nutmeg and clove, in various combinations, all make excellent sweet buttery bun fillings. The dough element – one a baking powder quick dough, one leavened with yeast and one laminated – is where you'll find the most variation. There's even a sponge version for anyone worried I was neglecting cake here. With the exception of the laminated rolls, all others have a lightly sweet, vanilla cream cheese frosting to top them off. Of course you don't have to gild the lily, but if you've ever tried frosting the lily you know they taste even better.

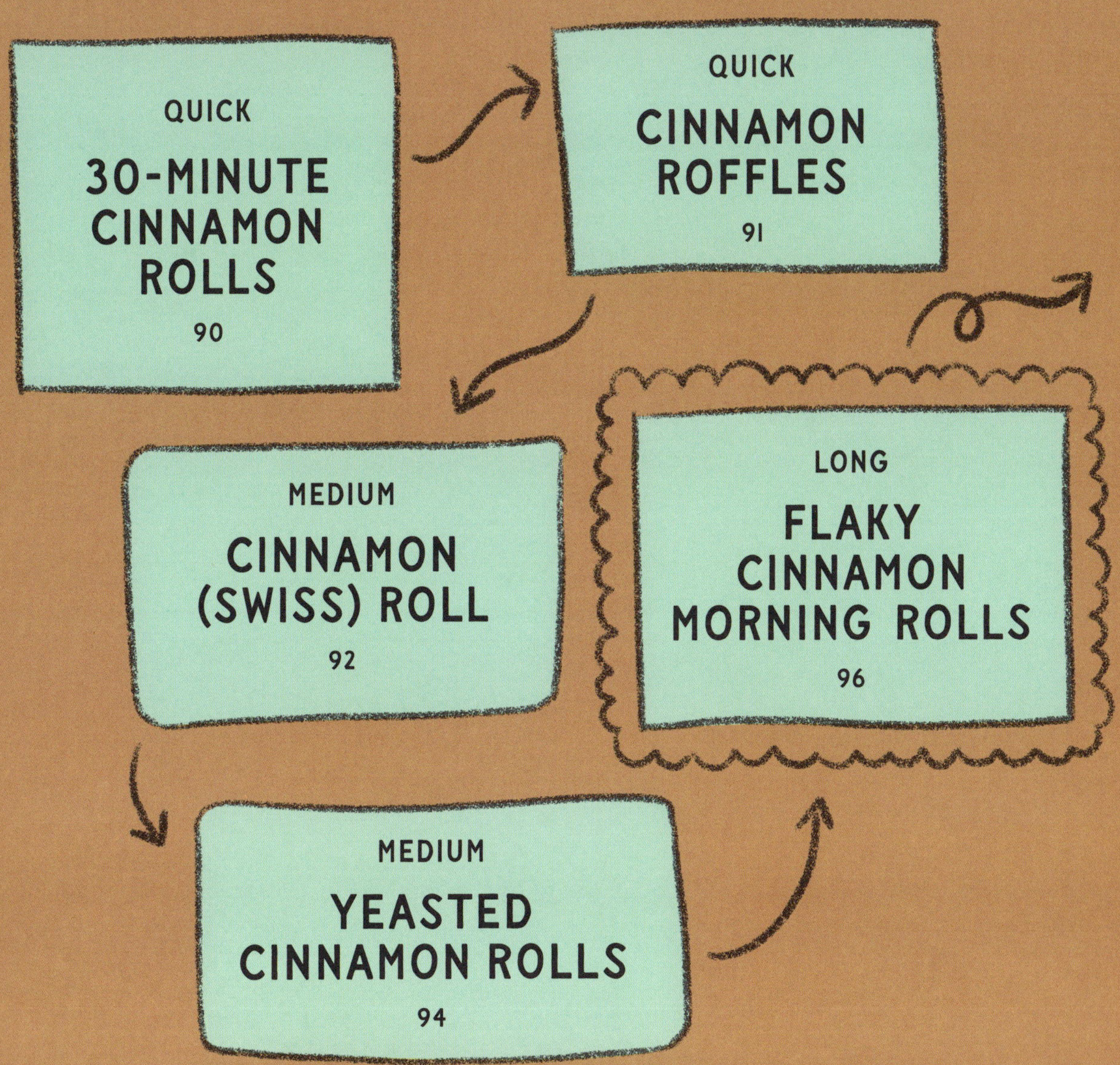

30-MINUTE CINNAMON ROLLS

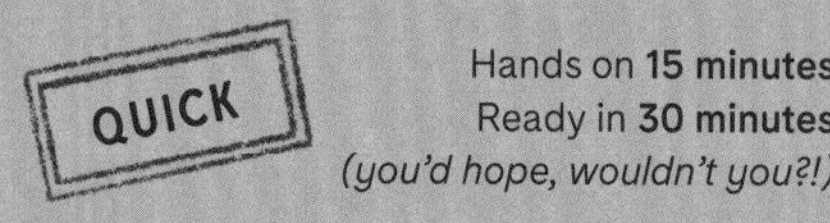

Hands on **15 minutes**
Ready in **30 minutes**
(you'd hope, wouldn't you?!)

MAKES
9 rolls

EQUIPMENT
20 x 30-cm (8 x 12-inch) brownie tin (pan)

These speedy cinnamon spirals use a quick dough, raised with baking powder, to deliver a cream cheese-frosted, spiced, buttery mouthful in just 30 minutes. You do have to get them into the oven swiftly to make the most of the baking powder's leavening power, but you don't have to stress about hitting the half-an-hour deadline. That's just there to shamelessly grab your attention. If they take you 35 or 40 minutes, they'll be just as good. If you manage to save some, they're even great the next day, by which point they will be 1,470-Minute Cinnamon Rolls.

FILLING

75g (2⅔oz) granulated sugar

2 tsp ground cinnamon

100g (3½oz) salted butter (dairy or plant-based), very soft

DOUGH

150g (5¼oz) plain (all-purpose) flour

150g (5¼oz) strong white bread flour

3 tsp baking powder

¼ tsp salt

240g (8½oz) full-fat plain yogurt (dairy or plant-based)

60g (2 oz) sunflower oil or any flavourless oil

TOPPING

50g (1¾oz) icing (confectioners') sugar

2 tsp vanilla extract

200g (7 oz) full-fat soft cheese or cream cheese (dairy or plant-based)

1. Set the oven to 175°C fan (375°F/gas 5) and line the brownie tin with baking paper.
2. First, make the filling. To a small bowl, add the sugar, cinnamon and butter, then use a spoon to mix it to an even, spreadable paste.
3. Next, make the dough. To a large bowl, add the dry ingredients and mix.
4. To a medium bowl or jug (pitcher), combine the yogurt and oil.
5. Pour the wet ingredients onto the dry and mix together with a table knife until you get ragged clumps of dough. Use your hands to pull the clumps together, incorporating any dry flour left in the bowl – don't knead it vigorously, just gently squash the dough enough to form a rough ball.
6. Generously flour your work surface, pat the dough into a vague oblong and then roll it out to 30 x 40cm (12 x 16 inches), orientated with the short side running from left to right.
7. Spread the filling over the dough, right up to the edges. Tightly roll up the dough from the short edge so you have a 30-cm (12-inch) long sausage.
8. Use a knife to lightly mark out 9 rolls: slip a piece of strong thread or plain dental floss (unused, please!) under the sausage, cross the ends over the top and pull in opposite directions to neatly garrotte the dough.
9. Place the buns in the lined tin, 3 x 3. Make sure the outer 'tails' of each bun face inwards so when they expand they are anchored by their neighbour and don't unravel. Lightly squash each bun to flatten slightly.
10. Bake straight away in the middle of the oven for 18 minutes or until puffed and golden.
11. Into a medium bowl, add the icing sugar, vanilla and a spoonful of the cream cheese, then mix to a smooth paste. Fold in the remaining cream cheese, being careful not to overwork it and turn it runny.
12. As soon as the buns are out of the oven, swirl the cream cheese topping over each roll. Leave them in their tray for 10 minutes to re-absorb the sweet cinnamon butter in the bottom of the tray.
13. Eat as soon as you like, although these do last really well for a few days when stored in an airtight container.

CINNAMON ROFFLES

Hands on **15 minutes**
Ready in **20 minutes**

SERVES 4

EQUIPMENT
Waffle maker

DOUGH

50g (1¾oz) plain (all-purpose) flour

50g (1¾oz) strong white bread flour

1 tsp baking powder

Pinch of salt

80g (2¾oz) full-fat yogurt (dairy or plant-based)

20g (¾oz) sunflower oil or any flavourless oil

FILLING

25g (¾oz) granulated sugar

1 tsp ground cinnamon

65g (2⅓oz) salted butter (dairy or plant-based), very soft

TOPPING

15g (½oz) icing (confectioners') sugar

1 tsp vanilla extract

65g (2⅓oz) full-fat soft cheese or cream cheese (dairy or plant-based)

Cinnamon rolls in a waffle maker. That's it!

1. Heat your waffle maker.
2. Using the quantities given here, make the dough, filling and topping following the instructions for the 30-Minute Cinnamon Rolls (opposite).
3. Roll out the dough to 12 x 40cm (5 x 16 inches) and add the filling. Roll up from the short edge so you have a 12-cm (5-inch) cylinder. Cut into four rolls. If your waffle maker isn't very non-stick, oil it before pressing a roll into it and cooking for 2 minutes or until puffy and golden. Spread each roffle with some topping once they're cooked and eat while warm.

CINNAMON (SWISS) ROLL

Hands on **30 minutes**
Ready in **1 hour 10 minutes**

MAKES
One 20-cm (8-inch) long Swiss roll (jelly roll)

EQUIPMENT
One 25 x 33-cm (10 x 13-inch) Swiss roll (jelly roll) tin (pan)

Flat baking sheet

This is sort of a cinnamon roll having a lie down, in cake form. It's a light and fluffy Swiss / jelly roll-style sponge rolled with melting cinnamon butter and finished with the requisite vanilla-infused, mildly sweet cream cheese topping. And as this is genuinely a sponge cake – which pastry pedants like to point out is not just another word for cake – it's one made solely without any fat added to the batter. Anyone really bothered by such distinctions probably just needs a lie down then a slice of lying down cake. That'll bring them round.

CINNAMON BUTTER

75g (2⅔ oz) salted butter

25g (¾ oz) granulated sugar

3 tsp ground cinnamon

CINNAMON SUGAR

20g (¾ oz) granulated sugar

1 tsp ground cinnamon

CAKE

75g (2⅔ oz) plain (all-purpose) flour or gluten-free flour + ¼ tsp xanthan gum

1¼ tsp baking powder

65g (2⅓ oz) granulated sugar

3 large (US extra-large) eggs

Pinch of salt

1 tsp vanilla extract

TOPPING

35g (1¼ oz) icing (confectioners') sugar

2 tsp vanilla extract

150g (5¼ oz) full-fat soft cheese or cream cheese

1. Set the oven to 175°C fan (375°F/gas 5) and line the Swiss roll tin with baking paper.
2. To a medium bowl, add the cinnamon butter ingredients and mix to a smooth spread. The butter should be really soft so the mix has the overall consistency of yogurt.
3. To a small bowl, add the sugar and cinnamon and mix.
4. In a separate small bowl, combine the flour and baking powder (and xanthan gum, if using gluten-free flour).
5. To a stand mixer or large bowl, add the sugar, eggs, salt and vanilla and beat until pale, thick and mousse-like. In a stand mixer this will take 2–3 minutes, although a hand mixer will probably take slightly longer.
6. Add one-third of the flour / baking powder to the eggs at a time, folding in after each addition, being careful not to knock out too much air. Stop mixing as soon as you are confident there are no dry patches of unmixed flour. Pour the batter into the lined Swiss roll tin and gently level the top.
7. Bake in the middle of the oven for 9–10 minutes, until the cake has risen, the top is evenly golden and a metal skewer comes out clean.
8. While the cake is baking, cut a sheet of baking paper just larger than the Swiss roll tin.
9. As soon as the cake is out of the oven, leave it in the Swiss roll tin and sprinkle the cinnamon sugar over the surface of the cake, reserving a teaspoon for the final decoration. Cover the cake with the baking paper followed by the flat baking sheet, hold the two trays together (with gloved hands or a dish towel) and flip everything upside down so the cake is now lying on the flat baking sheet.
10. Check the cinnamon butter is still very soft and spreadable; if it has cooled and firmed up, warm it to soften. Lift the Swiss roll tin off the cake and carefully peel away the baking paper – the warm cake will be fragile, so take great care. Working swiftly so the cake doesn't cool too much, spread the cinnamon butter over its surface so it melts in – go right to the edges and use up all the butter.

11. As soon as you have spread the butter over the sponge, roll the cake while it's still warm. Pick up the baking paper underneath the short edge and use it to roll the cake into a neat spiral. The cake needs to be tightly rolled so it holds together, but you don't want to squash the light, airy structure of the cake. Be firm but fair. Wrap the baking paper around the finished roll and leave it to cool completely on the baking sheet (a wire rack will mark the cake with ridges).
12. Make the topping. To a medium bowl, add the icing sugar and vanilla, mix to a smooth paste then fold in the cream cheese.
13. When the cake is completely cool, unwrap it and sit it on your serving plate. Using a very sharp knife, trim the ends of the roll to neaten it up. You don't have to do this, but it does mean you get to eat the offcuts. Saddle the top of the roll with the cream cheese topping, then sprinkle over a little of the reserved cinnamon sugar.

YEASTED CINNAMON ROLLS

Hands on **40 minutes**
Ready in **3 hours**

MAKES
12 rolls

EQUIPMENT
20 x 30-cm (8 x 12-inch) brownie tin (pan)

These cinnamon rolls use a standard dough rather than an enriched one. They don't need it because all their richness comes from their fillings and toppings. With options for both, they offer an embarrassment of riches *and* the luxury of choice. The first option uses cream cheese in the filling rather than the topping; the second takes the more traditional cinnamon butter route. Either can then be topped with a biscuity crumble or a classic cream cheese frosting. Think of them as haute couture cinnamon rolls, tailored to your whims and fancies (within reason).

DOUGH

210g (7½ oz) warm water (no warmer than 35°C/95°F)

1½ tsp fast-action dried yeast

20g (¾ oz) granulated sugar

330g (11⅔ oz) strong white bread flour

½ tsp salt

2 tsp vanilla extract

30g (1 oz) sunflower oil or any other flavourless oil

1 tsp flavourless oil, if using the pull-and-fold kneading method

FILLING OPTION 1 (CREAM CHEESE)

120g (4¼ oz) granulated sugar

20g (¾ oz) strong white bread flour

3 tsp ground cinnamon

75g (2⅔ oz) salted butter, softened

2 tsp vanilla extract

200g (7 oz) full-fat cream cheese

FILLING OPTION 2 (CINNAMON BUTTER)

150g (5¼ oz) salted butter, softened

115g (4 oz) granulated sugar

2½ tsp ground cinnamon

1. Line the brownie tin with baking paper.
2. Make the dough. To a large bowl, add the water, yeast and sugar, then swirl the bowl a few times to encourage everything to start dissolving. Add the flour, salt, vanilla and oil, mix to a ragged dough with a table knife and then use your hands to pull it together into a ball. If using the pull-and-fold kneading method, pour 1 teaspoon of the oil into the bowl, roll the dough around in it, then follow the instructions on page 212. Alternatively, knead the dough by hand for 12 minutes on an oiled work surface. Or use a dough hook in a stand mixer for 10 minutes until the dough is smooth and elastic.
3. Cover the dough bowl with a shower cap or cling film (plastic wrap) and leave to proof until doubled in size.
4. While the dough proofs, make the filling. For the Cream Cheese Filling, to a medium bowl add the sugar, flour and cinnamon and mix. Add the butter and vanilla and mix in, then gently work the cream cheese in until there are no lumps. For the Cinnamon Butter Filling, to a small bowl, add the butter, sugar and cinnamon, then mix to an even, spreadable paste. Set aside at room temperature until needed.

CREAM CHEESE FILLING

CINNAMON BUTTER FILLING

BISCUIT CRUMBLE TOPPING

CREAM CHEESE TOPPING

TOPPING OPTION 1 (BISCUIT CRUMBLE)

75g (2⅔ oz) strong white bread flour

60g (2 oz) light brown soft sugar

1 tsp ground cinnamon

½ tsp vanilla extract

60g (2 oz) salted butter, softened

TOPPING OPTION 2 (CREAM CHEESE)

50g (1¾ oz) icing (confectioners') sugar

2 tsp vanilla extract

200g (7 oz) full-fat soft cheese or cream cheese (dairy or plant-based)

5. Make the topping. For the Biscuit Crumble Topping, to a medium bowl, add the flour, sugar and cinnamon and mix, then the vanilla and butter in chunks. Work the butter into the flour with the back of a spoon then swap to your fingertips, rubbing the mix together to make small crumbly clumps. For the Cream Cheese Topping, to a medium bowl, add the icing sugar, vanilla and a spoonful of cream cheese. Mix to a smooth paste then fold in the remaining cream cheese. Keep refrigerated until needed.
6. When the dough has proofed, tip onto a lightly floured work surface, pat into a vague oblong with the long side running left to right, and roll to 40 x 30cm (16 x 12 inches). If the dough is very elastic and shrinks back as you're rolling, leave it to rest for 2 minutes before rolling again.
7. Leaving a 1-cm (⅓-inch) border along the far long edge, cover the rest of the rolled-out dough with your filling of choice. Wet the filling-free border with water then roll the dough up from the near long side into a 40-cm (16-inch) long cylinder. Gently press the wet end of the dough into the roll to seal the join. Mark the cylinder into 12 equal pieces, then cut into 12 rolls with a thread or sharp knife. Arrange them 3 x 4 in the brownie tin. Cover the top with oiled baking paper or cling film (plastic wrap) and leave to proof.
8. Set the oven to 185°C (400°F/gas 6).
9. When the rolls are proofed (see the pull-and-fold kneading method on page 212 for how to tell), scatter the crumble topping over the top, if using.
10. Bake on the second rung down in the oven for 25 minutes, or until the buns have puffed and the surface of the dough or the crumble topping is evenly golden brown. If you have a digital probe thermometer, the internal temperature should be at least 90°C (195°F).
11. Leave to cool for at least 20 minutes before topping with cream cheese frosting, if using, and eating.

FLAKY CINNAMON MORNING ROLLS

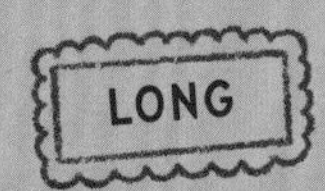

Hands on **1 hour**
Ready in **4 hours 30 minutes**
or up to 27 hours

MAKES
12 rolls

EQUIPMENT
12-cup muffin tin (pan)

You're forbidden from dolloping any topping on these rolls. That's my final word. The cinnamon butter I sweated over while devising this recipe – to get layers of flaky, golden, butter-laminated dough with a pillowy, cinnamon swirled middle – and the time and effort you'll put into achieving the same, doesn't deserve to be hidden by a dollop (a dollop?!) of anything. Their sugary, shattery, laminated leaves deserve to be seen and are worthy of a plinth in the National Gallery, works of art that they are.

DOUGH

180g (6⅓ oz) very cold salted butter (dairy or plant-based), for laminating

145g (5oz) water

2½ tsp fast-action dried yeast

35g (1¼ oz) granulated sugar

240g (8½ oz) plain (all-purpose) flour

120g (4¼ oz) strong white bread flour

¼ tsp salt

25g (¾ oz) sunflower oil or any other flavourless oil

1 tsp vanilla extract

FILLING

125g (4½ oz) granulated sugar

5 tsp ground cinnamon

75g (2⅔ oz) salted butter (dairy or plant-based), melted

1. Weigh out the butter for laminating and put it in the freezer until it's needed, to keep it really cold.
2. To a large bowl, add the water, yeast and sugar, then swirl the bowl a few times to encourage everything to start dissolving. Add the flours, salt, oil and vanilla, mix to a ragged dough with a table knife then use your hands to pull it together into a clump.
3. Tip out the dough onto the work surface and knead for just 1 minute to make a stiff ball of dough – you won't need any extra flour. It will look a bit dimpled but it should be pliable and not crack easily. Form into a thick sausage, about 20cm (8 inches) long, wrap in baking paper, cling film (plastic wrap) or an old cereal bag and leave to rest for 10 minutes.
4. To a medium bowl, add the sugar, cinnamon and melted butter and mix together. Set aside for later.
5. Flour the work surface, then roll out the dough to a 20 x 30-cm (8 x 12-inch) oblong, orientated in portrait (short side running from your left to your right).

Continued overleaf

6. Coarsely grate all the cold laminating butter over the top two-thirds of the dough, fold the unbuttered bottom one-third up over one-third of the butter, then fold up again to cover the top one-third of butter. This is known as a letter fold, which seems charmingly old fashioned, but I suppose you can't fold an email.
7. Re-wrap the slab of dough in the baking paper, cling film (plastic wrap) or old cereal bag as before, then mark it as 'FOLD 1' and put it in the freezer for 12 minutes. (A dry wipe marker is extremely useful for marking and re-marking the fold numbers.)
8. Place the dough on the floured work surface, orientated in portrait. Roll out to a 20 x 40-cm (8 x 16-inch) oblong. This time do a book fold (see Rough Puff Pastry on page 207). Fold the bottom one-quarter up to the centre and the top one-quarter down to the centre, then fold the top half down so your slab of dough has four layers. Re-wrap the dough, mark it as 'FOLD 2' and put it in the freezer for 12 minutes.
9. Repeat the last step, marking the dough as 'FOLD 3'. Put in the freezer for 12 minutes.
10. Place the dough on the floured work surface, this time orientated with the long side running from left to right, and roll out to 28 x 35cm (11 x 14 inches). It can be hard work rolling out the cold, stiff dough, but a long rolling pin (one longer than the dough is wide) will make things slightly easier. If the cinnamon sugar butter has cooled and set, warm it slightly so it is easily spreadable and use it to cover the rolled-out dough but leave a 1-cm (1⁄3-inch) border free from filling along the edge of the far long side. Wet the filling-free border then roll up the dough from the near long side so you have a 35-cm (14-inch) long cylinder. Gently press the wet end of the dough into the roll to seal the join. Tightly double wrap the cylinder in cling film (plastic wrap) and put it in the fridge.

NOTE ON TIMINGS

If you want to have these rolls ready as soon as possible, chill the dough in the fridge for 1 hour 30 minutes and then follow the instructions from step 11 onwards. If you want to have these rolls ready for the next morning, make the dough the day before and chill the tightly wrapped dough in the fridge for up to 24 hours and then follow the instructions from step 11 onwards. For the best, most reliable results don't leave the dough in the fridge for longer than 24 hours.

11. While the dough is chilling, cut twelve 12-cm (5-inch) squares of baking paper and press them over the base of a small glass to form a muffin case. (Store-bought muffin cases are rarely non-stick and will tear the finished roll.)
12. After the dough cylinder has chilled, mark it into 12 equal pieces and use a sharp knife to cut into 12 rolls.
13. Put each roll in a homemade muffin case and sit in the muffin tin. Lay a large piece of oiled cling film (plastic wrap) over the rolls and leave on the side for 2 hours to come up to at least 18°C (65°F), but don't let them get warmer than 20°C (68°F). The dough will expand and puff very slightly in the muffin cups.
14. Set the oven to 190°C fan (400°F/gas 6).
15. Sprinkle a little pinch of sugar over the top of each roll and bake on the second rung down in the oven for 18 minutes. Look for the rolls puffing, colouring a deep golden brown and the flaky layers emerging from the laminating process.
16. Lift the rolls out with their cases and leave them to cool for 10 minutes before eating. These keep well when stored in an airtight container for up to 2 days, or you can freeze any you don't eat, thaw and then warm briefly in the oven when you want one.

COCONUT MACAROONS

In this chapter I've taken everything I consider to constitute a coconut macaroon – golden toasted coconut, a sweet, chewy, moist middle, a touch of chocolate and a cherry on top – and not made a traditional coconut macaroon. To make matters worse, I have made a coconut macaron – the macaroon's finer, fancier, Frenchier cousin – because what's an errant 'o' between family. I've eaten many a coconut macaroon and I'm sad to say they haven't always been moist, so to avoid any potential for similar disappointment, I'm offering up a no-bake version. And is it moist? Well, if it threw a party, it would definitely be the hoistess with the moistest. In other iterations, coconut and chocolate go chewyly and fudgyly together as a plant-based blondie, and the aforementioned macaron, filled with milk chocolate ganache, is oh-so chic until you plonk a glacé cherry on top. Apologies if you've been put off by the use, indeed overuse, of the word 'moist' in this section, but these bakes really are m... Would you prefer 'succ-u-lent'? No, I thought not.

NO-BAKE COCONUT MACAROONS

Hands on **10 minutes**
Ready in **45 minutes**

MAKES
8–12 squares

EQUIPMENT
1-kg (2-lb) loaf tin (pan)

I'm calling these little squares of moist coconut heaven macaroons because, despite not being baked, they have all the sweet, chewy, golden, toasted nuttiness you'd demand of them. The desiccated coconut is toasted in a frying pan (skillet) and then it's simply a case of stirring in condensed milk, the heat helping it fully and deliciously absorb into the nutty shreds. Then finally, after a brief chill, spread on a dark (bittersweet) chocolate base and the cherry on top is... literally, a cherry on top.

200g (7 oz) unsweetened desiccated coconut

280g (10 oz) sweetened condensed milk

Pinch of salt

3 tbsp boiling water

70g (2½ oz) dark (bittersweet) chocolate (70% cocoa)

6 glacé cherries

1. Line the loaf tin with baking paper.
2. To a dry frying pan (skillet), add the coconut and put on a medium-low heat. Stir the coconut around the pan so it heats evenly for a few minutes.
3. As soon as the coconut starts to smell lightly toasty and just starts to turn very slightly golden, switch the heat off and pour over the condensed milk. Add the salt and boiling water and stir everything together. The coconut will quickly absorb the condensed milk and water in the residual heat. Keep stirring it in the pan until the mixture is damp and sticky rather than wet.
4. Tip the mix into the lined tin and press it down firmly with the back of a spoon, smoothing and levelling the top.
5. Break the chocolate into a microwave-safe bowl, then microwave in short bursts to melt. If you don't have a microwave, put the chocolate in a heatproof bowl set over a pan of hot water to melt. Spread the melted chocolate over the top of the warm coconut, then put the tin in the freezer for 30–40 minutes.
6. When the slab has chilled and firmed, lift it out of the loaf tin with the paper. Turn the slab over so the chocolate is on the base and cut into squares. Depending on the width of your loaf tin and how small you want the pieces, cut into 8 (2 x 4) or 12 (3 x 4). Cut each glacé cherry in two and sit a half on each square of coconut macaroon.

COCONUT BLONDIES

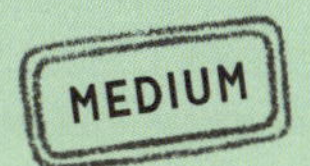

Hands on **25 minutes**
Ready in **1 hour 30 minutes**

MAKES
16 squares

EQUIPMENT
20 x 30-cm (8 x 12-inch) brownie tin (pan)

These plant-based, light-but-chewy blondies are so quick and easy you can have a batch in the oven in about the same time it takes to say 'damn, I've run out of butter and eggs'.* The creamed coconut block specified is finely milled coconut pressed into a solid slab and it gives this blondie most of its rich coconut flavour, as well as being a butter substitute. It's essential not only for the bake's taste but its structure, so don't be tempted to swap it for a can or carton of coconut cream.

***Ok, you'd have to be speaking really quite slowly.**

60g (2 oz) desiccated coconut

150g (5¼ oz) creamed coconut block

280g (10 oz) granulated sugar

160g (5⅔ oz) aquafaba – from a can of chickpeas (garbanzo beans), cannellini (white) beans or butter (lima) beans

½ tsp salt

100g (3½ oz) plain (all-purpose) flour or 220g (7¾ oz) gluten-free self-raising mix

½ tsp baking powder (omit if using gluten-free flour)

70g (2½ oz) dark (bittersweet) or milk chocolate, chopped into small chunks (optional)

1. Set the oven to 175°C fan (375°F/gas 5) and line the brownie tin with baking paper.
2. To a dry frying pan (skillet), add the desiccated coconut and put on a medium-low heat to toast until golden. Switch off the heat and add the creamed coconut block straight away and stir in to stop the desiccated coconut toasting further. When the coconut block has completely melted and blended with the desiccated coconut, scrape into a bowl to cool.
3. To a stand mixer or large bowl, add the sugar, aquafaba and salt, then beat on high with a whisk attachment until foamy and mousse-like. This may take up to 5 minutes depending on the power of your mixer. The aquafaba doesn't have to hold any meringue-like peaks, just be thick and airy.
4. Add the coconut mixture to the aquafaba, sliding it down the side of the bowl to avoid deflating the mix. Add the flour and baking powder, then fold the three components together.
5. Scrape the batter into the brownie tin and level, then scatter over the chocolate chunks. Bake in the middle of the oven for 30 minutes or until the surface looks set, not wet, and is lightly golden.
6. Leave the blondies in the tin to cool completely, then remove and cut into 16 squares.

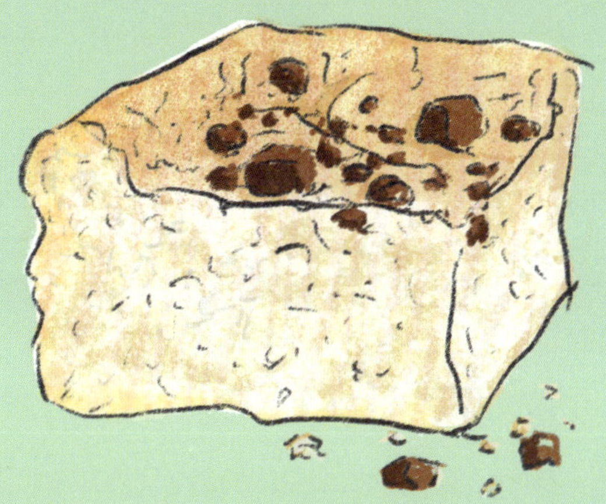

COCONUT MACARONS

Hands on **45 minutes**
Ready in **1 hour 55 minutes**
(although it might feel like 7 hours 45 minutes)

MAKES
10–12 macarons
(20–24 halves)

EQUIPMENT
Two flat baking sheets

To say I'm conflicted about making macarons is an understatement. Years ago, I wanted to have a go, but that go didn't go well. I'm not one to be defeated, particularly by a tiny biscuit, so I tried again. And again and again and again. For six months, my obsessional determination to conquer macaron making occupied a murky no-man's land between a keen interest in baking and something I should get help for. That I finally emerged being able to make a decent macaron isn't something I'm particularly proud of. The cost was high: I lost friends, I neglected my family, I wore out two balloon whisk attachments. Considering I only quite like macarons, was it worth it? All things considered, yes, if only so I can pass what I learned on to others tempted to take that precipitous path.

MACARONS

40g (1⅓ oz) sifted ground almonds (almond meal) – start with more as some will be discarded

60g (2 oz) icing (confectioners') sugar

1 large (US extra-large) egg white

Pinch of salt

25g (¾ oz) granulated or caster (superfine) sugar

¼ tsp vanilla extract

15g (½ oz) desiccated coconut

6 glacé cherries

GANACHE

60g (2 oz) double (heavy) cream

90g (3¼ oz) milk chocolate

This recipe uses French meringue. Perfect for a first-timer, it's quicker, simpler and removes the unnecessary pitfall of making an Italian meringue. When macarons fail, it's heart-breaking enough to have wasted time and ingredients without also subjecting yourself to the hoopla of precisely heating sugar. Some people swear by Italian meringue-based macaron recipes; I've never had any success with them, I can only swear *at* them.

While I find egg whites from a carton perfect for other meringue demands, I don't recommend them for macarons. In my experience, you are far more likely to suffer surface cracks. Using an egg white from an egg you've just cracked (ironically) gives a better chance of a pristine dome.

There's no point in being too uptight about this one, but if you're struggling to make good macarons, bear this point in mind: don't use very fresh eggs if you can help it. I'm not recommending rancid, rotten eggs, just ones that you bought one or two weeks ago. Older egg whites are less elastic, which means they 'relax' more easily when you're at the crucial folding stage, so you're less likely to overwork the batter. If you only have really fresh egg whites, you can 'age' them quickly, no, not by making them watch *The Human Centipede*. Put your egg white in a loosely covered, not airtight container in the fridge for 24 hours (up to 72 hours) and it will become runnier and less gloopy. Just make sure you leave the egg white to come up to room temperature before you use it.

Good luck and remember, I didn't make you do any of this.

Continued overleaf

1. Line the baking sheets with baking paper.
2. Fit a piping (pastry) bag with a 1-cm (⅓-inch) nozzle and clamp a small bag clip just above the nozzle to hold it closed. Sit the bag, nozzle down, in a pint glass or large mug and fold the top of the bag down the outside of the glass or mug, leaving a wide opening to make filling easier later.
3. Sit a medium bowl on your kitchen scales and sift the ground almonds into it until you have 40g (1⅓oz). (Save the larger pieces of almond left in the sieve for other baking.) Sift the icing sugar over the ground almonds and mix together.
4. To a large bowl, add the egg white and salt, then beat with a whisk attachment until the foam holds very soft peaks.
5. Add the sugar, ½ tablespoon at a time, beating after each addition until the egg white is glossy and holding stiff peaks. Beat a little longer if it isn't.
6. Add the vanilla and sifted almonds / icing sugar to the egg whites. Using a spatula, and as few folds as possible, evenly combine the dry ingredients into the egg. You're now at a critical stage of macaron making. At this point, you need to fold the mix so it slackens enough to form smooth domes when piped; however, if you over-mix, the macarons will crack in the oven.
7. Test the slackness of the mix by blobbing a teaspoon mound of it onto a plate and watching how long it takes to flatten slightly and lose any peaks. It's ready to use when it does this within 10 seconds of being blobbed onto a plate. The mixture will loosen with every fold of the spatula so go cautiously; it will take a few folds and test blobs to get the right consistency. If the blob runs, it's too loose and I'm afraid this batch has got away from you. Go back to the start, do not pass 'go', do not collect £200.
8. Carefully scrape the mix into your prepared piping bag. Do this delicately as over-handling the mix will make it looser than you need. Pipe directly down onto the lined baking sheet and don't lift the bag until the circle of batter is 3.5cm (1⅓ inches) in diameter. Space the macarons at least 2cm (¾ inch) apart.
9. When you have piped all the batter, hold the sheet 20cm (8 inches) above the work surface and drop it down flat three or four times. The impact will free any large air bubbles trapped in the macarons and you'll see small craters emerge and disappear as they work their way to the surface.
10. Sprinkle a pinch of desiccated coconut over each macaron so the surface is lightly covered. Leave them on the side for 30–60 minutes so the surface dries slightly and the distinctive frilly 'foot' will form in the oven. If you can, leave them in a breeze by an open window, but not in a wind so high it blows them off the baking sheet.*

*This absolutely happened to me.

11. Set the oven to 140°C fan (320°F/gas 2½).
12. Bake in the middle of the oven for 12–15 minutes. This is where it helps to know your oven: 14 minutes at 140°C fan is perfect in my current oven; however, in others I've owned they've taken up to 18 minutes. Look for the macarons rising slowly and developing the frilly foot, but don't let the domes darken in colour. They need to be baked long enough that their bases don't stick to the baking paper but you don't want to brown the tops. Try baking at a lower temperature if you find this is happening. It'll probably take some trial and error to get the timing and temperature perfect for your oven. With this coconut sprinkled version, don't worry if the desiccated coconut goes slightly golden so long as the surface of the macaron stays pale.
13. While the macarons bake, make the ganache. Add the cream and chocolate to a microwave-safe bowl and microwave in short bursts to gently melt the chocolate. If you don't have a microwave, sit the bowl over a pan of hot water. Mix the melted chocolate with the cream until fully blended. Leave the ganache to cool to a soft, pipable consistency, then scrape into a piping bag fitted with a 1.5-cm (½-inch) nozzle.
14. Remove the baking sheet from the oven and slide the macarons, on their paper, onto a wire rack to cool. Don't attempt to lift them until they're fully cooled or you risk leaving the bottoms stuck to the paper.
15. Carefully peel the macarons off the paper and pair them into matching sizes. Pipe a blob of ganache (approximately 10g/⅓oz) on one macaron and then top with its matching partner. Decorate the top of each paired macaron with half a glacé cherry.
16. Eat, enjoy and then decide if it was all worth it.

LEAVE TO DRY IN A GENTLE BREEZE

GINGERBREAD MEN

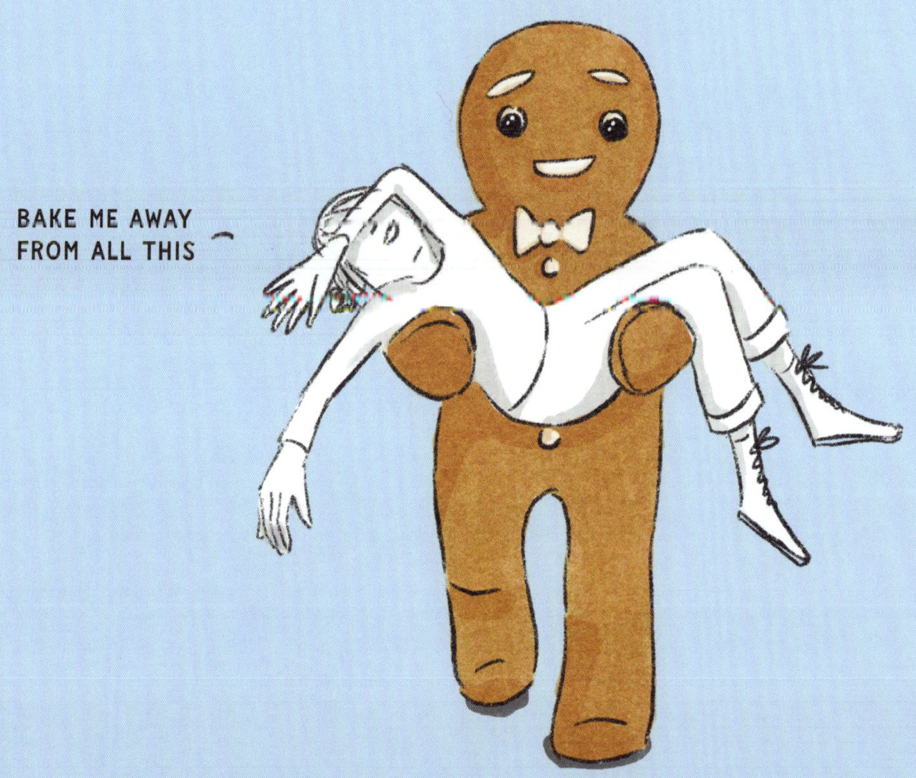
BAKE ME AWAY
FROM ALL THIS

Snappy and spicy, not 100% what I'm looking for in a dating profile, but exactly what I want in a gingerbread man biscuit. With other gingerbread men in this chapter, you get less of a snap and more of a crunch in their toast and choux versions. But then there's absolutely no snap or crunch for my literal ginger bread, just the softly chewy resistance of an enriched ginger-flavoured dough in the form of a sticky finger bun (gingerbread men are notorious for their sticky fingers). As far as flavour goes, tradition has been stuck with and ginger is represented throughout as either ground spice or syrup-soaked, candied stem. Of course, you can add whatever flavour you prefer, or indeed call them any name you prefer. I stuck with Gingerbread Men, not to assume their gender, even though they do look like they're not keen on asking directions, but because Gingerbread People is too much of a mouthful for me. I love words, but I'd rather my mouth was full of biscuit not syllables.

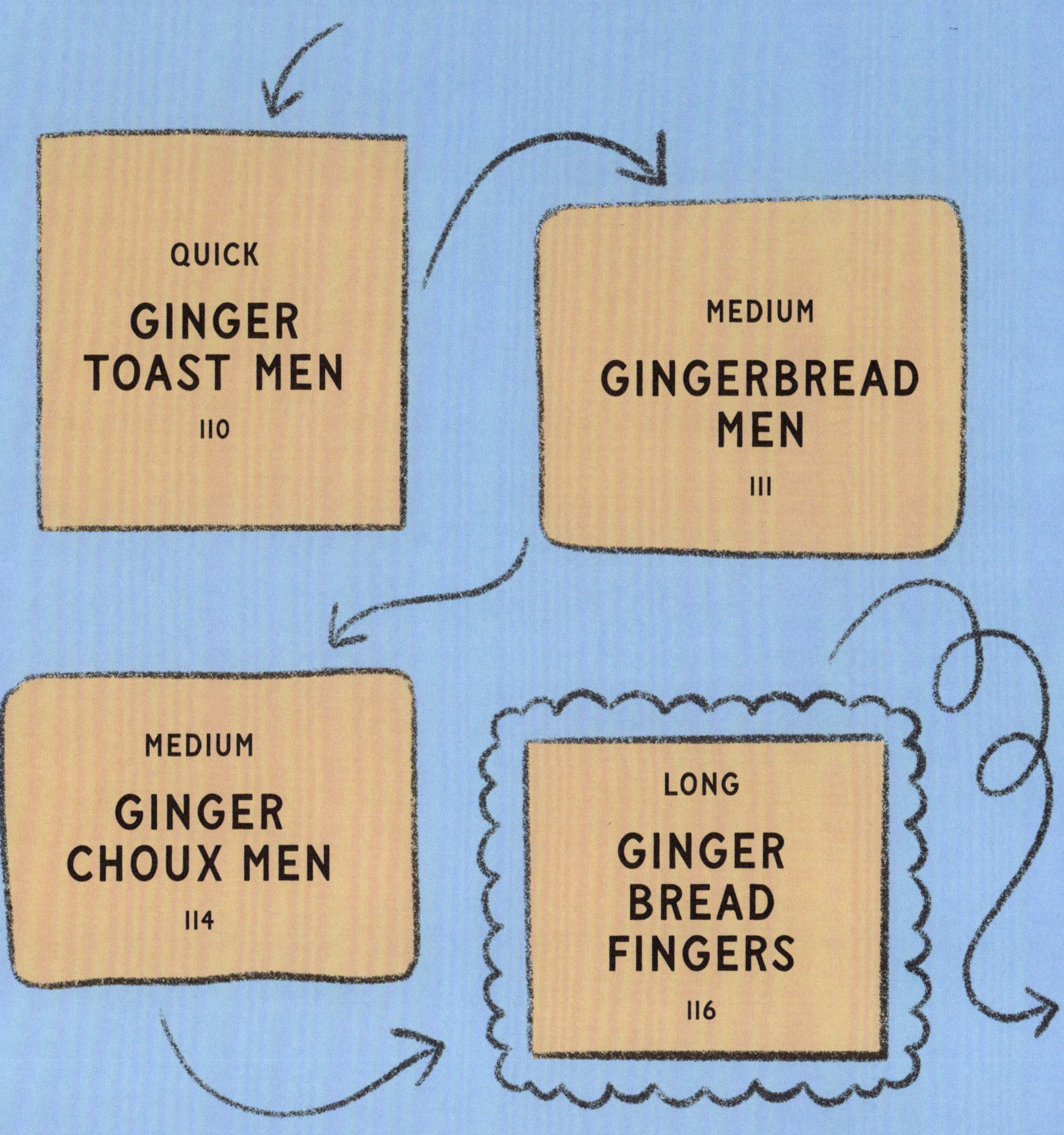

GINGER TOAST MEN

Hands on **15 minutes**
Ready in **30 minutes**

SERVES 4

EQUIPMENT

Flat baking sheet

Gingerbread man cookie cutter

Cut gingerbread men out of brown bread, spread with sweet ginger butter, bake briefly and decorate with icing faces and sweet buttons. These guys are the fast track to the fun bit of gingerbread men: the decorating and the head biting. If you're fond of biting someone's head off, particularly in the morning, these can be repurposed into a relatively wholesome breakfast. I don't want to sound preachy – eat sweets for breakfast, if you like – but if you swap the icing for cream cheese and the sweets for raisins or cereal shapes then you'll risk less of a sugar crash by 9am.

4 large slices of brown bread

GINGER BUTTER

30g (1 oz) dark brown soft sugar

1 tsp ground ginger

1 tsp vanilla extract

50g (1¾ oz) salted butter, softened

WATER ICING

75g (2⅔ oz) icing (confectioners') sugar

1–1½ tsp lemon juice or water

TO DECORATE

Sweets of your choice

1. Set the oven to 165°C fan (350°F/gas 4) and line the baking sheet with baking paper.
2. Make the ginger butter. Add the sugar and ginger to a small bowl and mix together. Add the vanilla and butter and mix to a smooth paste.
3. Spread the spiced butter over each side of the bread, concentrating on the area that will be pressed out with the cutter. Cut the gingerbread men shapes out of the bread. (You can always bake and eat the offcuts too to avoid food waste. It's not greed, it's activism.)
4. Put the shapes on a lined baking sheet and bake in the middle of the oven for 12 minutes or until a rich toasted brown. Turn them over halfway through to brown and crisp on the other side. Leave them to cool completely.
5. To decorate, mix the icing sugar with just enough lemon juice or water to make a thick but pipable consistency. Scrape the icing into a piping (pastry) bag fitted with a 1 mm (1/16 inch) nozzle or use a disposable bag and snip off a tiny end. Pipe faces onto the men and glue on sweets for buttons, or whatever extra decoration you fancy.

GINGERBREAD MEN

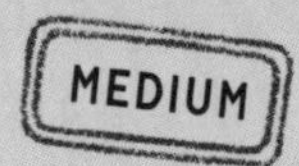

Hands on **40 minutes**
Ready in **1 hour 30 minutes**
(including decoration)

MAKES
Approximately 20 x 12-cm (5-inch) gingerbread men

EQUIPMENT
Two flat baking sheets

Gingerbread man cookie cutter

110g (3¾ oz) salted butter (dairy or plant-based)

110g (3¾ oz) granulated or caster (superfine) sugar (caster will dissolve faster)

110g (3¾ oz) golden syrup

275g (9¾ oz) plain (all-purpose) flour or gluten-free self-raising mix

¾ tsp bicarbonate of soda (baking soda), omit if using gluten-free flour

2 tsp ground ginger (or your spice of choice or citrus zest)

This foolproof gingerbread recipe, robust but still light and snappy, is perfect for gingerbread men but also great for cutting any biscuit shapes. It can also be easily veganised with plant-based butter, and the dough works brilliantly with gluten-free flour. I'll stop singing its praises now in case it sounds like I've got a thing for it.

1. To a heavy-bottomed pan, add the butter, sugar and golden syrup, put on a low heat and keep stirring while the sugar dissolves. Don't let the mixture boil; you don't want to evaporate any of the water from the butter, which is needed to make the dough pliable. When the sugar granules have almost all dissolved, remove from the heat and leave to cool a little while you weigh the dry ingredients.
2. Add the flour, bicarbonate of soda (if using wheat flour) and ground ginger (or other spice or grated zest) to a large bowl and mix well.
3. Pour the ingredients from the pan over the dry ingredients and stir together with a ridged spatula to form a soft ball of dough.
4. Tip the dough onto a sheet of baking paper, flatten it into a rectangle approximately 2cm (¾ inch) thick, cover with another sheet of paper and chill in the freezer for 15 minutes. The dough needs to cool to a firm, workable consistency but don't let it chill solid. It's best very slightly warm, between 20–25°C (70–77°F), when it will be easy to roll and still slightly pliable.
5. Set the oven to 150°C fan (325°F/gas 3).

STANDARD GINGERBREAD MEN AND SHAPES

6. Roll half the dough, for a manageable portion, between the two sheets of baking paper to 3–4mm (⅛ inch) thick, press out the shapes you want and peel away the excess. Lift the shapes with a fish slice and arrange them on lined baking sheets with plenty of space around them to spread. Lay the offcuts over each other in a pile, rather than squishing them together in a lump, cover with baking paper, re-roll and re-cut them. Repeat with the remaining half of the dough. Skip to step 8 for how to bake.

Continued overleaf

POSABLE GINGERBREAD MEN

7. To make gingerbread men in poses (as pictured) you need to use the dough when it's slightly warmer than for standard shapes, so it's extra pliable. This does make them harder to handle but much more fun to play with. After chilling for nearer 10 minutes, roll the dough as for standard shapes (step 6). Press out gingerbread men with a large cutter and lift the shapes onto the baking trays; as the dough is so soft it may stretch or tear, but you can patch it back together. Use a table knife to carefully nudge or lift the limbs and arrange them into the poses you want. You can stretch limbs by gently pulling and pressing the dough with your fingers. You can fold arms by crossing them over each other. You can add small pieces of dough to alter the shapes and silhouettes. If the dough cools and stiffens before you have finished shaping it, you can use a hair dryer to blow over some warm air to loosen it up. When you're happy with the shapes, bake as step 8.
8. Bake in the middle of the oven for 10–12 minutes or until they're just turning a light amber/ginger colour. Because of their high sugar content, they can burn easily. If they're colouring too much too early, turn the oven down slightly and rotate the sheet halfway through baking. There's very little difference in the baking time for gingerbread men of different sizes, just keep a close watch on them and remove when they reach the correct colour.
9. Straight from the oven the shapes will be soft and pliable, so you can re-cut their original shape by re-pressing with the cutter or re-pose their limbs before they harden. Or you can just leave them to cool as they are. Slide the baked shapes, on their paper, off the baking sheet and onto the work surface, then leave to firm for 3–5 minutes before lifting onto a wire rack to cool completely.
10. Decorate when completely cool. Make a quantity of water icing (page 110), fill a piping (pastry) bag with a fine nozzle and pipe on some personality. Undecorated biscuits will stay crunchy for many days when stored in an airtight container, decorated biscuits will start to soften within 48 hours.

GINGER CHOUX MEN

Hands on **55 minutes**
Ready in **1 hour 35 minutes**

MAKES
6 x 10-cm (4-inch) tall ginger choux men

EQUIPMENT
Large flat baking sheet

Approximately 7 x 9-cm (2¾ x 3½-inch) gingerbread man cookie cutter

Gingerbread men biscuits are great, although they can be a bit one-dimensional, lacking in depth, absolutely no emotional hinterland. If you've ever found yourself yearning for a gingerbread man with a more rounded personality, try these craquelin-covered choux pastry guys. Stick a batch in the oven and watch them come to life, growing in the promethean heat like you're some sort of baking Dr Frankenstein. You will have created monstrously good choux buns, so deep you can fill them with flavoured cream and have a really good chat about feelings.

CRAQUELIN

50g (1¾ oz) plain (all-purpose) flour or 70g (2½ oz) gluten-free plain (all-purpose) flour

50g (1¾ oz) salted butter, softened

50g (1¾ oz) granulated sugar

¼ tsp ground ginger

CHOUX PASTRY

35g (1¼ oz) plain (all-purpose) flour or 20g (¾ oz) gluten-free plain (all-purpose) flour + 15g (½ oz) gluten-free self-raising flour

17g (⅔ oz) salted butter

50g (1¾ oz) boiling water

1 large (US extra-large) egg

FILLING

20g (¾ oz) stem ginger in syrup (1 ball)

65g (2⅓ oz) speculoos spread (I use Biscoff; for gluten-free, use a chocolate-nut spread of your choice)

115g (4 oz) double (heavy) cream

1. Cut a piece of baking paper to fit the baking sheet.
2. Using the cookie cutter as a template, draw a pencil outline of six gingerbread men, spaced well apart. Turn the paper over so you don't end up with pencil on the bottom of the buns, and use it to line the baking sheet. If the outlines disappear, place a piece of white paper under the baking paper while you pipe the buns, but remove it before baking.
3. Make the craquelin. To a medium bowl, add all the craquelin ingredients and mix to a dough; the butter should be soft enough to do this with a spatula. Roll the dough between sheets of baking paper to a thickness of 3mm (⅛ inch). Chill flat in the freezer while you make the choux.
4. Using the given quantities, make the choux pastry (page 208). Scrape the dough into a piping (pastry) bag with a 1-cm (⅓-inch) nozzle.
5. Pipe the choux men. Start with a blob for the head, piping directly down until the choux is 2mm (1/16 inch) inside the pencil outline. For the arms, start piping down where the hand is and then drag the nozzle towards the centre of the body, lowering it as you go until it touches the paper at the torso. Repeat for the other hand. Use the same technique for the legs, then pipe a small mound for the belly. Pipe all six choux men then get the craquelin out of the freezer.
6. Using the gingerbread man cookie cutter, cut six shapes out of the craquelin dough. Lay a craquelin man over each choux man and very gently press down – don't squish the choux out of shape. If you need to reform the craquelin, press it together, re-roll it in the baking paper, re-freeze it and re-cut it. There's no rush, the choux can sit patiently while you get this bit done.
7. Set the oven to 175°C fan (375°F/gas 5). Bake in the middle of the oven for 20 minutes then drop the temperature to 150°C fan (325°F/gas 3) for 8–10 minutes or until the craquelin is evenly golden.
8. As soon as they're baked, turn them over onto a wire rack. Using the end of a chopstick, poke holes in the back of their heads, torsos, hands and feet to let the steam out. Leave them face down to cool completely.

9. Make the filling. Into a medium bowl, finely grate the ball of ginger to a purée, add the speculoos spread and mix together. Pour in the cream and lightly whip together until just thickened. Scrape into a piping bag with a 6-mm (¼-inch) nozzle and pipe the cream filling into all the holes. It takes approximately 30g (1 oz) of speculoos cream to fill each one. You'll notice the choux men plump up before your eyes, it's very satisfying.

10. Eat straight away or make up a quantity of water icing (page 110). Scrape into a piping bag fitted with a 2-mm (1⁄16-inch) nozzle and give them bow ties, buttons and enigmatic smiles.

GINGER BREAD FINGERS

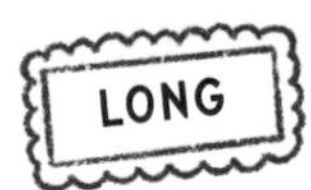

Hands on **1 hour**
Ready in **3 hours 10 minutes**

MAKES
6 finger buns (double all the ingredients to make 12)

EQUIPMENT
Baking sheet or Swiss roll tin (jelly roll pan)

A yeasted dough flavoured with ginger and dark brown sugar, rolled into finger buns, which are split and then filled with stem-ginger cream and topped with a zingy, orange water icing. Other recipes in this chapter have concerned themselves with the entirety of the gingerbread man, but here we're going to hyper-focus on his doughy digits. This recipe makes six fingers. I'm not sure whether it's polite to enquire as to what happened to the other four. Or is it two? Do gingerbread men have thumbs?

DOUGH

140g (5 oz) warm water (no warmer than 35°C/95°F)

2 tsp or 1 x 7-g (¼-oz) sachet fast-action dried yeast

50g (1¾ oz) dark brown soft sugar

250g (9 oz) strong white bread flour

2 tsp ground ginger

¼ tsp salt

50g (1¾ oz) salted butter (dairy or plant-based), melted

1 tsp flavourless oil, if using the pull-and-fold kneading method

GINGER CREAM

225g (8 oz) double (heavy) cream (dairy or whippable plant-based)

40g (1⅓ oz) stem ginger in syrup (approximately 2 balls)

15g (½ oz) syrup from stem ginger jar

ORANGE WATER ICING

100g (3½ oz) icing (confectioners') sugar

1 orange

Orange gel food colouring (optional)

1. Weigh the warm water into a large mixing bowl, add the yeast and sugar and give everything a quick mix to encourage them to start dissolving.
2. Add the flour, ginger, salt and melted butter and use a table knife to mix everything together, scraping the sides of the bowl to incorporate all the ingredients and stopping when a ball of dough has formed. This is a wet, sticky dough so I recommend using the pull-and-fold kneading method or a stand mixer. If using the pull-and-fold kneading method, pour 1 teaspoon of oil into the bowl, roll the dough around in it and then follow the instructions on page 212. For a stand mixer, use a dough hook on medium for 10 minutes or until the dough is smooth and elastic.
3. Cover the bowl with a shower cap or plastic bag and leave the dough to proof until doubled in size. This should take approximately 1 hour, but as an enriched dough it may take longer.
4. Tip the dough onto the work surface. If the dough is too sticky to handle, use a very light dusting of flour. Knock back the dough, folding it in on itself a few times, then divide into six pieces weighing approximately 83g (3 oz) each.
5. Roll each piece into a ball. Make a loose, low cage with your hand and fingers over the ball, and apply light pressure to the dough with your palm as you roll it over the work surface in a circular motion to form a neat ball. The dough should be just tacky enough that there's some purchase between your palm and the surface. If it's too sticky, use a little extra flour sparingly.
6. Once you've formed six even balls, turn each one into a 'finger' by rolling backward and forward under your palm until the dough is about 12cm (5 inches) long. They will shrink back slightly, but don't judge, maybe your kitchen is cold.
7. Arrange the fingers on a baking sheet lined with baking paper, allowing 2cm (¾ inch) between each one. Cover with an oiled piece of cling film (plastic wrap) or baking paper and leave to rise until they've puffed up and are just touching their neighbour.
8. Set the oven to 200°C fan (425°F/gas 7).

9. Bake in the middle of the oven for 14–16 minutes, or until they've puffed up and their tops have turned an even, rich amber. Rotate the tray after 10 minutes so they colour evenly. If you have a probe thermometer, the internal temperature should be at least 90°C (195°F).
10. Slide the fingers, on their paper, onto a wire rack. After 5 minutes remove the paper, carefully separate them and leave to cool for at least 30 minutes. Slice horizontally through each finger, open them out and leave to cool completely.
11. If using dairy, add the cream to a mixing bowl, finely chop or grate in the stem ginger and add to the cream with the ginger syrup. Beat until the cream has just thickened. If using plant-based whippable cream, beat the cream until thick then fold in the chopped ginger and syrup. Scrape the cream into a piping (pastry) bag fitted with a large star nozzle. If you don't want to pipe the cream, just leave it in the bowl and spoon it on when needed.
12. Add the icing sugar to a medium bowl and zest the orange into it. Squeeze the orange juice and add 4–6 teaspoons, one teaspoon at a time, mixing until you have a thick, smooth, slow-moving icing.
13. Pipe a 'rope' of ginger cream onto the bottom halves of the fingers; each one has a provision of 40g ($1\frac{1}{3}$ oz). Using a palette knife, spread the water icing over the tops of the fingers. Sandwich the tops with their matching bottoms.
14. Serve as they are or, if you have any icing left over, add a little orange food colouring, scrape into a piping bag with a 2-mm ($\frac{1}{16}$-inch) nozzle and zigzag or wobble a pattern over the white icing.

JAFFA CAKE

I haven't offered you a recipe for an actual Jaffa Cake because a Jaffa, even from the cheapest packet, is still a thing of rare beauty. Flavours and textures aside, they offer a whole funfair of ways to consume them. Although eating the sponge and chocolate first so you can dissolve the jelly circle on your tongue last is actually the best way. But enough about my hobbies. Instead of Jaffa dupes, there's everything you demand in the little cakey biscuit – or biscuity cake – but in different guises. The light vanilla sponge is present as pancakes and sheet cake. The sharp, zesty orange element appears as jelly, marmalade and curd. And chocolate declares itself present and correct by covering all bakes in varying consistencies of ganache. Now the only thing to say is... what Jaffa-ncy making first?

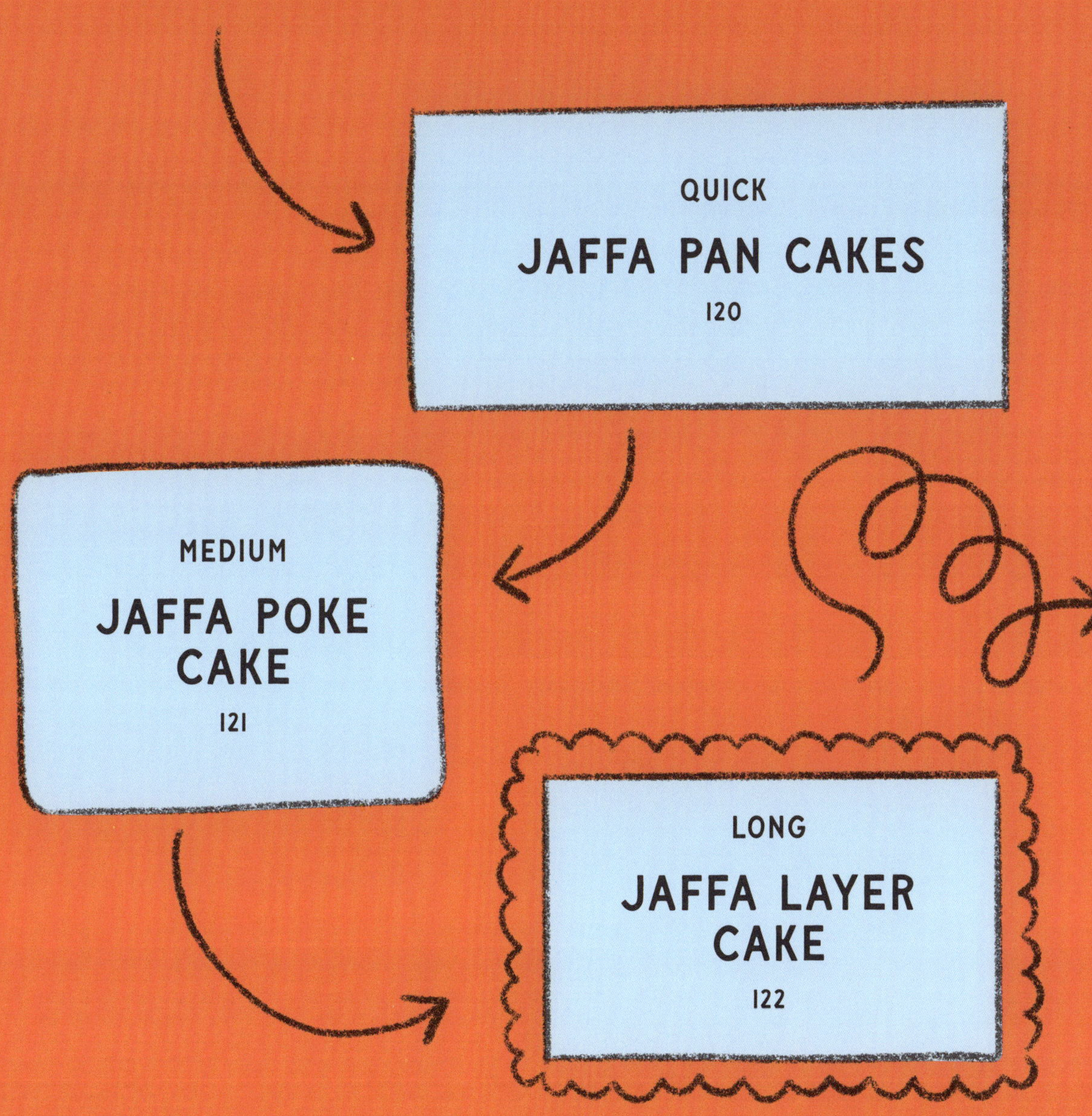

JAFFA PAN CAKES

Hands on **15 minutes**
Ready in **20 minutes**

MAKES
16 Jaffa Cake-sized pancakes

EQUIPMENT
Frying pan (skillet) with a lid

Right, no silly arguments over whether a Jaffa Cake is a cake or a biscuit – clearly this is breakfast. Fluffy little vanilla pancakes topped with your marmalade of choice and a generous dollop of ganache. If you're not sure about marmalade, think of it as an orange preserve and go for one that's light in colour. You can also sieve the shreds of peel out if that's a deal breaker, or simply buy a shredless variety. If you're still not convinced, that's ok. It just means all the more for me and Paddington.

1 tsp salted butter, for frying

DRY INGREDIENTS

80g (2¾oz) plain (all-purpose) flour or gluten-free self-raising mix

40g (1⅓oz) granulated sugar

1¼ tsp baking powder (omit if using gluten-free flour)

WET INGREDIENTS

40g (1⅓oz) salted butter, melted

40g (1⅓oz) milk

1 large (US extra-large) egg

2 tsp vanilla extract

GANACHE

100g (3½oz) milk chocolate

70g (2½oz) double (heavy) cream

150g (5¼oz) orange marmalade of your choice

1. Put a dry frying pan (skillet) on a low heat.
2. To a medium bowl, add the dry ingredients and dry whisk together.
3. To a separate medium bowl, add the wet ingredients and whisk together.
4. Add one-third of the dry ingredients to the wet and whisk well to work out any lumps. Slowly add the remaining dry ingredients in two goes, mixing as you go to make a thick, smooth batter.
5. Add ¼ teaspoon of butter to the warm pan and wipe it around with a piece of paper towel to lightly oil the base.
6. Using a teaspoon, rather than a teaspoon measure, drop teaspoons of batter into the pan, leaving 3cm (1 inch) between each one for spread. When you have 8 in the pan, put the lid on and leave for 5 minutes or until the pancakes puff up and bubbles break the surface. Carefully flip over and cook, lid off, for 1 minute or until just golden on the underside.
7. Put the first batch of pancakes on a wire rack to cool while you cook the remaining batter.
8. While the pancakes cook, prepare the ganache. Add the chocolate and cream to a microwave-safe bowl and microwave in short bursts to melt, then mix until blended. If you don't have a microwave, use a heatproof bowl over a pan of hot water.
9. Stir the marmalade to loosen it. Top each cool pancake with a teaspoon of marmalade then spoon over some ganache. Eat straight away.

JAFFA POKE CAKE

Hands on **25 minutes**
Ready in **1 hour 10 minutes**

SERVES 12–16
Makes one large traybake

EQUIPMENT
20 x 30-cm (8 x 12-inch) brownie tin (pan)

JUG (PITCHER)

2 large (US extra-large) eggs

30g (1 oz) sunflower oil or vegetable oil

30g (1 oz) / 2 tbsp water

2 tsp vanilla extract

MIXER

160g (5⅔ oz) plain (all-purpose) flour or gluten-free plain (all-purpose) flour + ½ tsp xanthan gum

120g (4 oz) granulated sugar

1½ tsp baking powder

Pinch of salt

60g (2 oz) salted butter, softened to the consistency of yogurt

30g (1 oz) sunflower oil or vegetable oil

JELLY

400g (14 oz) very good-quality orange juice

15g (½ oz) granulated sugar

1 x 6.5-g (¼-oz) sachet vegetarian jelly powder

GANACHE

150g (5¼ oz) milk chocolate

100g (3½ oz) double (heavy) cream

Light vanilla cake topped with a layer of orange jelly and finished with a glossy covering of ganache. This version of a poke cake uses vegetarian jelly because it thickens while still warm (unlike gelatine which has to be chilled), setting as a distinct layer rather than soaking in. But just because it's a vegetarian poke cake, don't get it confused with a vegetarian poke bowl. The two are at opposite ends of the nutritional spectrum.

1. Set the oven to 160°C fan (350°F/gas 4). Line the brownie tin with a single large piece of baking paper.
2. To a jug (pitcher), add the eggs, oil, water and vanilla. Roughly blend everything with a fork.
3. To a stand mixer (fitted with a whisk attachment) or large bowl, add the flour (and xanthan gum, if using gluten-free flour), sugar, baking powder and salt. Mix briefly then add the butter and oil. Start the mixer on slow to combine everything into a damp, breadcrumb-like mixture. Turn the mixer to fast and trickle in half the egg mixture. Beat for 30–60 seconds or until the batter is thick, fluffy and lump free. Stop the beaters and scrape down the sides of the bowl.
4. Mix again on fast and trickle in the remaining egg. Once it has all been added, beat for a further 30 seconds or until the batter is smooth.
5. Scrape the batter into the lined brownie tin. Level the top, particularly if making gluten-free, so it bakes evenly. Bake in the middle of the oven for 20 minutes – a metal skewer will come out clean when ready.
6. While the cake cools, add the orange juice and sugar to a pan. Whisk in the jelly powder and once dissolved, put the pan on a medium-high heat and stir until it comes to a full boil. Remove from the heat.
7. Leave the jelly for 5 minutes to thicken a little. Meanwhile, poke 1-cm (⅓-inch) deep holes, 3cm (1 inch) apart across the surface of the cake.
8. The jelly will be quite gelatinous by now. Stir it, pour over the cake and level the top. Put in the fridge to chill for 30 minutes.
9. To a microwave-safe bowl, add the chocolate and cream and microwave in short bursts to gently melt the two together. If you don't have a microwave, use a heatproof bowl over a pan of hot water.
10. When the ganache is still just pourable but not hot, pour over the cake and spread it across the jelly. Chill to set the chocolate before lifting the cake out of the tin, with the baking paper, and serving.

JAFFA LAYER CAKE

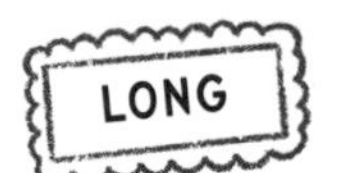

Hands on **2 hours**
Ready in **3 hours 10 minutes**

SERVES 12+

EQUIPMENT
Two 18-cm (7-inch) round cake tins (pans)

All the orange and chocolate flavours you're after only this time in an egg-free, dairy-free layer cake filled with ganache and orange curd. The cake is made with whole fruit, peel and all, and decorated with more citrus slices, dehydrated and dipped in chocolate. The only thing that could boast more satsumas and chocolate per square inch is my Christmas stocking. If you don't want or need a large layer cake, halve the ingredients to make a single cake. Or just do the decoration; it's a chewy, chocolatey revelation that's worth the entry fee alone.

CAKE

500g (17½ oz) small citrus fruit, such as easy peelers, mandarins, tangerines or clementines (approximately 10 fruits)

200g (7 oz) granulated sugar

80g (2¾ oz) ground almonds (almond meal)

150g (5¼ oz) mild olive oil or sunflower oil

Generous pinch of salt

300g (10½ oz) plain (all-purpose) flour or gluten-free self-raising mix

4 tsp baking powder (omit if using gluten-free flour)

GANACHE

Full quantity of Plant-Based Ganache (page 224)

ORANGE CURD

Full quantity of Orange Curd (page 125)

TO DECORATE

5 small citrus fruits (same as for the cake)

20g (¾ oz) granulated sugar

50g (1¾ oz) dark (bittersweet) or milk chocolate

1. Set the oven to 160°C fan (350°F/gas 4). Line the cake tin bases with discs of baking paper.
2. Wash and dry the fruit for the cake, but do not peel. Tear into rough quarters and add to a food processor.
3. Add the sugar, ground almonds, oil and salt and blitz to make a rough pulp. Don't completely puree the fruit until smooth, you want some small chunks of peel.
4. Add the flour and baking powder and pulse briefly to mix the flour in. If you don't have a food processor, you can blitz the fruit and oil in a blender in two or three batches, pour the pulp into a large bowl and mix the rest of the ingredients in by hand.
5. Divide the batter between the lined cake tins.

Continued overleaf

6. Bake for 32–36 minutes in the middle of the oven. A metal skewer will come out clean when the cakes are ready. Leave the cakes to cool in their tins for 5 minutes, then turn out onto a wire rack to cool completely. Drop the oven temperature to 120°C fan (275°F/gas 1).
7. While the cakes are baking, make the plant-based ganache (page 224) and orange curd (opposite).
8. Once the ganache has been made and thickened, scrape it into a piping (pastry) bag with a 1-cm (1⁄3-inch) nozzle. Scrape the orange curd into a separate piping bag also with a 1-cm (1⁄3-inch) nozzle.
9. While the cakes are cooling, start the decoration. Wash the fruit to decorate, but do not peel. Using a very sharp knife, cut into rounds no thicker than 5mm (1⁄5 inch) – you will probably get 3 from each. Very carefully remove and discard the peel from the cut slices. Sit the fruit on kitchen paper to soak up the juice while you cut the rest. When you have 12–15 good slices, pat both sides dry with more kitchen paper – don't press too hard or you will release more juice.
10. Line a flat baking sheet with baking paper. Arrange the fruit slices on the baking sheet and sprinkle a generous pinch of sugar over each one. Put the sheet in the oven, second rung down, and leave the fruit slices to dehydrate in the low heat for up to 1 hour 30 minutes. Turn over halfway through and sprinkle with sugar as before. If they are browning, drop the temperature and lower the tray. The slices are ready when they look thin and glassy and hold their shape when picked up – they may be slightly sticky, but they shouldn't be wet. Leave them to cool on a rack.
11. Melt the chocolate and half-dip each citrus slice, lay on a piece of baking paper then chill in the fridge to set.
12. When the cakes are completely cool, split each one into two layers (page 9). Place the first layer on your serving plate. Pipe a wall of ganache around the outer edge. Leave a 2-cm (3⁄4-inch) gap, then pipe another smaller circle of ganache. Leave another 2-cm (3⁄4-inch) gap, then pipe a third smaller circle. Finally, pipe a central blob of ganache. Pipe one third of the orange curd into the three circular gaps. Repeat this process with the second and third layers, then top with the fourth cake. Cover the sides and top of the cake with the remaining ganache. Arrange the chocolate-dipped citrus slices around the edge, and on top.

ORANGE CURD

MAKES
Enough to sandwich an 18-cm (7-inch) four-layer cake or fill a 300-ml (11-oz) jar

EQUIPMENT
Sterilised glass jar with lid

In a curd, orange is a much harder flavour to capture than lemon or lime. In comparison, it's subtler and far less intense. Using citric acid helps to bring out the brightness of the orange flavour that can get a bit lost during the heating of the juice, so although it's optional, it does make for a tastier curd. You can buy citric acid in small amounts from home-brewing shops. This is an egg-free curd that can be made with dairy butter if you're avoiding just eggs. The amount of cornflour (cornstarch) makes this curd stable as a cake filling; if you want to use it as a spread, reduce the cornflour to 12g ($\frac{1}{2}$ oz) for a softer set and pour the finished curd into a 300-ml (11-oz) jar that has been sterilised, then seal with a lid.

2 or 3 large oranges

15g (1 oz) cornflour (cornstarch)

40g ($1\frac{1}{3}$ oz) granulated sugar

80g ($2\frac{3}{4}$ oz) unsalted butter (dairy or plant-based)

Pinch of citric acid (optional)

Micro pinch of salt

1. Zest 2 of the oranges into a heavy-bottomed pan.
2. Squeeze the oranges and pass the juice through a sieve (fine-mesh strainer) into a jug (pitcher) until you have 200g (7 oz).
3. To the pan, add the cornflour and sugar.
4. Pour a little of the orange juice into the pan, then mix with the cornflour to make a smooth paste. Next, add the rest of the juice to the paste.
5. Put the pan on a medium-low heat and stir continuously until the curd thickens. Taste the curd; if there is any chalkiness from the cornflour, cook for a little longer until it has gone.
6. Remove the pan from the heat and stir in the butter until it has completely melted and emulsified with the curd.
7. Taste the curd, then add the citric acid, a small pinch at a time, until it sharpens up the flavour.
8. Add a micro pinch of salt to balance the flavours, then scrape the curd into a piping (pastry) bag with a 1-cm ($\frac{1}{3}$-inch) nozzle. Chill until needed to assemble the cake. Any leftover curd can be stored in the fridge for up to 2 weeks.

LEMON DRIZZLE

Despite lemons definitely not being British, Lemon Drizzle Cake is something of a British institution. How could a cake named after a type of rain not be? Bursting with zesty sweetness, a Lemon Drizzle should be as dreamily light and bright as a British summer isn't. Lemon is incontrovertible, as is a fluffy crumb made damp with a soaking of citrus juice, but when it comes to the drizzle, there are probably as many interpretations as there are recipes out there. On a cake I will always want a crisp sugar crust, left behind on the surface after the freshly squeezed, sweetened juice has soaked into the body of the cake. However, I'm all for equal opportunities, so in other iterations in this chapter you'll also find a drizzle translated into a cooked lemon syrup that soaks a sweet, knobbly focaccia, the crunchy top coming from a scattering of pearl sugar. Essentially, I'm treating 'drizzle' as an umbrella term for a sweet liquid that soaks into the bake. Later on, I'll be treating it as an actual umbrella, because it looks like it's just started raining.

LAZY LEMON DRIZZLE LOAF

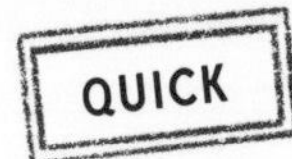

Hands on **10 minutes**
Ready in **1 hour 15 minutes**

SERVES 8–10
Makes one loaf cake

EQUIPMENT
1-kg (2-lb) loaf tin (pan)

This crunchy-topped, moist-middled lemon loaf has to be one of the lowest effort cakes to yield some of the highest praise. Just don't tell anyone it requires no creaming, no beating, no sifting, because it definitely tastes like you've slaved over it. Its moist crumb comes from using oil, so there's no need to get butter to the perfect consistency. Just throw everything into a bowl, whisk it all together and bake. You can have it in and out of the oven in 45 minutes and you can even transport it warm in its tin – perfect when you remember, slightly late, that you promised to bring the cake. It's certainly saved my bacon on many an occasion, and there's not even any bacon in it.

CAKE

2 large (US extra-large) eggs

150g (5¼ oz) mild olive oil, sunflower oil or any other flavourless oil

150g (5¼ oz) full-fat plain yogurt

170g (6 oz) granulated sugar

Grated zest of 4 lemons

¼ tsp salt

200g (7 oz) plain (all-purpose) flour or gluten-free plain (all-purpose) flour + ½ tsp xanthan gum

2 tsp baking powder

TOPPING

110–120g (3¾–4¼ oz) lemon juice (from 4 medium lemons)

150g (5¼ oz) granulated sugar

1. Set the oven to 175°C fan (375°F/gas 5). Line the loaf tin with a single piece of baking paper, scrunching and then unscrunching the sheet to make it easier to form it to the shape of the tin.
2. To a medium bowl, add the eggs, oil, yogurt, sugar, lemon zest and salt. Mix with a balloon whisk or fork until blended. It may look curdled, but that's normal, so don't panic.
3. Add the flour and baking powder and mix again, stopping as soon as the batter is evenly blended and there are no dry patches. If using gluten-free flour, combine the flour, xanthan gum and baking powder before adding.
4. Scrape the batter into the lined loaf tin. Bake in the middle of the oven for 40 minutes, nearer to 45 minutes for gluten-free, or until a metal skewer comes out clean. The cake will bake more quickly in a loaf tin with a wide base than in a tin with a narrower base as the batter will be shallower.
5. While the cake bakes, juice the lemons and set aside for later. Don't add the sugar to the juice now: the secret to the cake's crunchy top is adding the sugar last minute, so the grains don't dissolve.
6. Once the cake is out of the oven, leave it to cool for 5 minutes before using your skewer to poke holes all over the top. Now add the sugar to the lemon juice and mix to a wet paste. Spoon this paste over the hot cake, poking extra holes as you go to help it all soak in.
7. Using the paper, lift the loaf out of the tin and onto a wire rack to cool completely before eating.

LEMON DRIZZLE CREAM PIE

Hands on **35 minutes**
Ready in **1 hour 30 minutes**

SERVES 12–14
Makes one 21-cm (8½-inch) pie

EQUIPMENT
21-cm (8½-inch) fluted loose-bottomed tart tin (pan)

20-cm (8-inch) round cake tin (pan)

PASTRY BASE

320-g (11 oz) packet of ready-rolled shortcrust pastry (sweet or plain)

OR

Full quantity of Sweet Shortcrust Pastry (page 210)

OR

Full quantity of Gluten-Free Sweet Shortcrust Pastry (page 210)

LEMON DRIZZLE CAKE

1 large (US extra-large) egg

50g (1¾ oz) mild olive oil, sunflower oil or any other flavourless oil

75g (2⅔ oz) full-fat plain yogurt

85g (3 oz) granulated sugar

Grated zest of 2 lemons

Pinch of salt

100g (3½ oz) plain (all-purpose) flour or gluten-free plain (all-purpose) flour + ¼ tsp xanthan gum

1 tsp baking powder

It's difficult to have favourites, unless of course it's your kids, in which case it's easy.* But if pushed, when it comes to baking, I'd say the combination of lemon and cream is pretty much top of the flavour rankings for me. Add pastry into the mix and you've got this luscious Lemon Drizzle Cream Pie. Filled with lemon curd and whipped cream, capped with a crunchy layer of lemon drizzle cake and finished, just in case you doubted its credentials, with piped, lemony cream kisses.

1. If making your own lemon curd for the filling, prepare this first following the recipe on page 232. If your shop-bought lemon curd is a bit toothless, add 175g (6¼ oz) to a bowl and stir in some lemon juice, one teaspoon at a time, to give it some bite.
2. If making your own shortcrust pastry, follow the recipe on page 210 and roll it to a thickness of 3mm (⅛ inch). Otherwise, simply unroll the sheet of ready-rolled pastry.
3. Line the tart tin with the pastry. Leave 2cm (¾ inch) of excess pastry overhanging the rim of the tin to hold it in place while it bakes (it will be trimmed later). Prick the base all over with a fork. Scrunch and then unscrunch a sheet of baking paper and sit it over the pastry base and sides. Put the pastry case in the fridge to chill while you make the cake.
4. Set the oven to 175°C fan (375°F/gas 5).
5. Line the cake tin with a piece of baking paper that overhangs the rim of the tin. (This makes it easier to remove the warm cake from the tin later on.) With the quantities given here, make the batter for the lemon drizzle cake following the recipe on page 129. Scrape the batter into the lined cake tin. Remove the pastry case from the fridge and sit the cake tin on the baking paper inside the tart tin. Instead of baking beans or rice, the batter-filled cake tin will weigh the pastry down while it blind bakes.
6. Bake the stacked tins in the middle of the oven for 30 minutes or until the surface of the cake is a rich amber colour and the edges have shrunk away from the sides of the tin. It's almost impossible to over-bake this cake as it's so moist, plus it will be soaked with syrup later. Remove the stacked tins from the oven, lift the cake tin off the pastry and peel the baking paper from the pastry case. Raise the oven shelf up one rung and return the pastry to the oven for a further 15–20 minutes or until it has turned lightly golden and the surface looks dry and crisp.
7. Lift the cake from its tin using the overhanging baking paper and sit it on a wire rack to cool – you can leave it in the paper.
8. When the pastry case has baked, leave it in the tin to cool for 5 minutes, then run a sharp knife horizontally around the top of the tart tin to trim away the overhanging pastry. Pop the pastry case out of the tin and leave it on a wire rack to cool completely.

FILLING

100g (3½ oz) lemon curd (ready-made or see page 232)

20g (¾ oz) lemon juice (if needed)

250g (9 oz) double (heavy) cream

10g (⅓ oz) granulated sugar

LEMON 'KISSES'

75g (2⅔ oz) lemon curd (ready-made or see page 232)

Yellow food colouring (optional)

200g (7 oz) double (heavy) cream

5 or 6 mint leaves

TOPPING

80g (2¾ oz) granulated sugar

60g (2 oz) lemon juice (from 2 medium lemons)

9. Once the pastry is cool, prepare the pie filling. In a large bowl, beat the cream with the sugar until it forms stable peaks. Swirl 100g (3½ oz) of the lemon curd through the whipped cream filling, then spoon it over the pastry case and spread it out to fill the pie.
10. When the lemon drizzle cake is cool, peel away the baking paper and sit it on the whipped cream filling in the centre of the pastry case. There will be a small gap between the cake and the pastry case.
11. Make the lemon kisses. Add the lemon curd to a large bowl and mix in the yellow food colouring, if using. Pour the cream over the curd and beat until just holding firm peaks. Scrape the mixture into a piping (pastry) bag fitted with a 1.5-cm (½-inch) nozzle. Position the nozzle half over the edge of the cake and half over the gap. Pipe large 'kisses' down into the gap between the cake and the pastry case to resemble lemons – the lemon kisses should be large enough to conceal the join.
12. Now make the drizzle cake topping. Into a small bowl, add the sugar and lemon juice and mix briefly to a runny paste. Using a skewer, poke holes over the surface of the cake and spoon on the drizzle. Leave the drizzle to soak in before adding another spoonful so the cake gets an even soaking. Poke extra holes in as they fill with the juice and sugar. When all the drizzle has been used, smooth the surface with the back of a spoon to fill any remaining visible holes.
13. Cut the mint leaves to make small leaf shapes and stick one in the top of each lemon kiss. The pie can be served at room temperature or slightly chilled. Any leftovers can be stored in the fridge for up to 3 days.

* I may be joking, but I might also be keeping them both on their toes.

LEMON DRIZZLE FOCACCIA

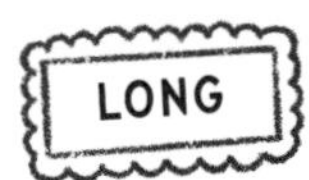

Hands on **1 hour 50 minutes**
Ready in **3 hours 10 minutes**

SERVES 16
Makes one 20 x 30-cm (8 x 12-inch) bread

EQUIPMENT
20 x 30-cm (8 x 12-inch) brownie tin (pan)

I once threw a book about baking yourself happy across the room. Some of my unhappiest times have been baking related;* it's just not a philosophy I'm on board with. So it's a bit awkward to admit making this focaccia might make you happy. Sticking fingers into a dough so wriggly and responsive it feels like play-wrestling a bath full of baby octopi, can't help but delight even the flintiest of hearts. And that's before the whole, bubbly, white chocolate-studded affair is soaked in lemon syrup after baking. Just imagine how happy eating a slice will make you.

DOUGH

250g (9 oz) warm water (no warmer than 35°C/95°F)

1¼ tsp fast-action dried yeast

35g (1¼ oz) granulated sugar

315g (11 oz) strong white bread flour

½ tsp salt

20g (¾ oz) sunflower oil or any other flavourless oil, plus an extra 20g (¾ oz) for oiling the dough and your hands

LEMON SYRUP

2 or 3 medium lemons

150g (5¼ oz) granulated sugar

300g (10½ oz) boiling water

PEARL SUGAR (OPTIONAL)

100g (3½ oz) granulated sugar

1½ tsp water

TO ASSEMBLE

75g (2⅔ oz) salted butter, melted

75g (2⅔ oz) white chocolate, chopped into 1-cm (⅓-inch) chunks

150g (5¼ oz) lemon syrup (see above)

MAKE THE DOUGH

1. To a bowl, add the warm water, yeast and sugar. Swirl the bowl a few times to encourage everything to dissolve. Add the flour, salt and oil to the bowl, then mix to a wet, sticky dough with a table knife. Using a rigid spatula or dough scraper, drag any stray dough from the sides into the amorphous mass in the bottom of the bowl.
2. If using the pull-and-fold kneading method to work the dough (page 212), leave the dough for its first 15-minute rest before pouring 1 tablespoon of the extra oil around the edges of the dough where it meets the bowl. Lightly oil your spatula or scraper and use it to work around the bowl, pulling the dough away from the sides and into the middle, allowing the oil to coat the bottom of the bowl. The dough should now be holding a very loose shape. Oil your hands and do the first pull and fold on the dough. It won't be very elastic to start, so just pull gently, pressing the pulled end firmly into the centre of the dough with your opposite hand. Rest for 15 minutes, then do the second pull and fold. Rest for 15 minutes, then do the third pull and fold. Re-oil your hands for these subsequent pulls and folds, but only oil the bowl again if the dough sticks to it.
3. If using a stand mixer fitted with a dough hook to knead the dough, knead for 8–10 minutes on medium speed. When the dough is smooth and elastic, oil both it and the bowl.
4. Cover the bowl with a clean dish towel or shower cap and leave the kneaded dough to double in size; this usually takes about an hour.

MAKE THE LEMON SYRUP

5. Using a citrus zester, remove very fine strands of peel from 2 lemons (or use a vegetable peeler and finely shred the peel with a sharp knife). Add the peel to a heavy-bottomed pan. Squeeze enough lemons to get 100–120g (3½–4¼ oz) of juice and set aside for later. Add the sugar to the pan with the lemon peel, then pour in the boiling water. Put on a medium-low heat and boil with the lid on for 10 minutes, by which time the peel should be tender. You will need at least 150g (5¼ oz) of cooled syrup for later, so top up with water if it's short.

FINISH THE DOUGH

6. When the dough has doubled in size, line the brownie tin with baking paper. Use a little melted butter to oil the baking paper. Scrape the dough into the lined tin. Drizzle a tablespoon of melted butter over the surface of the dough, getting some on your hands too. Press your buttery fingers into the dough to spread it out and fill the tin. Imagine you're playing chords on a buttery bread piano. Leave the dough for its second proof.
7. After about an hour, or when the dough has risen by half its height again, fish the candied lemon peel from the syrup and scatter it over the surface of the dough, along with the white chocolate. Drizzle a tablespoon of melted butter over the dough, getting a little on your fingers too. Press the lemon peel and chocolate down into the soft dough to bury them.

MAKE THE PEARL SUGAR (OPTIONAL)

8. While the dough is having its second proof, make the pearl sugar following the instructions on page 223.

BAKE THE FOCACCIA

9. Preheat the oven to 200°C fan (425°F/gas 7).
10. Bake the focaccia in the middle of the oven for 25 minutes or until risen and the top has evenly coloured to a pale golden brown.
11. While the focaccia bakes, make up the drizzle syrup. Weigh 150g (5¼oz) of the lemon syrup into a bowl. Tasting as you go, add the reserved lemon juice until it's a good balance of sweet and sour. I find 100g (3½oz) lemon juice is just right.
12. When the focaccia is baked, immediately pour over the remaining melted butter. Leave the focaccia to cool for 10 minutes, then spoon over the drizzle syrup – it will be quickly absorbed, but you can always poke in extra holes with a skewer to make sure everywhere gets a good soaking. Sprinkle over enough pearl sugar (about 50g/1¾oz) so that every bite has a crunch on top. Leave to cool completely before cutting and eating.

---

* See Coconut Macarons, page 104.

MERINGUE PIE

BOO-MERINGUE PIE

Comprising a crisp base, a fruit curd filling and a sweet cloud-like topping, no matter the flavours, a meringue pie is a stone-cold classic. (Although it's best eaten at room temperature.) As one of my favourite puddings, I've had fun playing around with all its component parts, but especially the meringue. French and Italian methods are included, however I left Swiss meringue out of the mix, sadly missing the opportunity to call into three Schengen countries in a single chapter. If you don't have time for a leisurely meringue tour of Alpine Europe, you'll also find shop-bought, ready-made meringue nests and a hacky little shortcut using marshmallow spread. Because marshmallow is really just meringue that's toned up at the gym. The curd filling is present in three iterations, from shop bought to made from scratch, and somewhere in between the two, my Any Jam Curd (page 233). When it comes to the base element, I've not excluded any reasonable contenders: shortcrust, shortbread, puff pastry. I've even included cake and biscuit in the Key Lime Pie Cake. I thought I might as well pay a visit to Florida, having skipped Switzerland.

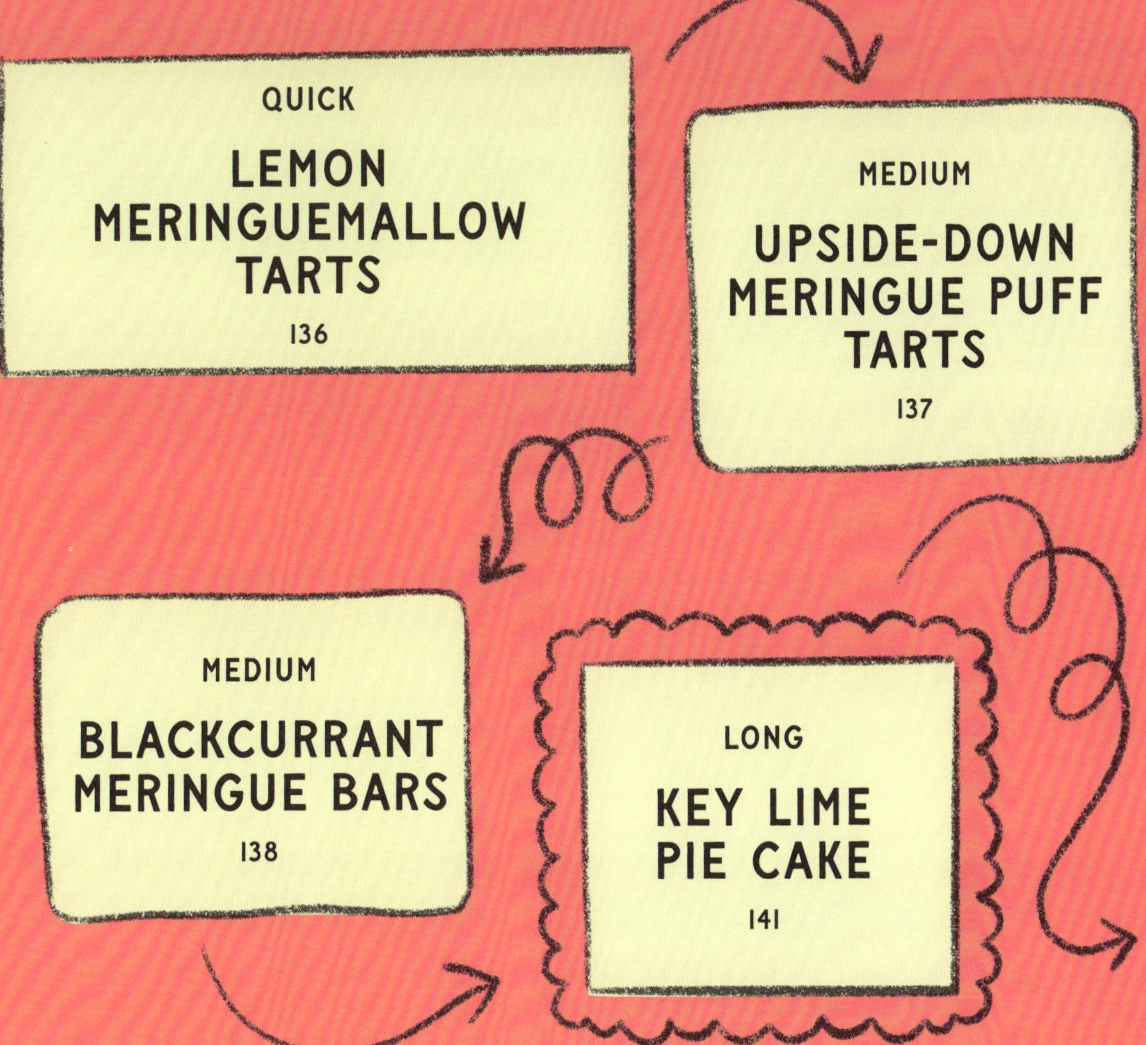

LEMON MERINGUEMALLOW TARTS

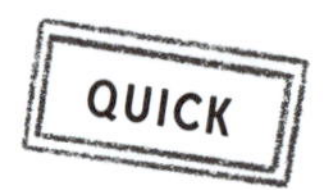

Hands on **20 minutes**
Ready in **50 minutes**

MAKES
8 individual tarts

EQUIPMENT
Shallow 12-cup bun tin (muffin pan)

8-cm (3-inch) round cookie cutter

Think of these as lemon meringue pies with an inferiority complex or as jam tarts with a superiority complex. Actually, there's nothing complex about them; they're stupidly simple. Cut out discs of ready-rolled shortcrust pastry, fill the tart cases with ready-made lemon curd, bake, top with marshmallow spread for a deliciously cheaty take on a classic LMP. These quantities make 8, but if you want to use up the pastry in the packet, double the filling and topping amounts.

160g (5⅔ oz) ready-rolled shortcrust pastry (sweet or plain)

OR

Half quantity of Sweet Shortcrust Pastry (page 210, omitting the baking powder)

OR

Half quantity of Gluten-Free Sweet Shortcrust Pastry (page 210)

160g (5⅔ oz) lemon curd (plus extra lemon juice, if required)

200g (7 oz) white marshmallow spread (I use Marshmallow Fluff)

1. Set the oven to 175°C fan (375°F/gas 5).
2. If making your own shortcrust pastry, follow the recipe on page 210 and roll it to a thickness of 3mm (⅛ inch). Otherwise, simply open the packet and unroll the sheet of pastry. Using an 8-cm (3-inch) round cookie cutter, press out 8 discs of pastry. Sit them in the cups of the bun tin.
3. Spoon 20g (¾ oz) of the lemon curd into each pastry case. To liven up a basic shop-bought curd, add what you need to a small bowl and stir in some fresh lemon juice to taste.
4. Bake on the second rung down from the top of the oven for 15 minutes or until the visible pastry has turned pale golden and the curd has melted and levelled.
5. Leave the tarts in the tin and let them cool for at least 5 minutes to allow the curd to set slightly.
6. Fill a mug or heatproof glass with boiling water and sit a dessert spoon in to warm up. Using the warm, wet spoon, take a scoop of marshmallow spread (approximately 10g / ⅓ oz) from the jar and, using a finger or a second warm, wet spoon, scrape it onto the curd filling. Use the end of the spoon or a table knife to encourage the spread into a neat mound that fully covers the curd and meets the pastry sides. Top all the tarts in this way.
7. Return the tray to the oven for 2–3 minutes or until the top of the marshmallow mound melts slightly so its surface becomes smooth and just set. If you prefer, you can use a blow torch to lightly toast the marshmallow spread rather than returning the tarts to the oven.
8. Leave to cool before eating. Any leftovers can be stored in an airtight container for up to 24 hours.

UPSIDE-DOWN MERINGUE PUFF TARTS

MEDIUM

Hands on **25 minutes**
Ready in **1 hour 5 minutes**
if using ready-made ingredients

MAKES
8 individual tarts

EQUIPMENT
12-hole muffin tin (pan)

9-cm (3½-inch) round cookie cutter

Lightweight baking sheet

Discs of puff pastry baked draped over the base of an upside-down muffin tin, filled with a curd of your choice and topped with cream and crushed shop-bought meringues. The only thing easier than baking individual tart cases over the cups of a muffin tin is buying them ready-made, but as these puff tarts already use shop-bought meringue, I didn't want us to get too lazy. Not only does this method give you generous tart cases without having to own lots of individual tart tins, there's also no need for fiddly little bits of paper and baking beans when blind baking.

320-g (11-oz) packet of ready-rolled puff pastry

250g (9 oz) double (heavy) or whipping cream

50g (1¾ oz) / approximately 4 ready-made meringue nests

320g (11¼ oz) ready-made curd or Any Jam Curd (page 233)

1. Set the oven to 175°C fan (375°F/gas 5).
2. Using a 9-cm (3½-inch) round cookie cutter, press out 8 discs of pastry.
3. Invert the muffin tin. Unless your tin has a very good non-stick surface, brush the exterior of the 'muffin cups' with a little oil or cake release. Sit a disc of pastry over each 'muffin cup' and gently press the edges of the pastry onto the mound. Repeat with the rest of the pastry discs. Chill the pastry in place on the muffin tin for 15 minutes.
4. Place a large piece of baking paper over all the pastry and then sit a baking sheet over that – this controls the rise and gives the cups a flat base. Use a lightweight baking sheet as a heavy-duty one can apply too much pressure and the pastry cases may develop splits. Bake in the middle of the oven for 12 minutes.
5. Remove the baking sheet and paper, then bake for a further 3 minutes or until the pastry is golden and dry-looking.
6. Leave the pastry to cool completely on the inverted muffin tin. Using a teaspoon, gently lift the tart cases off the muffin cups – be very careful as the puff pastry is quite fragile.
7. In a large mixing bowl, whip the cream to soft folds, stopping before it gets stiff. Roughly crush the meringues and fold them into the cream.
8. Spoon or pipe approximately 40g (1⅓ oz) of your chosen curd into each tart case, then top with a generous dollop of the meringue crumbled cream.
9. Decorate with an extra drizzle of warmed curd or fresh fruit. Or both.

BLACKCURRANT MERINGUE BARS

Hands on **40 minutes**
Ready in **1 hour 50 minutes**

MAKES
12 squares

EQUIPMENT
20 x 30-cm (8 x 12-inch) brownie tin (pan)

A buttery shortbread base covered with a blackcurrant curd, topped with baked French meringue and cut into bars. Blackcurrants might well be my favourite berry. Packing a tremendously deep sourness alongside a slightly unexpected whiff of tom cat, I've never identified more with one of my five a day. The easiest way to get your hands on blackcurrants is to grow your own. The plants are low maintenance and difficult to kill; even I've not managed it. Alternatively you can be very nice to someone who grows their own, buy them frozen online or use different, readily available berries. Blackberries or raspberries will give you the sharp, fresh contrast with the rich biscuit base and the light sweet meringue.

SHORTBREAD BASE

200g (7 oz) plain (all-purpose) flour or 250g (9 oz) gluten-free self-raising mix

1¼ tsp baking powder (omit if using gluten-free flour)

50g (1¾ oz) cornflour (cornstarch, omit if using gluten-free flour)

85g (3 oz) granulated sugar

Large pinch of salt

150g (5¼ oz) salted butter, melted

BLACKCURRANT CURD

400g (14 oz) fresh or frozen blackcurrants

300g (10½ oz) water

150g (5¼ oz) granulated sugar (plus extra, if necessary)

40g (1⅓ oz) cornflour (cornstarch)

2 egg yolks

MERINGUE TOPPING

2 large (US extra-large) egg whites

Pinch of salt

¼ tsp cream of tartar

110g (3¾ oz) granulated or caster (superfine) sugar

1. Set the oven to 165°C fan (350°F/gas 4) and line the brownie tin with baking paper.
2. Make the shortbread. Combine the dry ingredients in a large bowl, pour over the melted butter and mix to bring everything together as a dough.
3. Press the dough into the lined tin and level with the back of a spoon.
4. Bake in the middle of the oven for 40 minutes until the surface is lightly golden and crazed with tiny cracks.
5. Put the blackcurrants in a food processor or blender with the water and blitz to make a watery purée. Pass that purée through a sieve (strainer) into a heavy-bottomed pan. You will need 580g (20½ oz) of sieved purée, so add water to make up the weight if you don't have enough. Add the sugar to the pan and stir into the purée.
6. In a small bowl, mix together the cornflour, egg yolks and a few spoonfuls of the purée from the pan, stirring to make a smooth 'slurry', then stir that back into the rest of the fruit. Don't start cooking the fruit curd until about 5 minutes before the shortbread comes out of the oven – it needs to be poured over the base as soon as it's ready so it doesn't set in the pan.
7. Put the pan on a medium heat. Keep stirring while it comes just up to the boil, then remove from the heat once the first big bubble pops in the mixture. Taste the curd and add more sugar if needed. Pour the curd immediately over the baked shortbread base and level it out. (The shortbread doesn't need to cool, it can be covered straight from the oven.)
8. Drop the oven temperature to 150°C fan (325°F/gas 3).
9. Using the quantities given here, make the French meringue (page 216). Spread the meringue over the blackcurrant curd, pulling peaks up with a spatula so there's more surface area to crisp up in the oven.
10. Bake in the middle of the oven for 30 minutes. The meringue should develop a very lightly golden crust.
11. Leave to cool and then cut into squares. These are best eaten within 48 hours, but I doubt that will be a struggle.

PLANT-BASED / EGG-FREE BLACKCURRANT MERINGUE BARS

With just a few easy swaps you can make these bars egg-free or completely plant-based. The meringue comes courtesy of aquafaba, a name I struggle with, but it's slightly better than 'bean juice'. It's the liquid drained from cans of pulses which contains proteins that make it whippable in a similar way to egg whites. Chickpeas (garbanzo beans) make a very stable meringue but aquafaba from other pulses can be used similarly. It's pretty fabulous stuff, not interchangeable with egg white for all baking requirements but it does make an excellent meringue.

PLANT-BASED SHORTBREAD BASE

Follow the recipe on page 138, but use plant-based butter

PLANT-BASED BLACKCURRANT CURD

400g (14 oz) fresh or frozen blackcurrants

300g (10½ oz) water

150g (5¼ oz) granulated sugar (plus extra, if needed)

45g (1½ oz) cornflour (cornstarch)

20g (¾ oz) coconut oil or plant-based butter

PLANT-BASED MERINGUE TOPPING

80g (2¾ oz) chickpea (garbanzo bean) aquafaba

¼ tsp cream of tartar

Pinch of salt

110g (3¾ oz) granulated or caster (superfine) sugar

1 tbsp vanilla extract

1. Make the shortbread, substituting plant-based butter, following the recipe on page 138, steps 1–4.
2. Make the curd filling, following the recipe on page 138, steps 5 to 7, but omit the eggs and mix the cornflour to a smooth slurry with a little fruit purée from the cold pan. Add the coconut oil or plant-based butter to the pan at the same time as the cornflour slurry – it will melt into the curd as you heat the filling.
3. For the plant-based version, it's preferable that the filling cools for about 15 minutes before it's topped with the meringue.
4. For the meringue topping, use the quantities given here to make the Plant-Based French Meringue (page 217). Spread the meringue over the slightly cooled blackcurrant curd, pulling up peaks of meringue with a spatula so there's more surface area to crisp in the oven, and bake as per the egg version.
5. Similarly, these bars are also best eaten within 48 hours.

KEY LIME PIE CAKE

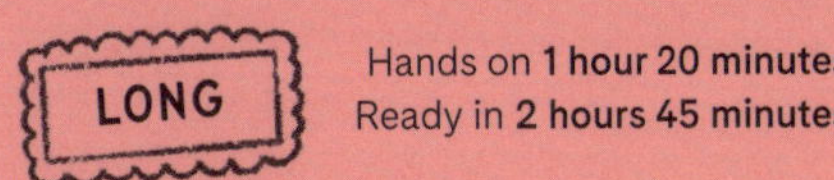

Hands on **1 hour 20 minutes**
Ready in **2 hours 45 minutes**

SERVES 12+
Makes one 18-cm (7-inch) four-layer cake

EQUIPMENT
Two 18-cm (7-inch) round cake tins (pans)

Based on a meringue-topped Key Lime Pie, this cake is four layers of light lime cake sandwiched with lime curd and cream cheese frosting. Then, for good measure, it's topped with digestive biscuit crumble and covered in toasted Italian meringue. For this to be a Key Lime Pie (or cake), it should really use Key limes, but I sense my whole concept is at breaking point so just use regular limes and go with it. Key limes are smaller, thinner skinned and much more acidic, so it's a shame they're not readily available in the UK because we've got a lot in common.

JUG (PITCHER)

4 large (US extra-large) eggs

60g (2 oz) sunflower oil or vegetable oil

60g (2 oz) / 4 tbsp water

MIXER

240g (8½ oz) granulated sugar

320g (11 oz) plain (all-purpose) flour or gluten-free plain (all-purpose) flour + 1 tsp xanthan gum

1 tbsp baking powder

Pinch of salt

Grated zest of 4 limes

120g (4¼ oz) salted butter, softened to the consistency of yogurt

60g (2 oz) sunflower oil or vegetable oil

LIME CURD

100g (3½ oz) granulated sugar (plus extra to taste)

10g (⅓ oz) cornflour (cornstarch)

2 large (US extra-large) egg yolks

100g (3½ oz) lime juice (from 4 or 5 limes)

Green food colouring (optional)

100g (3½ oz) unsalted butter

Micro pinch of salt

CREAM CHEESE FROSTING

170g (6 oz) salted butter

90g (3¼ oz) icing (confectioners') sugar

225g (8 oz) full-fat cream cheese or soft cheese

TO ASSEMBLE

100g (3½ oz) digestive biscuits (graham crackers) or make your own (page 215, make a half quantity and enjoy the leftovers with a cup of tea)

ITALIAN MERINGUE

110g (3¾ oz) granulated sugar

35g (1¼ oz) water

1 tsp golden syrup or glucose syrup

2 large (US extra-large) egg whites

Pinch of salt

¼ tsp cream of tartar

Continued overleaf

MAKE THE CAKE

1. Set the oven to 160°C fan (350°F/gas 4) and line the bases of the cake tins with discs of baking paper.
2. To a jug (pitcher), add the eggs, oil and water. Using a fork, break up the eggs and blend everything together.
3. To a stand mixer (fitted with a whisk attachment) or large bowl, add the sugar, flour (plus xanthan gum for gluten-free), baking powder, salt and lime zest. Mix briefly to evenly combine the dry ingredients. Add the butter and oil and start the mixer on slow. The dry ingredients will combine with the butter and oil to make a damp, breadcrumb-like mix.
4. Increase the mixer speed to fast and slowly pour in half the egg mix. Beat for 30 seconds to 1 minute or until the batter becomes thick, fluffy and lump free. Stop the beaters and scrape down the sides of the bowl so everything gets mixed in.
5. Start the mixer again to fast and trickle in the remaining egg mix. Once it has all been added, beat for a further 30 seconds or until the batter looks smooth. Divide equally between the two cake tins and level the tops. If using gluten-free flour, carefully level the top of the batter in the tin – the added xanthan gum means this cake won't completely self-level in the oven. Bake in the middle of the oven for 32 minutes, or until a metal skewer comes out clean.
6. Leave the cakes in their tins for 5 minutes, then turn out onto a wire rack to cool completely.

MAKE THE LIME CURD

7. If you haven't already, separate the eggs, saving the whites for the Italian Meringue, and juice the limes. To a heavy-bottomed pan, add the sugar and cornflour, then mix. Add the egg yolks and a little of the lime juice to make a runny paste and whisk until there are no lumps.
8. Whisk the rest of the lime juice into the pan, put on a medium-low heat and stir continuously until the curd thickens. Taste the curd; if it's too sour, add more sugar a little at a time. If there is any chalkiness from the cornflour, cook for a little longer until it has gone. Add a few drops of green colouring now, if using.
9. Remove the pan from the heat and stir in the butter until it has completely melted and emulsified with the curd. Add a micro pinch of salt to balance the flavours. Scrape the curd into a piping (pastry) bag with a 1-cm (1/3-inch) nozzle and chill for use later.

MAKE THE CREAM CHEESE FROSTING

10. Using the quantities given on page 141, make the cream cheese frosting (page 222). Scrape into a piping bag with a 1-cm (1/3-inch) nozzle and leave at room temperature for use later.

ASSEMBLE THE CAKE

11. Split each cake into two so you have four layers (page 9). Set the first layer on your serving plate and pipe a wall of cream cheese frosting around the top edge of the cake. Pipe a ring of lime curd next to the frosting. Alternate concentric rings of cream cheese frosting and lime curd until you reach the centre of the cake. Repeat this with the next two layers of cake, finishing with the fourth cake layer flat side facing up. Leaving a 2-cm (3/4-inch) border free, cover the rest of the cake top with cream cheese frosting and crumble the digestive biscuits in a thick layer over that. Leave the sides free from frosting.

MAKE THE ITALIAN MERINGUE

12. Using the quantities given on page 141, make the Italian meringue (page 218). Scrape 75g (2 2/3 oz) into a piping bag with a 1.5-cm (1/2-inch) plain nozzle. Leave the rest of the meringue in the bowl. Pipe meringue kisses around the frosting-free border of the cake top.
13. Using a palette knife, generously coat the sides of the cake with the meringue from the bowl and anything left in the piping bag. To finish the cake sides, either lightly blow torch the meringue on the sides until just golden or throw more digestive crumbs around the base and a little up the sides.
14. Serve at room temperature. Any leftovers can be stored in an airtight container in the fridge for up to 3 days. Cut slices and leave them to reach room temperature before eating.

MILLIONAIRE'S SHORTBREAD

Also known as caramel shortbread or caramel slice, millionaire's shortbread is a rags to riches story. Well, a shortbread to riches story. Starting out as a humble, buttery shortbread base, it pulled itself up by its bootstraps, speculated on a thick caramel filling, then when that paid off, added a chocolate topping to its delicious portfolio. Seeing as this is a recipe book, all the millionaires in this chapter have to be self made, but they range from quick scrappy start-ups to oligarch extravagance, so they're accessible to all. Even the really big rich ones are made to share. How refreshing! The crisp base appears, not surprisingly, as shortbread, both as ready-made and from scratch but also as choux pastry. Caramel comes as a filled chocolate bar, a microwaved shortcut, caramel condensed milk and, the richest of creams, salted caramel pastry cream. As required by the dessert ombudsman, chocolate tops all these bakes, from a no-nonsense topping to a yielding ganache, an airy mousse and a glassy glaze. And good news for consumers, you may eat all of these with your fingers or a fork. No silver spoon required.

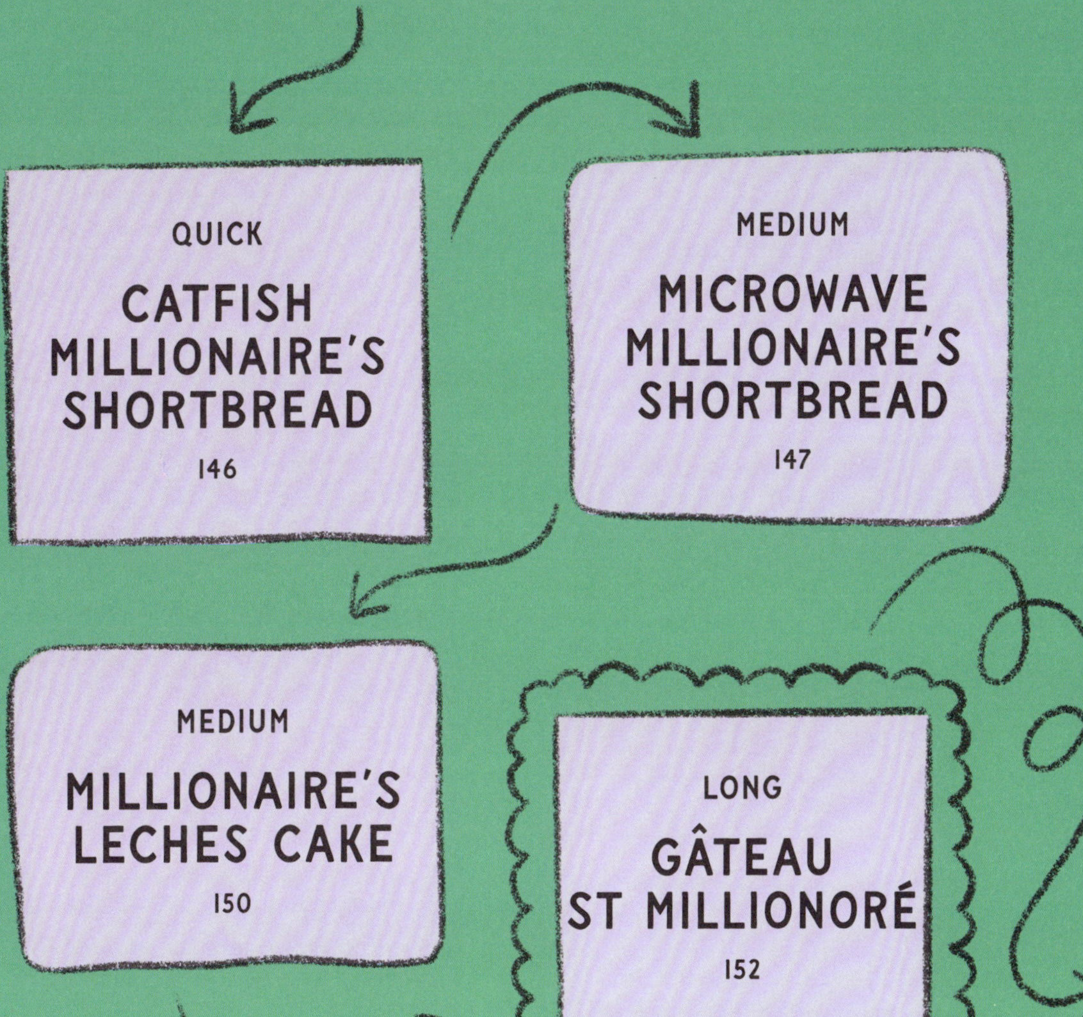

CATFISH MILLIONAIRE'S SHORTBREAD

Hands on **10 minutes**
Ready in **30 minutes**

MAKES
24 single bites or
12 double bites

EQUIPMENT
1-kg (2-lb) loaf tin (pan)

You'll forgive these bars for not being quite what they seem when you eat one. The base is ready-made biscuits crushed and pressed with melted butter, the topping a caramel-filled chocolate bar. The residual heat of the base partially melts the underside of the chocolate bar and the two bond together when chilled. If you have a few more minutes, you can make and bake your own shortbread in the microwave or oven. Either way this is such a cheat's route to a millionaire's shortbread you might want to hand yourself over to the authorities.

75g (2⅔ oz) salted butter

150g (5¼ oz) shortbread or malted milk biscuits

180g (6⅓ oz) or 200g (7 oz) bar of caramel-filled chocolate

1. Line the loaf tin with baking paper.
2. To a heavy-bottomed pan, add the butter and put on a low heat to melt. Turn the heat off as soon as the butter is liquid – don't allow it to bubble.
3. While the butter is melting, crush the biscuits to fine crumbs. Put them in a bowl and crush under the base of a sturdy glass or seal them in a strong plastic food bag and crush with a rolling pin.
4. Tip the crumbs into the pan and stir into the butter over a medium-low heat. Keep stirring the crumbs until you start to hear a little sizzle; this means the crumbs are hot enough for the next step.
5. Working swiftly, press the crumbs into the base of the lined loaf tin, levelling and firming them down with the back of a spoon.
6. While the base is warm, sit the chocolate bar on top. Leave for 2 minutes so the flat underside of the chocolate melts a little in the heat. So you don't squash the caramel pockets, press down gently on the chocolate, giving it a little wiggle so it bonds to the base as it cools.
7. Chill in the fridge for 20 minutes. Once set, cut along the chocolate bar's lines into uniform single or double bites.

Alternatively, make your own shortbread base from scratch; it won't take much longer. Use the shortbread base recipe for the Microwave Millionaire's Shortbread opposite. Bake in the oven in a 1-kg (2-lb) loaf tin at 160°C fan (350°F/gas 4) for 15–20 minutes or until just turning golden at the edges. Or cook in the microwave in a microwave-safe container that fits the chocolate bar, following the chart opposite. Leave the baked shortbread base to cool for 10 minutes and then follow the instructions above from step 6.

MICROWAVE MILLIONAIRE'S SHORTBREAD

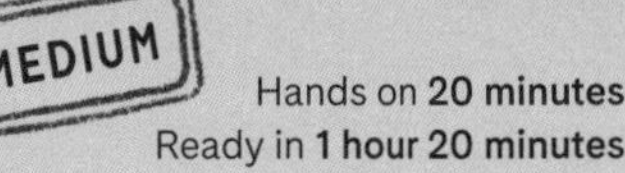

Hands on **20 minutes**
Ready in **1 hour 20 minutes**

MAKES
8 squares

EQUIPMENT
12 x 20-cm (5 x 8-inch) ovenproof glass or ceramic dish

I know it sounds wrong, but it is possible to make a crisp, light shortbread in the microwave. And if you've got a shortbread base, it would be wrong not to top it with caramel. And it would be wrong not to cook the caramel in the microwave, seeing as you're already standing in front of it. A bake of this relatively modest size might not justify switching the oven on, but when you can cook all the component parts in about 10 minutes in the microwave, I'm afraid there's absolutely no excuse not to make a batch.

SHORTBREAD BASE

80g (2¾ oz) salted butter, melted

100g (3½ oz) plain (all-purpose) flour or 150g (5¼ oz) gluten-free plain (all-purpose) flour

50g (1¾ oz) cornflour (cornstarch, omit if using gluten-free flour)

40g (1⅓ oz) granulated sugar

CARAMEL

35g (1¼ oz) granulated sugar

40g (1⅓ oz) light brown soft sugar

185g (6½ oz) sweetened condensed milk

100g (3½ oz) salted butter

Large pinch of salt

CHOCOLATE TOPPING

50g (1¾ oz) dark (bittersweet) or milk chocolate, chopped

1. Line the ovenproof dish with baking paper.
2. To a medium bowl, add all the ingredients for the shortbread and mix well to make a dough. Press the dough into the lined dish, then level the surface with the back of a spoon.
3. Cook and rest the shortbread according to the chart below, following the timings listed for your wattage of machine. Just like ovens, all microwaves, even the same wattage, heat slightly differently, so the below timings are a guide. The resting times are important in preventing any part of the shortbread superheating and burning; set a timer so you know when to start the next heat.

MICROWAVE WATTAGE	700W	800W	900W	1000W
COOK	1 minute 10 seconds	1 minute	55 seconds	50 seconds
REST	20 seconds	20 seconds	20 seconds	20 seconds
COOK	1 minute 10 seconds	1 minute	55 seconds	50 seconds
REST	20 seconds	20 seconds	20 seconds	20 seconds
COOK	1 minute 10 seconds	1 minute	55 seconds	50 seconds

4. After its final cook, gently compress the surface of the shortbread all over with the back of a spoon – this will help to stop it crumbling when cut. For gluten-free, lightly press down the shortbread with the back of the spoon after each cook.
5. As soon as the shortbread is cooked, start making the caramel. (The base doesn't need to cool before being topped.) Choose the tallest microwave-safe glass or plastic bowl that will fit in your microwave to contain the bubbling, molten caramel. Add all the ingredients for the caramel, except the salt, to the bowl, chopping the butter into chunks so it melts more quickly.

Continued overleaf

6. Make caramel using the chart below, following the timings for your wattage of machine. The first cook is to melt all the ingredients. Give everything a stir before returning to the microwave. After the second cook the caramel will be bubbling. Give it another quick stir and return to the microwave before the bubbling subsides.

MICROWAVE WATTAGE	700W	800W	900W	1000W
FIRST COOK	2 minutes 20 seconds	2 minutes	1 minute 45 seconds	1 minute 25 seconds
SECOND COOK	1 minute 45 seconds	1 minute 30 seconds	1 minute 20 seconds	1 minute 10 seconds
THIRD COOK	1 minute 45 seconds	1 minute 30 seconds	1 minute 20 seconds	1 minute 10 seconds

7. After the third cook, the caramel will look quite lumpy and porridgy, but just mix vigorously with a heatproof spatula and it will come back to a smooth caramel. Stir in the salt, pour over the shortbread and level the surface. Leave for 10 minutes so the surface of the caramel firms a little.
8. Scatter over the chopped chocolate and leave to melt in the residual heat for 10 minutes. Once melted, spread the chocolate evenly over the caramel. Chill in the freezer for 40 minutes or until firm and set. Cut into 8 squares.

FOR THE HOB AND OVEN

To make it worth the extra energy (both yours and the oven's) you can double the ingredients and use a square 20-cm (8-inch) cake tin (pan). Otherwise, use the same size dish and quantities given above.

1. Set the oven to 160°C fan (350°F/gas 4) and line the dish. Make the shortbread as above. Bake in the middle of the oven for 30 minutes, until just starting to turn golden at the edges.
2. Start the caramel 10 minutes before the base is baked, so the filling can be poured over the shortbread as soon as both are ready. Add the caramel ingredients, except the salt, to a heavy-bottomed pan and put on a medium-low heat. When the butter has melted and everything is blended, turn the heat up to medium. Any remaining sugar grains will dissolve as the mixture heats. Stir continuously as the mixture heats to a controlled bubble; keep it there for 5 minutes or until it reaches 120°C (250°F). Remove from the heat, add the salt and pour over the shortbread.
3. Top with chocolate as directed in step 8 above.

PLANT-BASED MICROWAVE MILLIONAIRE'S SHORTBREAD

PLANT-BASED SHORTBREAD BASE

80g (2¾oz) plant-based salted butter, melted

100g (3½oz) plain (all-purpose) flour or 150g (5¼oz) gluten-free plain (all-purpose) flour

50g (1¾oz) cornflour (cornstarch, omit if using gluten-free flour)

40g (1⅓oz) granulated sugar

PLANT-BASED CARAMEL

150g (5¼oz) light brown soft sugar

25g (¾oz) golden syrup

75g (2⅔oz) plant-based double (heavy) cream

90g (3¼oz) plant-based butter (hard block not soft spread)

Large pinch of salt

PLANT-BASED CHOCOLATE TOPPING

50g (1¾oz) plant-based dark (bittersweet) or milk chocolate

Plant-based condensed milk and coconut condensed milk are great for all sorts of plant-based baking (just as they are for eating straight out of the tin with a spoon, like their dairy counterpart), but I've never had success with them while conjuring a non-dairy millionaire's shortbread into life. Instead this recipe uses a combination of golden syrup and plant-based butter and cream instead of a straight swap for vegan-friendly condensed milk.

1. Cook the shortbread following the instructions for the dairy version on page 147, but substituting plant-based butter.
2. Add the caramel ingredients except the salt to a microwave-safe bowl, chopping the butter into chunks so it melts more quickly.
3. Make the caramel using the chart below, following the timings for your wattage of machine. After the first cook, to melt the ingredients, give a quick stir and return to the microwave. After the second cook the caramel will be bubbling; give it a quick stir and return to the microwave before the bubbling subsides. The caramel will be ready after the third cook. Add the salt, give it a quick stir and pour over the base.

MICROWAVE WATTAGE	700W	800W	900W	1000W
FIRST COOK	2 minutes 20 seconds	2 minutes	1 minute 45 seconds	1 minute 25 seconds
SECOND COOK	2 minutes 20 seconds	2 minutes	1 minute 45 seconds	1 minute 25 seconds
THIRD COOK	3 minutes 25 seconds	3 minutes	2 minutes 30 seconds	2 minutes 5 seconds

4. Leave the caramel to set; it will take a lot longer than the dairy version. When it is firm enough to support the topping, melt the chocolate, carefully spread it over and leave to set.

MILLIONAIRE'S LECHES CAKE

Hands on **25 minutes**
Ready in **1 hour 10 minutes**

SERVES 12–16
Makes one traybake

EQUIPMENT
20 x 30-cm (8 x 12-inch) brownie tin

Flat baking sheet

JUG (PITCHER)

2 large (US extra-large) eggs

30g (1 oz) sunflower oil or any other flavourless oil

30g (1 oz) / 2 tbsp water

2 tsp vanilla extract

MIXER

120g (4¼ oz) granulated sugar

160g (5⅔ oz) plain (all-purpose) flour or gluten-free plain (all-purpose) flour + ½ tsp xanthan gum

1½ tsp baking powder

Pinch of salt

30g (1 oz) sunflower oil or any other flavourless oil

60g (2 oz) salted butter, softened to the consistency of yogurt

SHORTBREAD RUBBLE

20g (¾ oz) icing (confectioners') sugar

50g (1¾ oz) plain (all-purpose) flour or 60g (2oz) gluten-free plain (all-purpose) flour

¼ tsp baking powder

30g (1 oz) cold salted butter

CARAMEL MILK

180g (6⅓ oz) caramel condensed milk

150g (5¼ oz) milk (any type)

100g (3½ oz) double (heavy) cream

GANACHE

200g (7 oz) milk chocolate

175g (6¼ oz) double (heavy) cream

With a base of caramel cream-soaked vanilla sponge, topped with chocolate ganache and shortbread rubble, this tres leches-inspired cake is undeniably rich. But it's a traybake that can be quickly divided into equal pieces and easily shared out so maybe it should be called Millionaire Philanthropist's Cake.

1. Set the oven to 160°C fan (350°F/gas 4) and line the brownie tin with a single large sheet of baking paper.
2. In a jug (pitcher), roughly blend the eggs, oil, water and vanilla with a fork.
3. To a stand mixer (fitted with a whisk attachment) or large bowl, add the sugar, flour (and xanthan gum, if making gluten-free), baking powder and salt. Mix briefly to evenly combine. Add the oil and butter. Start the mixer on slow to combine everything to a damp breadcrumb-like mix.
4. Turn the mixer to fast and slowly pour in half the egg mix. Beat for 30–60 seconds or until the batter becomes thick, fluffy and lump free. Stop the beaters and scrape the sides of the bowl.
5. Start the mixer again on fast and trickle in the remaining egg mix. Once it has all been added, beat for 30 seconds or until the batter looks smooth. Scrape into the lined brownie tin, level the top and bake in the middle of the oven for 20 minutes or until a metal skewer comes out clean.
6. While the cake bakes, make the shortbread rubble. Line a flat baking sheet with baking paper. Mix the dry ingredients together in a bowl. Coarsely grate over the butter and work it in with your fingertips to make small crumbs. Squash handfuls of the crumbs in your fists, then crumble onto the baking sheet so the clumps are a mix of sizes. When the cake is out of the oven, drop the temperature to 150°C fan (325°F/gas 3). Bake the rubble on the middle shelf for 15 minutes or until golden. Leave to cool.
7. Leave the cake to cool for 15 minutes, then make the caramel milk. Add the ingredients to a heavy-bottomed pan and whisk together on a medium heat. Bring just to the boil, then remove from the heat. Using a chopstick, poke deep holes across the surface of the cake. Spoon half the caramel milk into the holes. Once that has soaked in, repeat with the remaining milk. Using the paper, lift the cake from its tin onto a wire cooling rack.
8. While the cake cools, start the ganache. To a medium bowl, add the chocolate and cream and microwave in short bursts to gently melt the two together. Pour 75g (2⅔ oz) of warm ganache into a separate small bowl and leave at room temperature. Put the medium bowl in the fridge to chill. When firm, beat until thick, pale and fluffy. Spread over the cooled cake. Scatter the shortbread rubble over the top.
9. Warm the reserved ganache until just runny. Wobble the ganache over with a teaspoon. Serve at room temperature. Any leftovers can be stored in an airtight container in the fridge.

GÂTEAU ST MILLIONORÉ

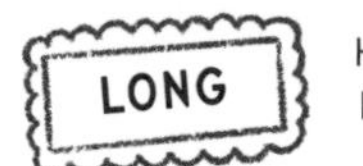

Hands on **2 hours 15 minutes**
Ready in **2 hours 45 minutes**

SERVES 12–14
Makes one 20-cm (8-inch) dessert

EQUIPMENT
Two large flat baking sheets

20-cm (8-inch) plate or cake tin (pan)

This symphony of choux and caramel is based on a Gâteau St Honoré, a patisserie salute to the patron saint of bakers and pastry chefs. With a shortbread base, caramel-topped, chocolate mousse-filled choux, a layer of salted caramel pastry cream and a chocolate glaze, this is a true celebration of the patron saint of millionaire's shortbread. Whomever or whatever you choose to celebrate with this bake, it's worth every step required to get it onto your serving plate then into your mouth.

CHOUX PASTRY

70g (2½ oz) plain (all-purpose) flour or 40g (1⅓ oz) gluten-free plain (all-purpose) flour + 30g (1 oz) gluten-free self-raising mix

100g (3½ oz) boiling water

35g (1¼ oz) salted butter

2 large (US extra-large) eggs

SHORTBREAD BASE

120g (4¼ oz) butter, softened

100g (1¾ oz) icing (confectioners') sugar

170g (6 oz) plain (all-purpose) flour or 180g (6⅓ oz) gluten-free plain (all-purpose) flour + ¼ tsp xanthan gum

1 tsp baking powder

Ingredients continued overleaf

MAKE THE CHOUX

1. Set the oven to 175°C fan (375°F/gas 5). Using the quantities given here, follow the recipe on page 208 to make the choux pastry dough. Scrape the dough into a piping (pastry) bag with a 1.5-cm (½-inch) nozzle. Keep the leftover beaten egg for use later.
2. Using a 20-cm (8-inch) plate or cake tin (pan) as a template, draw a circle on a sheet of baking paper. Turn the paper over and use it to line the baking sheet; if the pencil line isn't visible, slide a piece of white paper between the baking paper and the baking sheet to make it stand out. Weigh the choux-filled piping bag before using then, following the pencil guide, pipe a ring of choux using 100g (3½ oz) of the dough. If necessary, pipe a double ring and use a wet finger to smooth the two together. Remove the sheet of white paper if used.
3. On a separate lined baking sheet, pipe the rest of the choux pastry dough as profiteroles, using 10g (⅓ oz) of pastry for each one. You should have enough dough to pipe 15 profiteroles.
4. Bake on the middle and second rung down of the oven for 35 minutes, until the choux is puffed and golden. Remove from the oven and immediately use the pointy end of a chopstick to poke a hole in the base of each profiterole and at 4-cm (1½-inch) intervals around the inside top of the choux ring. Transfer the choux ring and profiteroles to a wire rack to cool, sitting the profiteroles upside down to help the steam escape.

MAKE THE SHORTBREAD BASE

5. As soon as the choux is baking, make the shortbread dough. To a medium bowl, add the butter that has been softened to a yogurt-like consistency. Sift in the icing sugar. Using a rigid spatula, mix the two together until smooth. Add the flour and baking powder and stir in to make a ragged dough. Pull the dough into a rough ball with your hands.

Continued overleaf

CHOCOLATE MOUSSE

200g (7 oz) milk chocolate

300g (10½ oz) double (heavy) cream

CARAMEL PASTRY CREAM

30g (1 oz) cornflour (cornstarch)

1 large (US extra-large) egg

½ tbsp vanilla extract

200g (7 oz) whole (full-fat) milk

40g (1½ oz) unsalted butter, cubed

125g (4½ oz) Salted Caramel Sauce (dairy or plant-based, page 230) or ready-made spreadable sauce from a jar (not runny from a squeezy bottle)

DRY CARAMEL (TO ASSEMBLE)

100g (3½ oz) granulated sugar

DARK CHOCOLATE GLAZE

40g (1⅓ oz) dark (bittersweet) chocolate (40% cocoa)

80g (2¾ oz) double (heavy) cream

6. Knead the dough briefly on the work surface to make a smoother ball, then sit the dough on a sheet of baking paper. Cover the dough with another sheet of paper and roll to 5mm (¼ inch) thick and at least 20cm (8 inches) in diameter. Sit the plate or cake tin (pan) on the dough, cut around it and peel away the small amount of excess. Crumble the excess dough into 1-cm (⅓-inch)-ish pieces on a separate sheet of baking paper; don't spread the crumbs out, they should be just touching each other so they bake back together in a random fashion in the oven.

7. When the choux comes out of the oven, drop the oven temperature to 150°C fan (325°F/gas 3). Slide the shortbread base on its paper onto one of the baking sheets and the crumbled excess dough onto the other. Bake the base on the middle shelf and excess dough on the shelf below for 12 minutes. Remove the excess dough and leave to cool on its sheet; the pieces will have puffed and fused together. Remove the base; it will have spread slightly in the oven.

8. If you want to neaten up the circle, sit the plate or cake tin over it and trim the shortbread that's spread. Neatening the base is optional, but you do need to brush the surface with the egg left over from making the choux. Return to the oven to bake fully for 8 minutes, or until just starting to colour at the edges, then leave on its sheet to cool completely.

MAKE THE CHOCOLATE MOUSSE

9. Finely chop the chocolate and add to a medium bowl. Heat 100g (3½ oz) of the cream to almost boiling point, then pour over the chocolate and leave for 2 minutes to melt. Mix to a smooth ganache. Set aside to cool. You can start the pastry cream while you're waiting for the chocolate mixture to cool to 35°C (95°F).

10. Once cool, lightly whip the remaining cream until just holding soft peaks, then fold into the chocolate mixture. Scrape the mousse into a piping (pastry) bag with a 6-mm (¼-inch) nozzle.

MAKE THE CARAMEL PASTRY CREAM

11. Using the quantities given here, make the caramel pastry cream following the instructions on page 220. (The white sugar is left out because of the amount of caramel that will be added.) When the custard is cool and firm, beat in the salted caramel sauce (instead of cream). Leave to chill in the fridge while you start to assemble the gâteau.

ASSEMBLE THE GÂTEAU

12. Fill the choux ring and profiteroles with the chocolate mousse, piping into the holes made with the chopstick to let the steam out. Wipe away any overspill of mousse with paper towels.
13. Using the quantity given here, make a dry caramel following the instructions on page 227.
14. Sit the biscuit base on your serving plate and place the choux ring on top. When the caramel is ready, lift one side of the ring and dribble a teaspoon of caramel onto the biscuit base and stick the ring down. Repeat at two or more points around the ring so it is secured to the base. Dip the base of each profiterole, one at a time, into the caramel then swiftly press it on top of the choux ring. Attach as many profiteroles round the ring that will fit.

MAKE THE CHOCOLATE GLAZE

15. Finely chop the chocolate and add to a medium bowl. Heat the cream to almost boiling point, then pour over the chocolate. Leave for 2 minutes, then stir to blend the cream and chocolate together.
16. Spread the caramel pastry cream onto the biscuit base, smoothing it out to the choux ring border, then level the top. Spoon the chocolate glaze over and use the back of a spoon to encourage it to spread and completely cover the pastry cream. There will be a few tablespoons left.
17. Break the excess shortbread into abstract shapes, 3–4cm (1–1½ inches) in size, then pick out 15 good pieces for decoration. Re-warm the caramel in the pan if it has hardened and, one at a time, spoon a little over the top of each profiterole and stick on a piece of shortbread. Repeat until each profiterole has been decorated. Drizzle a little of the leftover chocolate glaze over the shortbread.
18. Serve straight away or store somewhere cool for up to 3 hours. Any leftovers can be stored in an airtight container in the fridge; however, the choux will gradually lose its crispness.

PEANUT
BUTTER
AND
JELLY

Although it's a well-established combination, I'm relatively new to enjoying the fruity, nutty pairing of peanut butter and jelly (read jam). In my childhood it spoke of exotic, brown paper bag-wrapped lunches, eaten at recess in North American schools we only ever visited via our TV screens. While the kids at Degrassi Junior High ate their PBJs, I enjoyed my own peanut butter mash-up, but in a more British fashion as PBM. The 'M' being Marmite. So this chapter is really about making up for lost time. If you've never tried it, consider other great fruit and nut combinations – raspberries and almond, apple and walnut, hazelnut and... chocolate, and it will make more sense. The peanut appears as both peanut butter and whole nuts, the jelly as berry-based jams and fresh fruit, and as for the sandwich, well, what's a doughnut if it isn't the best jam sandwich you've ever eaten?

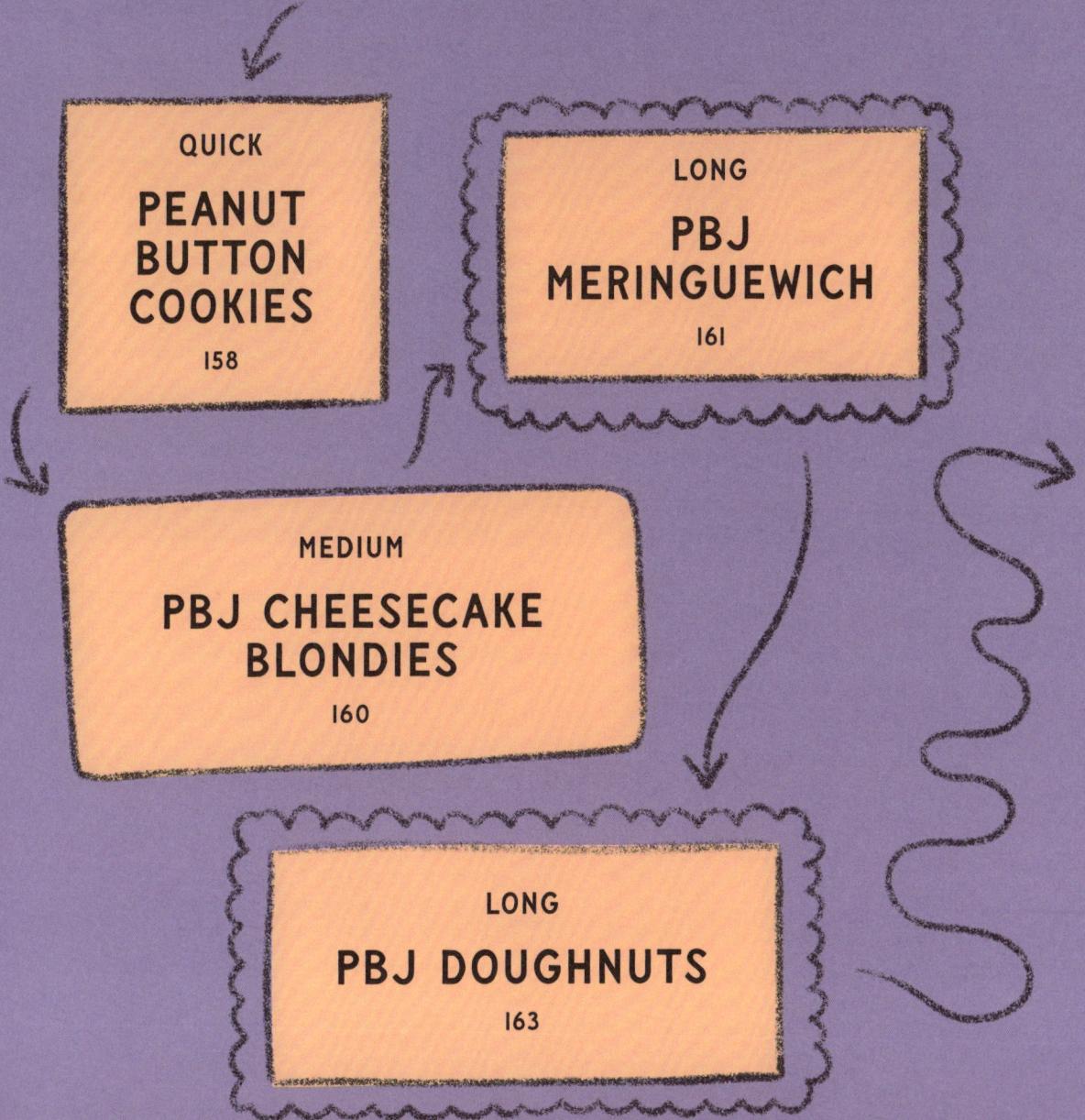

PEANUT BUTTON COOKIES

Hands on **15 minutes**
Ready in **30 minutes**

MAKES
16 cookies or 8 sandwiches

EQUIPMENT
Large flat baking sheet

These delicious, soft, little peanut butter cookies may be as cute as buttons, but they are useless for holding up your trousers. Filled or sandwiched with jam, they are however perfect for delivering a sweet and swift solution to a PBJ craving. You can choose to fill them with jam, like a thumbprint cookie, by pressing the back of a measuring teaspoon into the just-baked dough, or you can leave them to cool and sandwich them with jam instead. (If you want to swap the jam for chocolate spread, I'm happy to look the other way, provided you let me try one.)

80g (2¾oz) peanut butter* (either smooth or crunchy)

80g (2¾oz) golden syrup

Large pinch of salt

25g (¾oz) plain (all-purpose) flour or gluten-free plain (all-purpose) flour + a pinch of xanthan gum

½ tsp baking powder

75g (2⅔oz) jam (jelly or preserve) of your choice (such as strawberry, raspberry, etc)

1. Set the oven to 150°C fan (325°F/gas 3) and line a flat baking sheet with baking paper.
2. To a medium bowl, add the peanut butter, golden syrup and salt and mix with a spoon or a rigid spatula until well blended.
3. Add the flour and baking powder, then stir in until all the dry ingredients have been incorporated. If using gluten-free flour, combine the flour, xanthan gum and baking powder before adding.
4. Wet your hands, then scoop up 10g (⅓oz) of the dough at a time. Lightly roll into a ball and place on the prepared baking sheet. If you prefer, you can spoon teaspoons of dough onto the sheet. Leave space in between each cookie to allow for their slight spread.
5. Bake in the middle of the oven for 8–10 minutes or until the cookies have puffed, their surfaces are lightly crazed with tiny cracks and they have turned a very pale golden colour. Don't leave them to colour more than that or they won't be softly chewy when cooled.
6. To make filled cookies, gently press the back of a ½ teaspoon measure into the soft dough to make an indentation in each one. Fill the indentations with a small blob of jam. Leave to cool for 10 minutes on the baking sheet before transferring to a wire rack to cool completely.
7. To make sandwiches, do not make any indentations in the cookies; leave them to cool on the baking sheet before transferring to a wire rack to cool completely. Spread a little jam on the flat underside of one cookie, then sandwich together with a second cookie.

---

*You can make these with any type of peanut butter: whole nut, with or without added sugar, with or without added oil, etc. Cookies made with a peanut butter that has added oil may spread slightly further than those without, but overall there's very little difference in the results, so just use whatever you have in the cupboard.

PBJ CHEESECAKE BLONDIES

Hands on **15 minutes**
Ready in **1 hour 15 minutes**

MAKES
16 squares

EQUIPMENT
20 x 30-cm (8 x 12-inch) brownie tin (pan)

With a crisp, crackly top and a light, chewy middle, with just a hint of fudginess, these peanut butter blondies are great as just peanut butter blondies. But what bake isn't improved by adding a fruity cheesecake element? Particularly when it's so shamefully easy to achieve. When the blondies are baked and cooled, simply cover them with a generous layer of cream cheese and swirl over lashings of your favourite jam for an almost-instant conversion to PBJ Cheesecake Blondies.

PEANUT BUTTER BLONDIE

75g ($2\frac{2}{3}$ oz) salted butter

210g ($7\frac{1}{2}$ oz) peanut butter (either crunchy or smooth)

3 large (US extra-large) eggs

300g ($10\frac{1}{2}$ oz) granulated sugar

Pinch of salt

75g ($2\frac{2}{3}$ oz) plain (all-purpose) flour or 125g ($4\frac{1}{2}$ oz) gluten-free self-raising mix

$\frac{1}{4}$ tsp baking powder (omit if using gluten-free flour)

CHEESECAKE TOPPING

300g ($10\frac{1}{2}$ oz) full-fat cream cheese or soft cheese

120g ($4\frac{1}{4}$ oz) jam (jelly or preserve) of your choice (such as blackcurrant, raspberry or strawberry)

1. Set the oven to 175°C fan (375°F/gas 5) and line the brownie tin with baking paper.
2. To a medium bowl, add the butter and peanut butter. Gently warm in the microwave to melt the two, then mix together until blended. If you don't have a microwave, melt the two together in a pan over a very low heat.
3. To a stand mixer or large mixing bowl, add the eggs, sugar and salt. Beat for 2 minutes until thick and mousse-like. Using a handheld mixer may take slightly longer.
4. Pour the peanut butter mixture into the foamy egg, then add the flour and baking powder (if using wheat flour). Fold the dry ingredients into the wet, stopping as soon as everything is evenly combined. Scrape the batter into the lined tin and level the top.
5. Bake in the middle of the oven for 28 minutes or until a skewer inserted into the centre of the blondie comes out clean.
6. Leave the blondie to cool in the tin for 10 minutes. Using the edges of the paper, lift it onto a wire rack to cool completely.
7. Spread the cream cheese over the cooled blondie. Stir the jam with a spoon to loosen it up, then dot it over the cream cheese and swirl it in just a little – don't blend it, you want generous patches of jam.
8. Cut the blondie into 16 squares. Leftovers will keep well for several days when stored in an airtight container in the fridge.

PBJ MERINGUEWICH

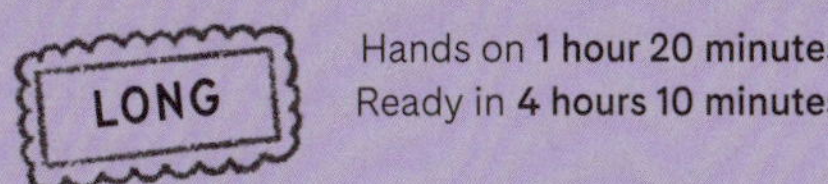

Hands on **1 hour 20 minutes**
Ready in **4 hours 10 minutes**

SERVES 8–10
Makes one 18 x 23-cm (7 x 9-inch) meringue cake

EQUIPMENT
Two large flat baking sheets

I could have called this a sandwich-shaped peanut strawberry pavlova, but I saw the opportunity to torture some words into a pun and so I took it. Sandwich = Meringuewich. I have no shame. What I do have is options for filling these deliciously nutty meringues. Strawberries and strawberry jam are a must, but you can choose whether to layer them with a pastry cream or just whipped cream to save a little time. For pastry cream, use the yolks left over from the meringue, or if you've used egg white from a carton, and haven't got any yolks, use a whole egg. And of course you don't have to shape the meringues as a sandwich; a roundwich or a squarewich will taste just as good.

PEANUT MERINGUE

200g (7 oz) salted peanuts

190g (6⅔ oz) granulated or caster (superfine) sugar

30g (1 oz) dark brown soft sugar

4 large (US extra-large) egg whites or 160g (5⅔ oz) chickpea (garbanzo bean) aquafaba

¼ tsp cream of tartar

PASTRY CREAM

20g (¾ oz) cornflour (cornstarch)

25g (¾ oz) granulated sugar

4 egg yolks (or 1 whole egg)

½ tbsp vanilla extract

200g (7 oz) whole (full-fat) milk

40g (1⅓ oz) unsalted butter, at room temperature

OR

350g (12⅓ oz) double (heavy) cream, whipped to soft folds (instead of pastry cream)

TO ASSEMBLE

100g (3½ oz) strawberry jam (jelly or preserve)

250g (9 oz) fresh strawberries, hulled and sliced

1. Set the oven to 100°C fan (210°F/gas ¼).
2. On a sheet of baking paper, draw a 'slice of bread' approximately 18 x 23cm (7 x 9 inches). Copy that shape onto another sheet of baking paper so you have two identical 'slices'. Use these pieces of baking paper to line the baking sheets, placing the drawn-on sides facing downwards.
3. Finely chop the peanuts to roughly the size of grains of rice. You can use a food processor but don't blitz the nuts too small or the oils will be released and affect the meringue later.
4. To a medium bowl, add both sugars and mix well.
5. In a stand mixer or a separate bowl, use the egg whites, cream of tartar and sugar mix to make a French meringue (page 216). Carefully fold the peanuts into the meringue, stopping when they are evenly distributed.

Continued overleaf

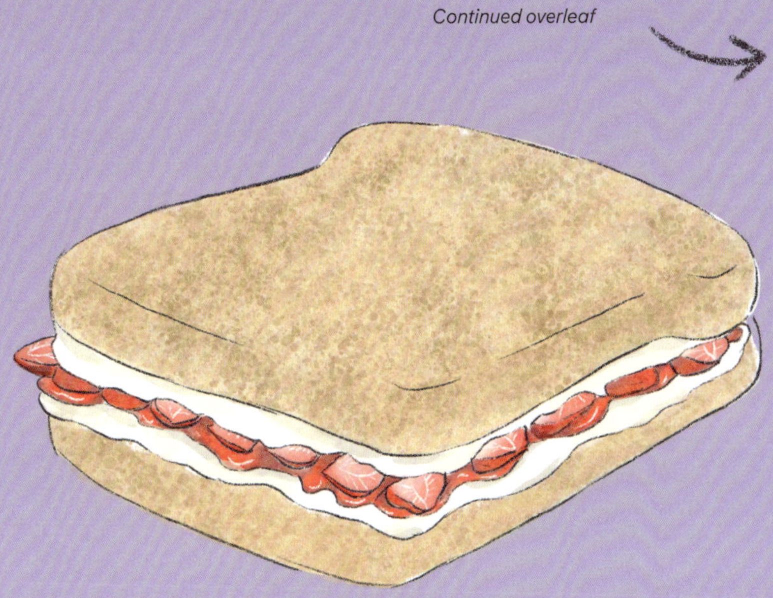

6. Spoon half the meringue onto each lined baking sheet and use a palette knife or back of a spoon to smooth it into the 'slice' shape. Level the surface. The meringue should end up about 2cm (¾ inch) high.
7. Bake on the middle shelves of the oven for 2 hours or until the meringues are crisp and dry. Once baked, switch off the oven and leave the door propped open until the 'slices' are completely cool.
8. While the meringues bake, make the pastry cream. Follow the instructions on page 220 but use the 4 egg yolks left over from the meringues in place of the whole egg.
9. When the meringues are cool and the pastry cream has chilled, start assembling the Meringuewich. Carefully peel the baking paper off the base of the meringues and set one 'slice' right side up on your serving plate and spread over half the pastry cream. Stir the jam with a spoon to loosen it up, swirl it over the cream and then layer on the sliced strawberries. Spread the remaining pastry cream over the top of the second 'slice' so when you invert it over the sliced strawberries the visible top is the flat underside of the meringue. If your meringue has misbehaved, stuck to the baking paper and is not looking great, you can do it the other way round.
10. Assemble the Meringuewich an hour before serving so the meringue softens slightly and cuts easily into neat slices. All the components can be made in advance, if you have an airtight container to fit the meringues.

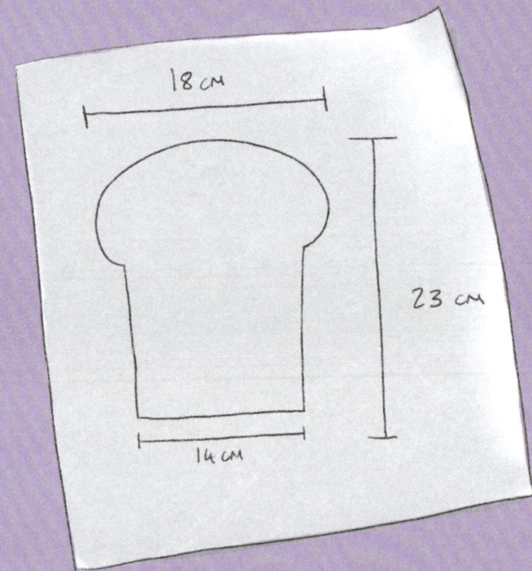

PLANT-BASED PBJ MERINGUEWICH

1. For the meringue, make a plant-based French meringue (page 217), swapping the egg whites for aquafaba, then follow the directions given for the egg version. Aquafaba meringue is fragile, so rather than the 'slice' shape, you might prefer to spread it into two 20-cm (8-inch) circles, which will be structurally more robust.
2. For the filling, make a full quantity of plant-based pastry cream (see page 221) or use 350g (12⅓ oz) of whippable plant-based double (heavy) cream.

PBJ DOUGHNUTS

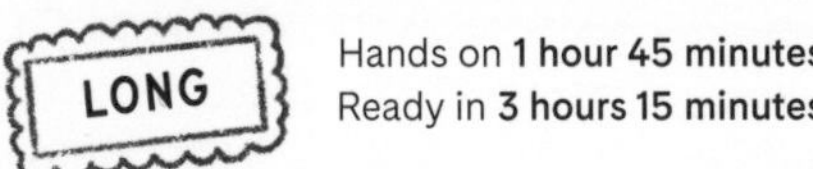

Hands on **1 hour 45 minutes**
Ready in **3 hours 15 minutes**

MAKES
9 doughnuts

EQUIPMENT
Large flat baking sheet

Just to be clear, these doughnuts are baked to avoid the associated smell and clear up that comes with deep-fat frying rather than any attempt to sidestep extra calories. Dipped in a sweet, buttery syrup after baking, then rolled in sugar and filled with caramel pastry cream and jam, no one is going to assume they are a salad. Or indeed that they are baked. The dough uses tangzhong paste, which is flour cooked with liquid to form a custard-like paste, that gives a fluffier, lighter texture to the finished bake. It also keeps the dough fresher for longer, robbing you of the excuse to eat them all in one go. Sorry.

TANGZHONG PASTE

30g (1 oz) plain (all-purpose) flour

255g (9 oz) milk (whole/full-fat dairy or plant-based)

35g (1¼ oz) salted butter (dairy or plant-based)

DOUGHNUT DOUGH

1 tsp fast-action dried yeast

20g (¾ oz) granulated sugar

250g (9 oz) strong white bread flour

½ tsp salt

1 tsp flavourless oil, if using the pull-and-fold kneading method

CARAMEL PEANUT PASTRY CREAM

20g (¾ oz) cornflour (cornstarch)

10g (⅓ oz) granulated sugar

½ tbsp vanilla extract

120g (4¼ oz) milk (whole/full-fat dairy or plant-based)

25g (¾ oz) coconut oil or dairy unsalted butter

100g (3½ oz) salted peanuts

110g (3¾ oz) Salted Caramel Sauce (dairy or plant-based, page 230), or ready-made spreadable sauce from a jar (not runny from a squeezy bottle)

Ingredients continued overleaf

1. Line the baking sheet with baking paper.
2. To make the tangzhong paste, add the flour to a heavy-bottomed pan. Slowly pour in 175g (6¼ oz) of the milk, whisking out any lumps. Add the butter and put the pan on a medium-low heat. Stir continuously until the mixture becomes as thick as softly whipped cream; this only takes a minute or so. Scrape into a large bowl and whisk in the remaining 80g (2¾ oz) of milk until you have a smooth paste with a custard-like consistency. Leave to cool to no more than 35°C (95°F).
3. Whisk the yeast and sugar into the cooled tangzhong paste. Add the flour and salt, then mix to a ragged dough with a table knife.
4. Next, pull the dough into a ball with your hands. This is a sticky dough so I recommend using the pull-and-fold kneading method or a stand mixer. If using pull and fold, you'll find it's more a case of folding than pulling as the dough isn't very elastic until after its first proof. For pull and fold, pour 1 teaspoon of oil into the bowl, roll the dough around in it and then follow the instructions on page 212. For a stand mixer, use a dough hook and mix for 10 minutes. Cover the bowl with a shower cap or cling film (plastic wrap) and leave to proof until doubled in size.
5. While the doughnut dough is proofing, make the egg-free pastry cream (page 221) using the quantities given here, but using the peanuts and salted caramel sauce (in place of cream) in the next step.
6. When the pastry cream is firm and cold, add the peanuts to a food processor and process until very finely ground and almost peanut butter. Scrape the peanuts from the sides and base of the processor then add the cold pastry cream and blitz until it becomes a smooth paste. Add the salted caramel sauce and beat until thick and smooth. Scrape into a piping (pastry) bag with a 6-mm (¼-inch) nozzle and set aside at room temperature until needed.

Continued overleaf

JAM FILLING

150g (5¼ oz) strawberry jam (jelly or preserve)

SOAKING SYRUP

100g (3½ oz) granulated sugar

300g (10½ oz) water

25g (¾ oz) salted butter (dairy or plant-based)

SUGAR FOR COATING

100g (3½ oz) granulated sugar

7. Stir the jam to loosen it. Scrape into a separate piping bag with a 6-mm (¼-inch) nozzle and set aside at room temperature until needed.
8. Tip the dough onto a lightly floured surface and divide it into 9 equal portions. (For accuracy, weigh the dough and divide the total weight by 9.) Roll each portion into a ball by making a loose, low cage with your hand over the ball. Roll the dough over the surface in a circular motion to form neat spheres, applying light pressure to the dough with your palm. The dough should be just tacky enough that there's some purchase between your palm and surface. If it's too sticky, use extra flour sparingly.
9. Place the balls on the lined baking sheet, leaving space between each one for them to expand. Press down to flatten into discs 1cm (⅓ inch) high and 8cm (3 inches) in diameter. Cover loosely with a sheet of oiled baking paper or cling film (plastic wrap) and leave to proof.
10. When the doughnuts are puffy and proofed (see page 213, step 7), preheat the oven to 175°C fan (375°F/gas 5).
11. Bake on the second shelf down in the oven for 15 minutes, until puffed and lightly golden
12. While the doughnuts are baking, make the soaking syrup. Add the sugar and water to a heavy-bottomed pan. Put on a medium heat until the sugar has dissolved, then boil for 5 minutes. Remove from the heat and stir the salted butter into the syrup; it will melt but not emulsify completely.
13. When the doughnuts are baked, leave them to cool on their baking sheet for 10 minutes. (Don't dip them too early as they will collapse.) Once cooled, using two dessert spoons, pick up a doughnut and lower it into the syrup, soak each side for 15 seconds, then remove and sit on a wire rack. Repeat for the remaining doughnuts.
14. As soon as they have been dipped and are still warm, fill the doughnuts. Starting with the first-dipped, use a chopstick to poke a hole into the centre of the doughnut, being careful not to pierce all the way through. Inject around 15g (½ oz) jam into the doughnut by pushing the tip of the piping bag a few mm into the hole. Cup the doughnut in one hand and pipe down into it so that you can gauge how much pressure is needed to fill them. Follow this with 40g (1⅓ oz) of the peanut pastry cream. You can weigh the doughnuts before and during filling to make sure they are being filled equally and no one's being diddled out of their fair share.
15. Add the sugar for coating to a shallow, wide bowl. Roll each doughnut in the sugar when filled. If the doughnuts aren't sticky enough for the sugar to cling to them, brush a little extra syrup over each one before coating. Eat straight away or within 24 hours.

RHUBARB AND CUSTARD

If you've never tasted rhubarb, it's sour. But not like lemon, which has a bright tartness. Rhubarb has a more intriguing, slightly metallic astringency that, as you can tell from this sentence, is quite hard to describe. Word waffle aside, the cool, vanilla creaminess of custard provides a delightfully straightforward foil to all of rhubarb's sour complexity. Rhubarb appears as a no-cook syrup, sugar macerated slices, softly baked stems and an airy mousse. Custard turns up as cookies, pastry cream and – sorry to be obvious – actual custard. As well as their flavour, the colour combination of the two is just as much of a pull for me. Whether it's pink and cream in their natural states or pink and bright yellow in their boiled sweet incarnations, both are fully honoured by my food colouring collection. Adding colouring is optional. I think it makes things more fun, but feel free to opt out if you've lost some capacity for joy.

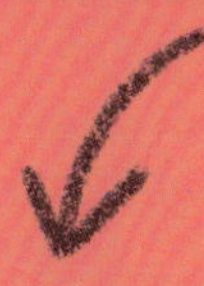

RHUBARB ROLL AND CUSTARD

Hands on **15 minutes**
Ready in **45 minutes**

SERVES
2 hungry people or
4 peckish ones

EQUIPMENT
Swiss roll tin (jelly roll pan) or large baking tray with a lip

Wrap a stalk or two of rhubarb in marzipan, then puff pastry, and then bake it. If you don't like marzipan, I won't spend too much time trying to convince you that it bakes into the pastry and its almondy sweetness is a delicious way to round out the sour rhubarb. If you're not convinced then all the more for the marzi'fans'. This is a great Sunday evening pudding, so easy to make and so packed with custard-topped comfort, it can ward off the dread of the worst Monday mornings.

200g (7 oz) rhubarb (1 very fat or 2 averagely built stalks)

200g (7 oz) marzipan

1 x 320-g (11-oz) packet of ready-rolled puff pastry

1. Set the oven to 175°C fan (375°F/gas 5) and line the Swiss roll tin or baking tray with baking paper.
2. Trim the ends of the rhubarb. If the stalks are very curved, make shallow cuts across the back of the rhubarb along its length so they lie flat and straight.
3. Roll out the marzipan into a rectangle the same length as the rhubarb and wide enough to wrap fully around the stalks with a narrow overlap. Roll up the stalks in the marzipan. Use a little water to moisten the marzipan at the join and press to seal.
4. Sit the marzipan-covered rhubarb on the pastry sheet. Roll to wrap the rhubarb in a single layer of pastry with overlap on the underside of the pastry roll. Cut away the excess pastry. Trim the pastry at the ends of the roll, leaving just enough to pinch together to seal the gap. This helps stop the juices running out of the sides.
5. Using a sharp knife, cut small slits through both the pastry and marzipan across the top of the roll and along its length, like a classic sausage roll. Sit on the lined tray and bake for 30 minutes in the middle of the oven until puffed and golden.
6. While the roll bakes, if making your own, start the custard (see opposite).
7. Once baked, leave the rhubarb roll to cool for 5 minutes and then cut up and serve with custard, cream or ice cream. (Or all three.)

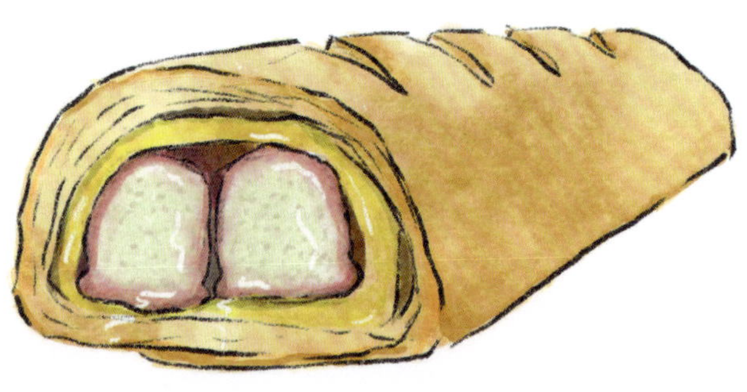

EGG CUSTARD

SERVES 4–6

15g (1/2 oz) cornflour (cornstarch)

30–40g (1–1 1/3 oz) granulated sugar (start with 30g/1 oz, then add more if you want it sweeter)

2 egg yolks

1/2 tbsp vanilla extract

500g (17 1/2 oz) milk (any)

50g (1 3/4 oz) double (heavy) cream

HOB: HANDS ON / READY IN 15 MINUTES

1. To a medium bowl, add the cornflour, sugar, yolks, vanilla and a little of the milk and mix to a loose, lump-free paste.
2. To a heavy-bottomed pan, add the remaining milk and put on a medium heat. Bring to the boil then trickle into the cornflour and egg mix, whisking continuously until all the hot milk has been combined. Pour back into the pan and stir in the cream.
3. Put on a medium-low heat and stir continuously with a silicone spatula to stop any lumps forming as the custard thickens. When the custard is a similar consistency to double (heavy) cream, taste to check the chalkiness of the cornflour has cooked out; if not, keep cooking until it has gone.
4. Serve immediately when ready or sit a piece of baking paper or cling film (plastic wrap) directly over the surface of the custard to stop a skin forming as it cools. Reheat gently when needed.

MICROWAVE: HANDS ON / READY IN 10 MINUTES

1. To a medium, microwave-safe bowl or a large jug (pitcher), add the cornflour, sugar, yolks, vanilla and enough milk to mix to a loose, lump-free paste, then mix in the remaining milk and cream.
2. Microwave in 90-second bursts, whisking after each one. When the custard starts to thicken, heat in shorter bursts. Once the custard is the consistency of double (heavy) cream, taste to check the chalkiness of the cornflour has cooked out; if not, keep cooking until it has gone.
3. Continue as directed in step 4 above.

PLANT-BASED CUSTARD

SERVES 4–6

25g (3/4 oz) cornflour (cornstarch)

30g (1 oz) granulated sugar

1/2 tbsp vanilla extract

425g (15 oz) plant-based milk

150g (5 1/4 oz) plant-based cream

HOB: HANDS ON / READY IN 15 MINUTES

1. To a heavy-bottomed pan, add the cornflour, sugar, vanilla and 50g (1 3/4 oz) of the plant-based milk, then mix until lump free. Add the remaining milk and cream, then mix well.
2. Continue as directed in steps 3 and 4 for the Hob Egg Custard.

MICROWAVE: HANDS ON / READY IN 10 MINUTES

1. To a medium, microwave-safe bowl or a large jug (pitcher), add the cornflour, sugar, vanilla and 50g (1 3/4 oz) of the plant-based milk, then mix until lump free. Add the remaining milk and cream, then mix well.
2. Continue as directed in steps 2 and 3 for the Microwave Egg Custard.

CANDIED RHUBARB AND CUSTARD COOKIES

Hands on **25 minutes**
Ready in **1 hour 10 minutes**
plus 5 days if you make the candied rhubarb

MAKES
8 cookies

EQUIPMENT
Flat baking sheet

These sweet vanilla cookies are balanced out by the sharp twang of candied rhubarb, the happy byproduct of making cheong (page 175). This bake relies on the miraculous properties that macerating with sugar bestows on the rhubarb, allowing it to keep its structure and flavour when heated. Please don't try making these cookies with fresh rhubarb; the fruit (yes, I know it's a vegetable) simply collapses into sour, mushy patches, ruining an otherwise great cookie. If you don't have any candied rhubarb, start the cheong now and in five days you can make these cookies. Which does add to the 'ready in' timing, but they're worth the wait, I promise.

150g (5¼ oz) Candied Rhubarb (page 175)

Pink food colouring (optional)

Citric acid (optional)

100g (3½ oz) salted butter, softened

40g (1⅓ oz) granulated sugar

60g (2 oz) golden syrup

1 tsp vanilla extract

25g (¾ oz) custard powder (I use Bird's; if you can't get custard powder, use cornflour/ cornstarch + 2 tsp vanilla extract)

125g (4½ oz) plain (all-purpose) flour or 135g (4¾ oz) gluten-free self-raising mix

1 tsp baking powder (omit if using gluten-free flour)

1. To a medium bowl, add the candied rhubarb and stir through the food colouring to make it pink, if you like. Add the citric acid to taste, if using, a pinch at a time, and stir through, then set aside.
2. To a large bowl, add the butter, sugar, syrup and vanilla. Mix with a spatula, then add the custard powder and stir that in.
3. Add the flour and baking powder (if using wheat flour) and start to mix until you have a crumbly dough – don't fully combine everything.
4. Add the candied rhubarb, mixing it in until evenly distributed. Bring everything together as a smooth dough.
5. Chill the dough in the fridge for 15 minutes. If using gluten-free flour, chill the dough for 30 minutes.
6. Set the oven to 175°C fan (325°F/gas 5) and line the baking sheet with baking paper.
7. Scoop about 64g (2¼ oz) dough for each cookie. Roll the dough into balls then slightly flatten each one onto the lined baking sheet. Leave space between each one for the cookies to spread.
8. Bake in the middle of the oven for 12 minutes until puffed and slightly golden at the edges.
9. Leave to cool on the baking sheet for at least 10 minutes before attempting to move them to a cooling rack. For gluten-free, leave the cookies on the baking sheet to cool completely (they're less robust than their wheaty cousins and more likely to break when warm).

RHUBARB AND CUSTARD MOUSSE CAKE

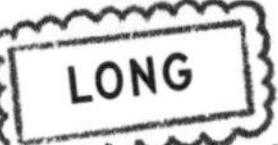

Hands on **2 hours**
Ready in **5 hours 40 minutes**

SERVES 12–14
Makes one 23-cm (9-inch) cake

EQUIPMENT
23-cm (9-inch) springform cake tin (pan)

10-cm (4-inch) wide acetate roll

If you've got rhubarb in your freezer that was frozen as fresh stalks, rather than stewed, this is a great use for it. The best way to preserve rhubarb's flavour is to cook it as little as possible; as freezing breaks down its structure, you only need to heat rhubarb very briefly to turn it into a punchy purée. This layered mousse cake – consisting of a layer of light almond sponge soaked with a strawberry compote, covered with thick, vanilla pastry cream, topped with an airy rhubarb and strawberry mousse, then finished with a ginger ganache glaze and mini meringues – makes the most of all that zingy, summery flavour. And if you think that description was a mouthful, wait until you try the cake.

RHUBARB AND STRAWBERRY COMPOTE

4 sheets of gelatine (6.5g/1⁄5 oz total weight)

400g (14 oz) rhubarb (fresh or frozen)

30g (1 oz) granulated sugar

200g (7 oz) strawberries (fresh or frozen)

Pink gel food colouring

1⁄2 tsp vanilla extract

VANILLA PASTRY CREAM

45g (1 1⁄2 oz) cornflour (cornstarch)

60g (2 oz) granulated sugar

1 whole egg

2 egg yolks

1 1⁄2 tbsp vanilla extract

300g (10 1⁄2 oz) whole (full-fat) milk

Yellow gel food colouring

60g (2 oz) unsalted butter, cubed

225g (8 oz) double (heavy) cream, to be beaten into the cooled custard

MAKE THE COMPOTE

1. To a medium bowl, add the gelatine sheets and cover with cold water. Leave to soak for up to 10 minutes while you stew the rhubarb.
2. If using fresh rhubarb, finely slice it no thicker than 5mm (1⁄5 inch). The thinner you can cut it, the faster it will stew. Add it to a wide frying pan (skillet) with a lid with 15g (1⁄2 oz) of the sugar. If using frozen rhubarb, there's no need to defrost it first unless it needs to be chopped, just add to the pan with the sugar. Put on a medium-high heat, stir the rhubarb and after a minute or so, when the water starts to release from the cut stalks, put the lid on, turn the heat to low and simmer gently just until the rhubarb starts to soften. For frozen, this usually only takes a minute. For fresh, this takes about 4–5 minutes. Switch off the heat, keep the lid on and leave to sit for 5 minutes; the rhubarb will soften further in the residual heat.
3. The rhubarb should be almost completely collapsed by now, but use a masher or fork to make sure all of it has broken down to a pulpy purée. Wring the water from the gelatine sheets, add to the pan and stir well to ensure all the gelatine dissolves into the warm rhubarb. (Make sure you retrieve all four sheets of gelatine from the water, they're completely transparent and can be easily missed.)
4. Defrost the strawberries, if using frozen, then blitz to a purée with a food processor or blender.
5. Add 100g (3 1⁄2 oz) of the strawberry purée to the rhubarb and mix well, then add enough pink colouring to deepen the colour – it will lighten slightly when the meringue is folded through it later. Scrape into a large bowl and leave on the side to cool.
6. Add the remaining strawberry purée to a small bowl, stir in the other 15g (1⁄2 oz) of sugar and the vanilla extract.

ALMOND SPONGE CAKE

JUG (PITCHER)

1 large (US extra-large) egg

25g (3/4 oz) sunflower oil or vegetable oil

15g (1/2 oz) / 1 tbsp water

2 tsp vanilla extract

MIXER

60g (2 oz) granulated sugar

70g (2 1/2 oz) plain (all-purpose) flour or gluten-free plain (all-purpose) flour + 1/8 tsp xanthan gum

20g (3/4 oz) ground almonds (almond meal)

3/4 tsp baking powder

Pinch of salt

35g (1 1/4 oz) sunflower oil or vegetable oil

MERINGUE

2 egg whites

Pinch of salt

1/4 tsp cream of tartar

110g (3 3/4 oz) caster (superfine) or granulated sugar

Pink gel food colouring

GINGER GANACHE GLAZE

40g (1 1/3 oz) syrup from stem ginger

50g (1 3/4 oz) double (heavy) cream

25g (3/4 oz) unsalted butter

75g (2 2/3 oz) white chocolate, finely chopped

Yellow gel food colouring

Pink gel food colouring

MAKE THE PASTRY CREAM

7. Using the quantities given here, follow the recipe on page 220 to make a pastry cream, adding the yellow food colouring to the milk in step 2. Leave the hot custard to cool in step 5; you will beat the cream in later to finish the pastry cream.

MAKE THE CAKE

8. Set the oven to 160°C fan (350°F/gas 4) and line the base of the springform cake tin with baking paper.

9. To a jug (pitcher), add the egg, the 'jug' oil, water and vanilla and roughly blend everything with a fork.

10. To a stand mixer (fitted with a whisk attachment) or large bowl, add the sugar, flour, ground almonds, baking powder, salt and xanthan gum (if using). Mix briefly then pour in the 'mixer' oil. Start the mixer on slow to make a damp, clumpy, breadcrumb-like mix.

11. Turn the mixer to fast and slowly pour in half the egg mix. Beat for 30–60 seconds or until the batter becomes thick, fluffy and lump free. Stop the beaters and scrape down the sides of the bowl.

12. Start the mixer again on fast and trickle in the remaining egg mix. When all the egg has been added, beat for a further 30 seconds or until the batter looks smooth. Pour the batter into the cake tin and level it well, particularly for gluten-free.

13. Bake in the middle of the oven for 14 minutes or until the cake looks matt and set, and springs back a little when gently pressed. Leave in its tin for 5 minutes, then remove to a wire rack to cool completely.

FINISH THE PASTRY CREAM

14. Break up the firm, cooled custard into a stand mixer or a large bowl and beat with a whisk attachment until it breaks down to a fine scrambled egg texture. Add the cream and beat; it will quickly become thick and smooth; stop as soon as it does. Scrape into a piping (pastry) bag fitted with a large nozzle; 1.5–2cm (1/2–3/4 inch) is ideal.

Continued overleaf

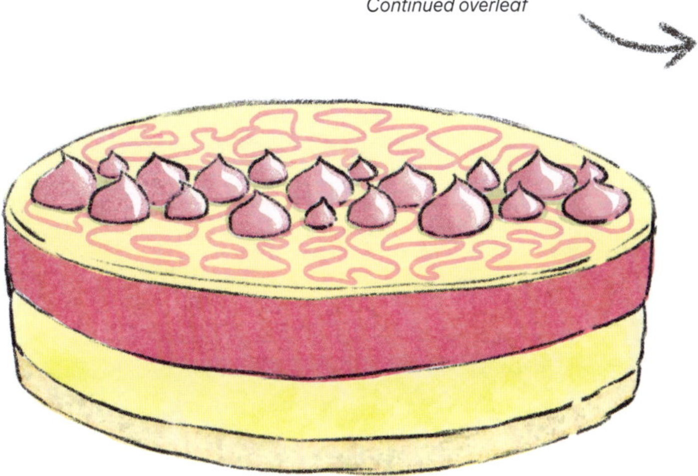

ASSEMBLE THE CAKE

15. Invert the cake onto your serving plate so the flat base faces up. Sit the closed springform tin side around the cake to act as a mould. Tuck a long strip of acetate inside the tin to line it, overlapping the ends – the cake will hold it in place. Alternatively, use strips of baking paper.

16. Spread the remaining strawberry purée evenly over the cake. Pipe the pastry cream over the soaked cake in a spiral from the outer edge inwards. Level the pastry cream with an offset spatula or the back of a spoon and put the cake in the fridge to chill.

MAKE THE MERINGUE

17. Using the quantities given here, follow the recipe on page 216 to make a French meringue. Add the pink colouring after the last addition of sugar.

MAKE THE MOUSSE

18. Check the rhubarb and strawberry compote has cooled to at least 35°C (95°F) then add 150g (5¼oz) of the meringue to the bowl. Using a large silicone spatula, carefully fold the compote together with the meringue, stopping as soon as both are evenly combined. Pour the mousse over the pastry cream. Return to the fridge for 3 hours or until the mousse has set firm. Start the mini meringues immediately.

19. Set the oven to 100°C fan (210°F/gas ¼). Line a baking sheet with baking paper. Scrape the remaining meringue into a piping (pastry) bag fitted with a 1-cm (⅓-inch) nozzle. Pipe kisses of meringue in varying sizes from 1cm to 3cm (⅓ to 1 inch) wide, with gaps in between, until the sheet is filled or the meringue is used up. Bake in the middle of the oven for 1 hour, or until dry enough to lift off the paper. Prop the door open with the handle of a wooden spoon and leave the meringues there to cool completely.

20. When the mousse has set firm, but is bouncy when lightly pressed, start the ganache glaze. To a microwave-safe bowl, add the ginger syrup, cream, butter and finely chopped white chocolate. Microwave in short bursts until the chocolate has melted. If you don't have a microwave, use a heatproof bowl over a pan of hot water. Stir until smooth and glossy. Remove 25g (¾oz) of the ganache to a small bowl and stir in a little pink colouring to match the meringues, then scrape into a piping (pastry) bag with a 2-mm (1/16-inch) nozzle. Add yellow colouring to the ganache in the bowl. When the pink ganache has slightly cooled but is still pourable, pour over the mousse and level with an offset spatula. Wiggle a random thread of pink ganache all over the yellow.

21. Put the cake back in the fridge for at least 30 minutes to set the glaze. You can chill the cake at this stage for up to 24 hours, if you want to make it ahead of time. If so, keep the meringues in an airtight container until needed.

22. Just before serving, run a hot sharp knife around the acetate where it meets the ganache glaze then carefully peel the strip away. Decorate the top with the meringue kisses, then serve. The cake will be stable at room temperature but is best served chilled and eaten within 24 hours. Any leftovers can be kept covered and stored in the fridge.

GANACHE DECORATION

GINGER GANACHE GLAZE

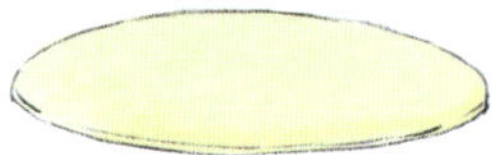

RHUBARB AND STRAWBERRY MOUSSE

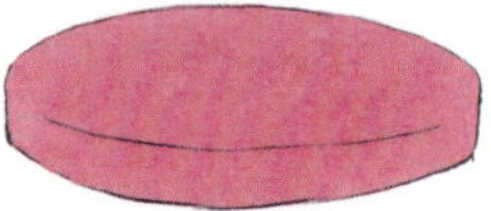

VANILLA PASTRY CREAM

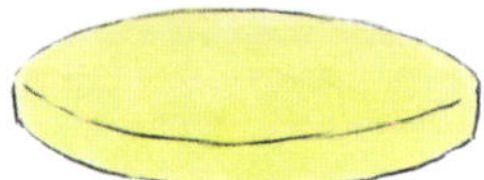

STRAWBERRY PURÉE

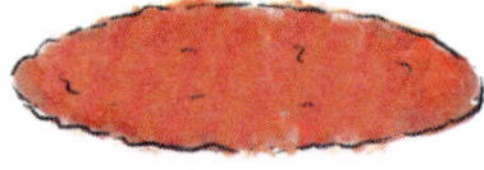

ALMOND SPONGE CAKE

RHUBARB CHEONG AND CANDIED RHUBARB

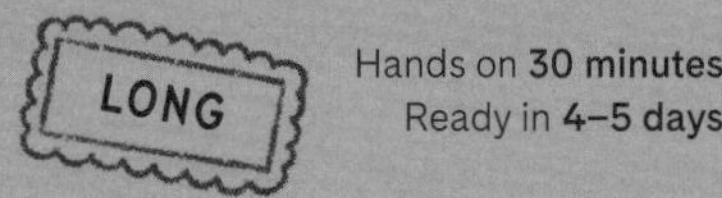

Hands on **30 minutes**
Ready in **4–5 days**

MAKES
350g (12⅓ oz) syrup

EQUIPMENT
Sterilised glass jar with lid

Cheong is a Korean method of making flavoured no-cook syrups by macerating equal weights of fruit and sugar, and it works perfectly with rhubarb. Even though rhubarb is a vegetable. The rhubarb and sugar simply sit together in a jar for a few days, during which time the juices leach from the cut stalks, dissolve the sugar and create syrup. Because the flavours aren't diminished by heat, all the fresh, bright taste is preserved in both the syrup and the resultant candied rhubarb. Use the syrup as a cordial with sparkling water or add a dash to a G&T or a glass of fizz or just slosh some over vanilla ice cream. Use the candied rhubarb in the Candied Rhubarb and Custard Cookies on page 170–1.

Use an equal weight of fruit to sugar. To fill a 1-litre (1-quart) jar or bottle use:

400g (14 oz) fresh rhubarb

400g (14 oz) granulated sugar

Pink gel food colouring (optional)

Citric acid (optional)

1. Wash and dry the rhubarb, then cut the stalks into 1-cm (⅓-inch) slices.
2. Layer the rhubarb and sugar in the sterilised jar, making sure the final layer is sugar and the cut rhubarb is well covered. Seal the jar with a lid. Leave it somewhere dark and cool, such as a cupboard.
3. After a couple of days, stir the rhubarb and syrup to encourage any remaining sugar to dissolve. If using, add the pink food colouring and stir in so the rhubarb can fully absorb it.
4. After 5 days, all the sugar will have dissolved so drain the rhubarb and syrup through a jelly bag or a fine sieve (strainer). Leave it draining for a couple of hours to catch all the syrup.
5. If you want to give the syrup a little extra zing, stir in citric acid, a pinch at a time, until it's as sour as you want it. If your citric acid is granular rather than powdered, gently heating the syrup will encourage it to dissolve.
6. Bottle the syrup in a sterilised jar or bottle, then store in the fridge or freezer (the sugar content means it won't freeze solid).
7. Unless using straight away, keep the candied rhubarb in an airtight tub or sealable plastic food bag in the freezer until needed.

ROCKY ROAD

Just like life, Rocky Road is what you make of it. Only you really can't screw up Rocky Road because it's supposed to be a beautiful mess of broken things. And isn't that a bit like life? Enough fridge magnet philosophy, let's get back to the baking. I say baking, this chapter is actually a no-bake affair. If you want to go the extra mile, down the Rocky Road, you'll find recipes in the Foundation Recipes chapter to make your own biscuits (pages 214–215) and marshmallow (page 219). After mandatory biscuits for crunch and marshmallows for chew, everything else is really up to you. Nuts, seeds, dried fruit, other chocolate treats, whatever you like. Break them up, throw them in and stick the whole delicious jumble together with a chocolatey, buttery, syrupy mortar. The result is beauty emerging from chaos, like a slab of confectionery terrazzo.

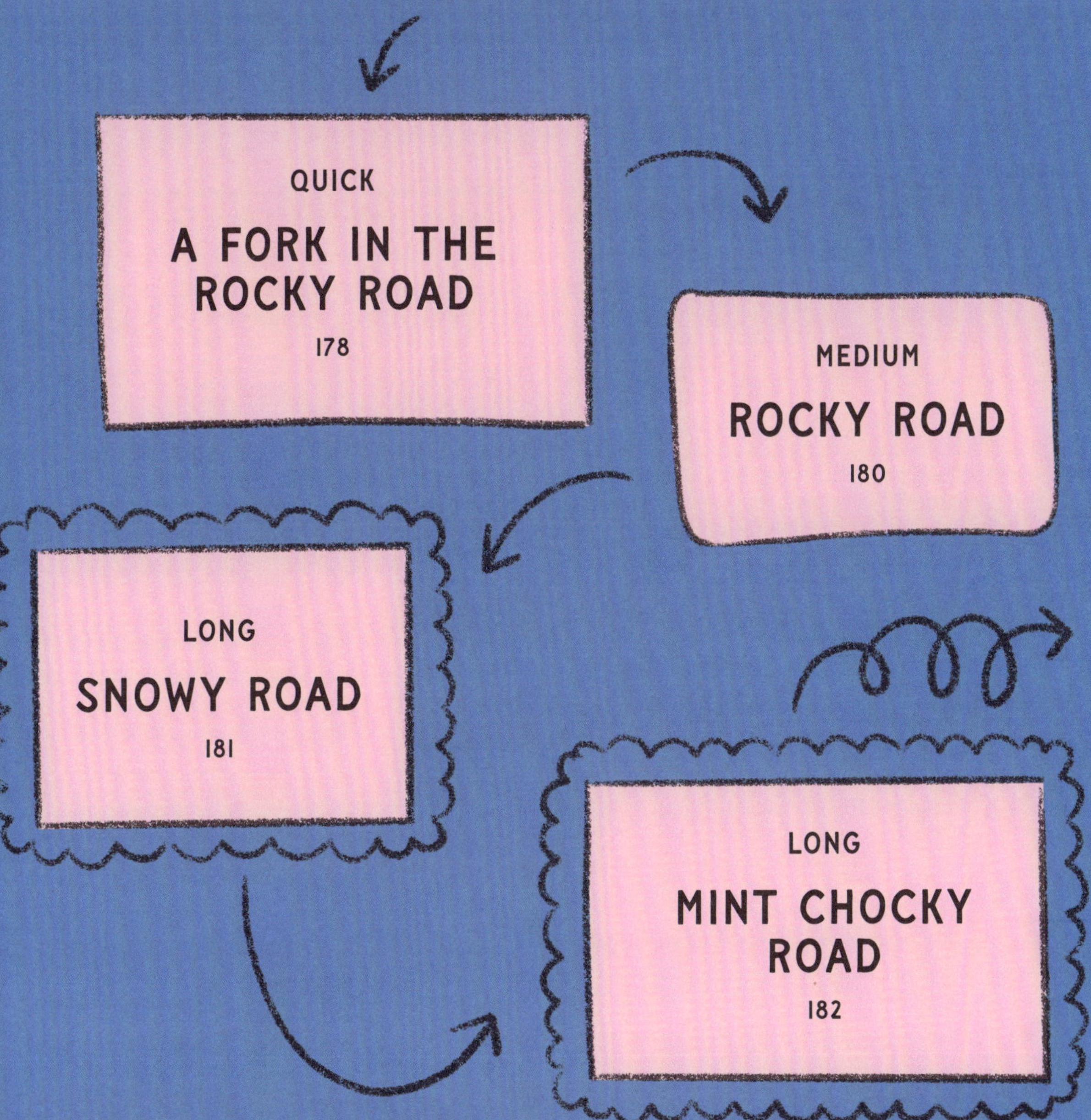

A FORK IN THE ROCKY ROAD

Hands on **10 minutes**
Ready in **25 minutes**

MAKES
12 large or 24 small

EQUIPMENT
Flat baking sheet

12 forks

When you come to a fork in the road, don't worry about the one less travelled. Choose the one that leads to a shop where you can buy chocolate, marshmallows and biscuits. If you're hankering for a Rocky Road hit, these are the quickest of fixes. Just a few minutes of melting, dipping and crumbing and you'll have all the chocolatey, marshmallowy chew and biscuity crunch you're after. And as these are served on a fork... Why! They're practically dinner.

150g (5¼ oz) milk or dark (bittersweet) chocolate

20g (¾ oz) coconut oil

12 giant marshmallows or 24 large marshmallows

25g (¾ oz) biscuits of your choice – digestives (graham crackers), ginger nuts, speculoos, shortbread, etc.

25g (¾ oz) nuts of your choice

25g (¾ oz) dried fruit of your choice

25g (¾ oz) mini marshmallows

1. Line the flat baking sheet with baking paper.
2. To a medium microwave-safe bowl, add the chocolate and coconut oil. Microwave in short bursts to melt the two, then mix them together. If you don't have a microwave, put the bowl over a pan of hot water.
3. Spear one giant or two large marshmallows with each fork.
4. Crush the biscuits and roughly chop the nuts and fruit of your choice, then add each to their own small bowl.
5. Dip a marshmallow in the melted chocolate so it's fully coated and lay it with its fork on the lined baking sheet. Sprinkle over the biscuit crumbs, then the chopped nuts and fruit. Leave the coated and loaded marshmallow on the baking sheet and drizzle over more chocolate, add more biscuit crumbs, nuts and fruit or stick on a few mini marshmallows. Repeat with the remaining marshmallows. Chill them on the baking sheet for 15 minutes to set the chocolate.
6. Eat straight away or store at room temperature.

ROCKY ROAD

Hands on **20 minutes**
Ready in **40 minutes–1 hour**

MAKES
12–16 squares

EQUIPMENT
20 x 30-cm (8 x 12-inch) brownie tin (pan)

Is the name Rocky Road an ironic one? Because the journey you take in making this low-stakes, no-bake slab of biscuit, chocolate and marshmallow yum couldn't be smoother. It's just melting, crushing, stirring and chilling. Nothing's going to go soggy, nothing's going to overbake, nothing's going to collapse because you don't know what folding means. Your only potential obstacle is someone getting to the chocolate before you do, so you'd better crack on.

200g (7 oz) milk chocolate

125g (4½ oz) dark (bittersweet) chocolate (40% cocoa)

200g (7 oz) salted butter

75g (2⅔ oz) golden syrup

400g (14 oz) digestive biscuits (graham crackers), rich tea, malted milk or shortbread biscuits OR source gluten-free alternatives OR make your own gluten-free digestives (page 215) and Vanilla Mini Biscuits (page 214)

45g (1½ oz) mini marshmallows

125g (4½ oz) chopped nuts / chopped dried fruit (optional)

TO DUST (OPTIONAL)

2 tsp icing (confectioners') sugar

½ tsp cornflour (cornstarch)

1. Line the brownie tin with baking paper.
2. In a medium microwave-safe bowl, melt both chocolates, the butter and syrup gently in the microwave. If you don't have a microwave, put the ingredients in a heavy-bottomed pan on a very low heat and stir until melted and mixed.
3. Crush half of the biscuits to fine crumbs. You can add them to a large bowl and crush them with the base of a glass or seal them in a strong plastic food bag and roll a rolling pin over them.
4. Break the remaining biscuits into approximately 1.5-cm (½-inch) pieces.
5. Add the marshmallows and the nuts and/or dried fruit, if using, to the biscuit bowl. Pour the warm chocolate mixture over and mix well until all the biscuits etc. are well coated.
6. Scrape into the lined brownie tin and roughly level the mixture. Chill for 20 minutes in the freezer or 45 minutes in the fridge until completely set.
7. If using, mix the icing sugar with the cornflour, put in a fine-mesh sieve (strainer) and dust the top of the Rocky Road.
8. Cut into 12–16 squares. Store in an airtight container at room temperature.

PLANT-BASED ROCKY ROAD

Simply swap the chocolate, dairy butter and marshmallows for plant-based versions. Most ready-made digestive biscuits are plant-based anyway, but you can make your own digestives (page 215) or vanilla mini biscuits (page 214) with plant-based butter.

SNOWY ROAD

Hands on **50 minutes**
Ready in **up to 2–3 hours**

MAKES
12–16 squares

EQUIPMENT
20 x 30-cm (8 x 12-inch) brownie tin (pan)

Full quantity of Rocky Road (page 180)

Full quantity of Marshmallow (page 219)

TO DUST

1 tbsp icing (confectioners') sugar

1 tbsp cornflour (cornstarch)

If you think marshmallow is the best bit of a Rocky Road, this is the version for you. Not only is the thick, chocolatey base riddled with mini marshmallows but the whole thing is covered in a deep, snowy blanket of marshmallow topping for you to plough your way through.

1. Make the Rocky Road following the instructions opposite. When chilled and set, remove from the fridge or freezer, but don't cut it into pieces yet. Leave it at room temperature while you make the marshmallow.
2. Make a batch of Marshmallow following the instructions on page 219. Pour it over the top of the Rocky Road and then leave it to set at room temperature.
3. Mix the icing sugar and cornflour, add to a small, fine-mesh sieve (strainer) and lightly dust the surface of the marshmallow.
4. Cut into 12–16 pieces. Store in an airtight container at room temperature.

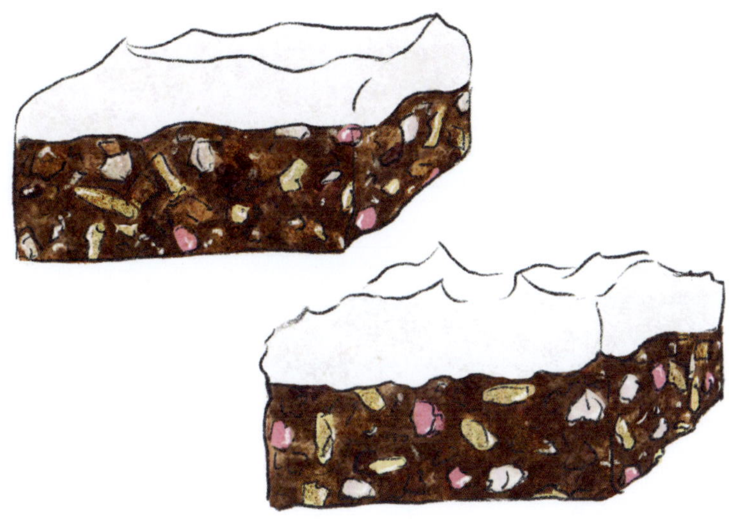

For a bit of a S'mores vibe, if you're so inclined, you can sully the pristine, virgin white 'snow' by lightly blow-torching its surface after it has set. One should always steer clear of yellow snow, but in this case toasted, golden snow is more than acceptable.

MINT CHOCKY ROAD

Hands on **55 minutes**
Ready in **4 hours 15 minutes**

SERVES 12–14
Makes one tall 21-cm (8½-inch) pie

EQUIPMENT
21-cm (8½-inch) loose-bottomed tart tin (pan)

A crunchy, chewy, chocolatey rocky road base, filled with lurid mint choc chip ice cream (yes, it does have to be green, it's the law) topped off with a cartoonishly tall bouffant of meringue. This big old ice-cream pie is very much my outer adult feeding my inner child the pudding it always wanted but was never allowed. Whether it can handle the excitement, or ends up needing a time out, we'll have to see.

BISCUIT BASE

105g (3¾ oz) milk chocolate

85g (3 oz) salted butter

35g (1¼ oz) golden syrup

250g (9 oz) digestive biscuits (graham crackers), shortbread, rich tea or malted milk*

20g (¾ oz) mini marshmallows (optional)

NO-CHURN MINT CHOC CHIP ICE CREAM**

250g (9 oz) sweetened condensed milk

375g (13¼ oz) double (heavy) cream

2–3 tsp peppermint extract

Light green and yellow food colouring

75g (2⅔ oz) mint chocolate or dark (bittersweet) chocolate, chopped into small chunks

ITALIAN MERINGUE***

165g (5¾ oz) granulated sugar

50g (1¾ oz) water

10g (⅓ oz) / ½ tbsp golden syrup or glucose syrup

3 egg whites (120g/4¼ oz from a carton)

Pinch of salt

¼ tsp cream of tartar

1. Start with the biscuit base. Gently melt the chocolate, butter and syrup together in a microwave-safe bowl in the microwave or in a heavy-bottomed pan on a very low heat.
2. Crush the biscuits to fine crumbs. You can use a food processor or put them in a large bowl and crush them with the base of a glass or seal them in a strong plastic food bag and roll a rolling pin over them.
3. If using, snip the marshmallows into 5-mm (¼-inch) pieces and stir into the melted chocolate mix. Pour the chocolate over the crushed biscuits straight away and mix in well.
4. Press the mixture into the base of the tart tin so it's about 1cm (⅓ inch) thick and then up the sides to the rim. Put in the freezer to set.
5. While the base sets, make the ice cream. To a large mixing bowl, add the condensed milk and cream and give them a gentle stir together. Add the peppermint extract half a teaspoon at a time, mixing and tasting after each one, but bearing in mind that flavours taste less strong when frozen so you can be relatively bold.
6. Add the green food colouring. If your colouring is a dark green, use it sparingly and add a little yellow to make it a light minty green.
7. Start to beat everything together with an electric hand mixer. The mixture will become paler as it thickens, so add more colour if needed. Stop beating when the ice cream holds soft peaks and fold in the chopped chocolate. Scrape the ice cream into the chilled biscuit base, smooth the top into a shallow dome and return to the freezer.
8. The ice cream will be frozen after approximately 4 hours; however, you can leave it in the freezer, covered, for up to 48 hours.
9. About 45 minutes before you want to serve, using the quantities given here, make the Italian meringue following the instructions on page 218.
10. When the meringue has cooled to room temperature, remove the pie from the freezer and, using a large palette knife, pile it onto the mound of ice cream. Use the palette knife to shape the meringue up and over the ice cream – you can smooth it, swirl it or pull it up into spiky peaks. When you're happy with the finish, you can lightly toast the marshmallow with a blow torch or leave it pristine and white.

11. Serve the pie within 15 minutes of removing it from the freezer. Covering it in meringue will take 5–10 minutes so that only leaves about 5 more minutes to wait until you can eat it. And that's plenty of time to dig out the cake forks.
12. Any leftover pie can be wrapped in cling film (plastic wrap) and frozen, however the meringue will deteriorate and so it's best eaten within 3 days.

---

*If you want to make your own biscuits, or you can't source gluten-free biscuits, you'll need one quantity of Digestive Biscuits (page 215) or a double quantity of Vanilla Mini Biscuits (page 214). Or make one quantity of each.

**You can use 1 litre (1 quart) of store-bought ice cream instead of making your own, but the No-Churn Mint Choc Chip is so quick and simple there isn't really much difference timewise.

***Italian meringue is perfect for this because of its impressive stability, however, if you want to save a little time you can use French meringue (page 216). Use the same amount of egg whites and sugar, but omit the water.

STICKY TOFFEE PUDDING

Discovering Sticky Toffee Pudding is actually made with dates is a rite of passage. I went through it as a teenager when I wanted to make my first one. Being told I had to start by soaking dates in boiling water felt like nothing less than a betrayal. I had assumed, not unreasonably, I'd been scarfing down a light sponge pudding that was sticky with toffee, but you're telling me I've been eating fruit this whole time? Worse, dried fruit? My youngest son went through his own loss of innocence while I was devising this chapter's recipes. Poor thing had to put his spoon down and take a few deep breaths as reality hit him. So dates are mandatory and fully represented throughout these recipes, all of which are egg-free. Dates' superpower to provide structure in the absence of egg means no one will miss them and the recipes can be easily veganised. The toffee is present as caramel-filled chocolate, but mostly as brown sugar-flavoured sauce. If you're still finding the truth about Sticky Toffee Pudding hard to swallow, washing it down with plenty of sticky toffee sauce will definitely help, I promise.

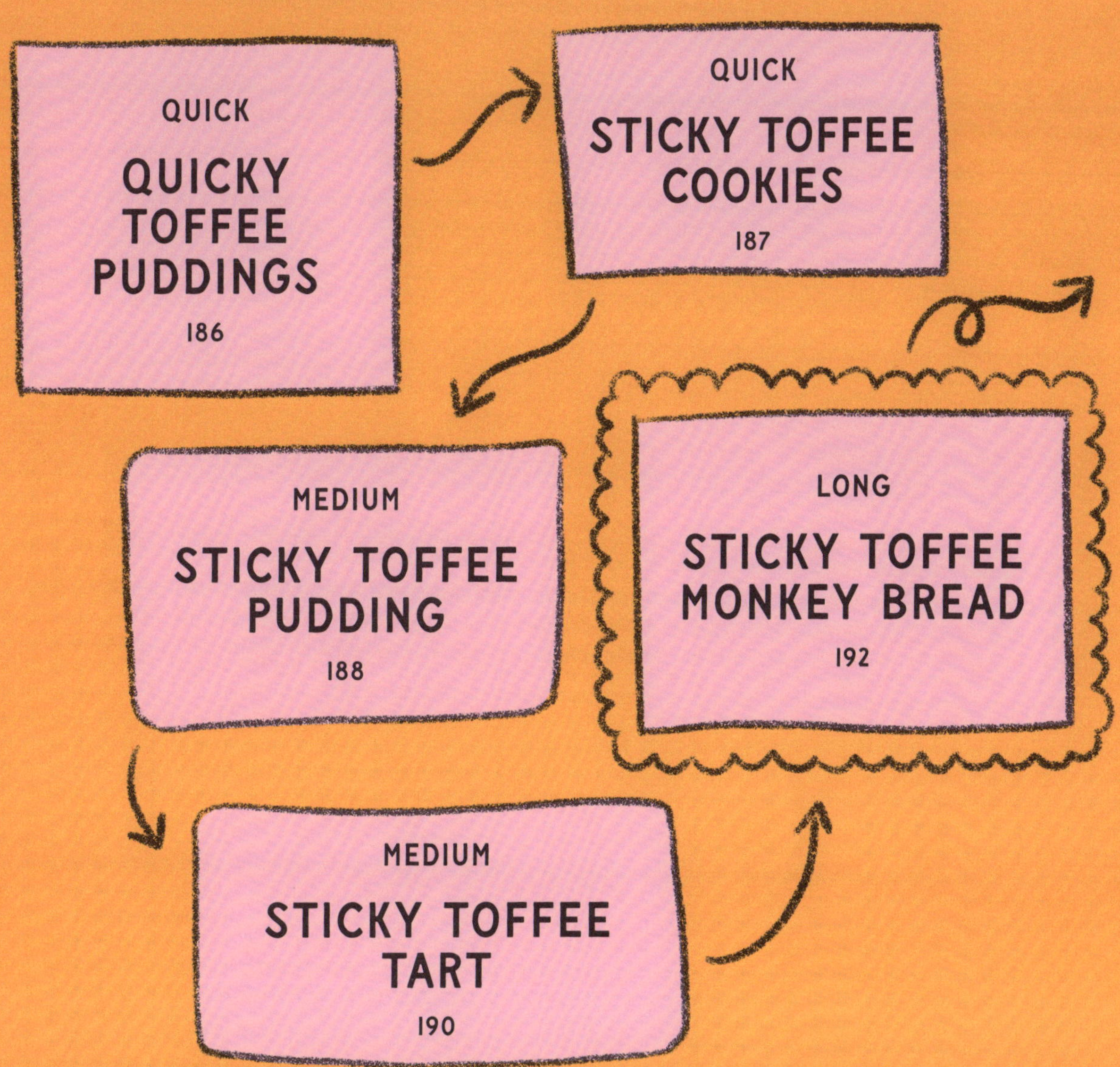

QUICKY TOFFEE PUDDINGS

Hands on **15 minutes**
Ready in **20 minutes**

SERVES 4

EQUIPMENT
4 x 120-ml (4-fl oz) ramekins

These quick microwave puddings, with a cakey exterior and saucy centre, are perfect for any small dessert-shaped void in your tum tum. There's no added sugar in the batter of dates, butter and flour, but that's more than made up for by serving them with a glug of toffee sauce and a scoop of ice cream. It's all about balance: balancing the pudding, the ice cream and the sauce on your spoon.

100g (3½ oz) blocked stoned dates or pressed dates, crumbled

1 tsp bicarbonate of soda (baking soda)

¼ tsp instant coffee powder

50g (1¾ oz) salted butter (dairy or plant-based)

100g (3½ oz) boiling water

40g (1⅓ oz) plain (all-purpose) flour or gluten-free plain (all-purpose) flour

¼ tsp baking powder

Half quantity of Sticky Toffee Sauce (page 189)

1. Roughly chop the dates and add them to a food processor along with the bicarbonate of soda, coffee powder, butter and boiling water. Blitz to a smooth runny paste. (If you don't have a food processor, see page 188.) The butter can be added cold straight from the fridge as it will melt in the heat of the water.
2. Add the flour and baking powder, then blitz until the dry ingredients are fully mixed into the batter.
3. Divide the batter equally between the ramekins (store-bought glass pudding pots are the perfect size for this). Microwave each one for 30–35 seconds* or until the puddings have puffed up and the surface looks set but the middle is slightly soft.
4. Spoon 1–2 tablespoons of the Sticky Toffee Sauce over each pudding and top with a scoop of vanilla ice cream. Keep the remaining sauce in a jug (pitcher) to hand for when you need a top up.

* This timing is for an 800 watt microwave. If using a lower-powered machine, the puddings require a longer cooking time; for higher powered machines, shorten the cooking time.

WITHOUT A MICROWAVE

These puddings are best cooked in the microwave; if you don't have one, try them in your oven. By comparison, they'll take longer to cook, which renders them Not-Very-Quicky-Toffee-Puddings, but I'll leave the option here for any microwave refuseniks. Sit the ramekins on a baking sheet and bake at 175°C fan (375°F/gas 5) for 16–18 minutes or until the puddings have puffed, the top and sides are set, but the middles are slightly soft.

STICKY TOFFEE COOKIES

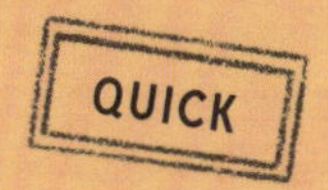

Hands on **15 minutes**
Ready in **45 minutes**

MAKES
12 cookies

EQUIPMENT
Large flat baking sheet

All the STP flavours but in a chewy cookie. The toffee component is represented by a square of caramel-filled chocolate; wrapped in the date dough, it becomes the cookie's concealed core. Baked until they puff and then banged on the work surface so they collapse and wrinkle into a classic cookie, their hidden centre of caramel chocolate is only revealed when bitten into. Collapsed and wrinkled, but hiding a sensational secret – it's everything I wish for in my dotage.

200g (7 oz) blocked stoned dates or pressed dates

1 tsp bicarbonate of soda (baking soda)

1 tsp instant coffee powder

2 tsp vanilla extract

45g (1½ oz) / 3 tbsp boiling water

100g (3½ oz) salted butter (dairy or plant-based), at room temperature

125g (4½ oz) light brown soft sugar

Pinch of salt

200g (7 oz) plain (all-purpose) flour or 215g (7½ oz) gluten-free (all-purpose) flour + ¼ tsp xanthan gum

12 squares of caramel-filled chocolate

1. Set the oven to 175°C fan (375°F/gas 5) and line the baking sheet with baking paper.
2. Roughly chop the dates and add them to a food processor along with the bicarbonate of soda, coffee powder, vanilla and boiling water. Blitz to a smooth runny paste. (If you don't have a food processor, see page 188.)
3. Add the butter, sugar and salt, then blitz until evenly combined. Add the flour (and xanthan gum, if using). Pulse until fully mixed into the dough.
4. Very lightly oil your hands to make the dough easier to handle. Scoop up 55g (2 oz) of the dough, roll it into a satsuma-sized ball and sit it on the lined baking sheet. Repeat with the remaining dough, spacing them well apart so they have space to spread in the heat. Press a square of caramel-filled chocolate half way into each ball, pull the dough up from the sides and over the top of the chocolate to conceal it.
5. Bake in the middle of the oven for 13 minutes, or until they have puffed, slightly spread and their surface looks matt and set. As soon as the tray is out of the oven, drop it flat down onto the work surface from a height of about 15cm (6 inches) to jolt the cookies and encourage them to collapse and wrinkle. Leave to cool on the tray for 5 minutes before transferring to a wire rack to cool completely.

STICKY TOFFEE PUDDING

Hands on **20 minutes**
Ready in **45 minutes**

MAKES
One 20-cm (8-inch) square pudding or one half-sized loaf

EQUIPMENT
1 x 20-cm (8-inch) square ovenproof dish

Of course Sticky Toffee Pudding is delicious, however, for me its main function is as a sauce mule. It's there to smuggle as much Sticky Toffee Sauce into my mouth as possible without drawing attention. Until eating a bowl of sauce like a consommé is socially acceptable, I will continue to accompany it with a bit of pudding. This pudding, made from an egg-free batter, is packed full of datey, caramelly, toffee flavour and, bearing in mind it's a mule, it's delightfully light in texture.

PUDDING

200g (7 oz) blocked stoned dates or pressed dates, crumbled

1 tsp bicarbonate of soda (baking soda)

1 tsp instant coffee powder

2 tsp vanilla extract

150g (5¼ oz) boiling water

100g (3½ oz) salted butter (dairy or plant-based)

60g (2 oz) light brown soft sugar

Large pinch of salt

200g (7 oz) plain (all-purpose) flour or gluten-free plain (all-purpose) flour + ¼ tsp xanthan gum

4 tsp baking powder

SAUCE

Full quantity of Sticky Toffee Sauce (opposite)

1. Preheat the oven to 175°C fan (350°F/gas 5). Butter the ovenproof dish.
2. Make the pudding batter. Roughly chop the dates and add to a food processor* with the bicarbonate of soda, coffee powder, vanilla and boiling water. Blitz until smooth. Add the butter, sugar and salt and blitz again until combined. Add the flour and baking powder and pulse until everything is fully mixed. Scrape the batter into the prepared dish and level the top.
3. Bake in the middle of the oven for 30 minutes; the pudding is ready when a metal skewer comes out clean from the middle and the top springs back when lightly pressed.
4. While the pudding is baking, make the sauce following the instructions opposite.
5. Once baked, poke holes all over the pudding with a chopstick. Spoon over some of the sauce to glaze the top and soak into the sponge.
6. Serve portions of the pudding with the remaining warm sauce in a jug (pitcher) for pouring over.

***WITHOUT A FOOD PROCESSOR**

Finely chop the dates, add to a large bowl with the bicarbonate of soda, coffee (if the recipe requires it), vanilla and boiling water. Mash everything roughly together with a fork and leave for 5 minutes to soften. Mash again to get as smooth a paste as you can, then add the butter (to make mixing easier, soften the butter slightly), sugar and salt. Beat with an electric hand mixer to combine the ingredients and break the dates down further. Add the flour and baking powder (if the recipe requires it) and stir in by hand until the dough is fully mixed.

HALF-SIZED STICKY TOFFEE PUDDING

For a smaller pudding, halve the above quantities and bake in a lined 1-kg (2-lb) loaf tin (pan) for 20 minutes. Serve with a half quantity of sauce.

STICKY TOFFEE SAUCE

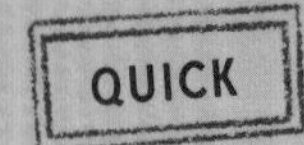

Hands on/Ready in **5 minutes**

MAKES
Enough sauce for a full-sized Sticky Toffee Pudding

All the toffee and caramel flavour in this sauce comes from using light and dark brown soft sugars, meaning there's no actual caramel to be sweated over and you can knock up a jugful in 5 minutes. What's more, it's very versatile. Not only does it adorn all the recipes in this chapter, it's also used in the Tiny Tart Tatins (page 198), and there's nothing stopping you pouring it over anything from ice cream to crumble. It's also incredibly useful for those awkward times when your waistband feels a bit loose.

40g (1⅓ oz) light brown soft sugar

90g (3¼ oz) dark brown soft sugar

150g (5¼ oz) double (heavy) cream (dairy or plant-based)

150g (5¼ oz) salted butter (dairy or plant-based)

1. Add the ingredients to a heavy-bottomed pan, put on a medium-high heat to melt the butter and dissolve the sugar, then bring to the boil.
2. Remove from the heat, taste and add a little salt if the salted butter hasn't provided enough.
3. Pour into a jug (pitcher) ready to serve.

(SERVING SUGGESTION)

STICKY TOFFEE TART

Hands on **25 minutes**
Ready in **1 hour 30 minutes**

SERVES 12
Makes one 21-cm (8½-inch) tart

EQUIPMENT
21-cm (8½-inch) loose-bottomed tart tin (pan)

I don't need to work too hard explaining this one; it's a tart with a sticky toffee pudding filling. Or do you want more? The pastry gives a short, crisp contrast to the dark, fudgy, datey, coffee, toffee-ness of the filling, which is topped with a glaze and a glug of sticky toffee sauce – there, you've covered all bases. Speaking of bases, there's no blind baking here. Just line the tart tin with pastry, spread in the filling, bake and eat.

PASTRY BASE

320g (11 oz) packet of ready-rolled shortcrust pastry

OR

Full quantity of Sweet Shortcrust Pastry (page 210)

OR

Full quantity of Gluten-Free Sweet Shortcrust Pastry (page 210)

FILLING

200g (7 oz) blocked stoned dates or pressed dates

1 tsp bicarbonate of soda (baking soda)

1 tsp instant coffee powder

2 tsp vanilla extract

75g (2⅔ oz) boiling water

75g (2⅔ oz) salted butter (dairy or plant-based), at room temperature

25g (1 oz) light brown soft sugar

Pinch of salt

65g (2⅓ oz) plain (all-purpose) flour or gluten-free plain (all-purpose) flour

1 tsp baking powder

SAUCE

Full quantity of Sticky Toffee Sauce (page 189)

1. If making your own pastry, follow the instructions on page 210. Note, the gluten version of this pastry does not use baking powder. Roll the pastry to 3mm (⅛ inch) thick.
2. Line the tart tin with the pastry and trim away any excess so nothing is overhanging the sides. Prick the base all over with a fork and chill in the fridge until the filling is ready.
3. Preheat the oven to 200°C fan (425°F/gas 7).
4. Make the filling using the quantities given here and following step 2 of the method for the Sticky Toffee Pudding (page 188).
5. Spoon the date filling into the chilled pastry case, spread out to the edges and level the top.
6. Put the tart in the middle of the oven. Immediately drop the temperature to 175°C fan (375°F/gas 5). This gives the pastry an initial blast of high heat to start it off, the oven cooling slowly for the rest of the baking time. Bake for 35 minutes until the pastry is golden brown and has shrunk slightly from the sides. The surface of the filling should look just set and have lost its gloss. The filling will be fudgy rather than springy and cake-like.
7. While the tart is baking, make the sauce following the instructions on page 189.
8. Once baked, leave the tart to sit for 5 minutes. Remove it from the tart tin (sides and base) and slide onto a cooling rack to allow the pastry to crisp as it cools. Spoon 3 or 4 tablespoons of the sauce over the hot tart to glaze the surface, then leave the tart to cool for 30 minutes. To serve, rewarm the sauce in the microwave or in a pan on the hob and pour over cut slices.

STICKY TOFFEE MONKEY BREAD

Hands on **55 minutes**
Ready in **3 hours**

SERVES 18
Makes one large bundt cake, 18 slices

EQUIPMENT
2.4-l (10-cup) bundt tin (pan)

DOUGH

320g (11¼ oz) warm water (no warmer than 35°C/95°F)

15g (½ oz) dark brown soft sugar

½ tsp instant coffee powder

1 tsp vanilla extract

2 tsp or 1 x 7-g (¼-oz) sachet fast-action dried yeast

500g (17½ oz) strong white bread flour

1 tsp salt

30g (1 oz) sunflower oil or any other flavourless oil

1 tsp flavourless oil, if using the pull-and-fold kneading method

FILLING

175g (6¼ oz) blocked stoned dates or pressed dates

½ tsp bicarbonate of soda (baking soda)

2 tbsp boiling water

1 tsp vanilla extract

75g (2⅔ oz) walnut pieces

SAUCE

60g (2 oz) light brown soft sugar

3 tbsp water

100g (3½ oz) salted butter

45g (1½ oz) double (heavy) cream (dairy or plant-based)

CINNAMON SUGAR

65g (2⅓ oz) granulated sugar

1 tsp ground cinnamon

TO ASSEMBLE

75g (2⅔ oz) walnut pieces

A gloriously sticky crown of monkey bread made from little buns of date and walnut-filled vanilla dough, rolled in cinnamon sugar and baked in a bundt tin with extra nuts and toffee sauce. For this, I offer two serving suggestions. Slice it up and present it on a doily-bedecked plate or lean into your primate ancestry and tear it apart with your fingers, then eat it swinging from the light fitting by your prehensile tail like an actual cheeky monkey. Let me know how you get on.

1. Making sure it is no more than 35°C (95°F), weigh the warm water into a mixing bowl. Add the sugar, coffee and vanilla, then give it a brief stir. Sprinkle in the yeast and swirl the bowl to encourage it to dissolve.
2. Add the flour, salt and oil. Use a table knife to mix everything together, scraping the sides of the bowl to incorporate all the ingredients. Stop when a ball of soft dough has formed. If using the pull-and-fold kneading method, pour 1 teaspoon of oil into the bowl, roll the dough around in it, then follow the instructions on page 212. Alternatively, knead the dough by hand for 12 minutes on a lightly oiled work surface or use a stand mixer with a dough hook for 10 minutes until the dough is smooth and elastic.
3. Cover the bowl with a shower cap or plastic bag and leave the dough to proof until doubled in size.
4. Once the dough has started its first proof, begin preparing the filling. Roughly chop the dates and add to a food processor with the bicarbonate of soda, boiling water and vanilla. Pulse to start to break the dates down. Add the walnuts and blitz to finely chop the nuts and make a paste with the dates. Scrape the filling into a bowl and chill in the fridge.
5. Next, make the sauce. Add the sugar to a heavy-bottomed pan with the water and put on a low heat. Stir together to dissolve the sugar. Once the sugar is mostly dissolved (it doesn't need to have disappeared completely), add the butter and cream. Stir to blend together, then turn up the heat slightly, bring up to the boil and remove from the heat.
6. Add the granulated sugar and cinnamon to a wide pasta bowl and mix.
7. Brush the inside of the bundt tin with cake release.

Continued overleaf

8. Once the dough has proofed, tip it onto your work surface – it shouldn't need any flour or oil – and roll into a long sausage. It will eventually be divided into 25 pieces, but work on five at a time. If you want to be uptight about it (I always am, it's actually quite fun), each one should weigh 35g (1¼ oz). Roll a piece of dough into a ball, then flatten into a disc. Spoon 10g (⅓ oz) of filling into the middle and pinch the dough around the filling to seal it. Roll the ball in the cinnamon sugar and leave, pinched side down, in the bowl while you roll, fill and coat the next four.
9. To assemble the bread, you will need two-thirds of the sauce – you can either eye it or pour off and reserve 85g (3 oz) to glaze the baked bread later. Drizzle 2 tablespoons of the sauce into the oiled tin, scatter in a few walnut pieces, then arrange the first five dough balls. Don't worry about their placement as they will expand and fill the space. However, do make sure that, for the first layer of balls, the pinched side is facing up, so when the bread is upturned, you only see smooth dough. Continue to roll, fill, coat the dough balls and arrange them in the tin with the walnuts and generous drizzles of sauce. When adding the final balls, make sure their pinched side is facing down so no filling will be exposed when they expand during baking.
10. Leave the dough for a short, second proof, approximately 15 minutes or until the exposed dough is puffy (see page 213, step 7).
11. Preheat the oven to 175°C fan (375°F/gas 5).
12. Bake in the middle of the oven for 40 minutes. The internal temperature of the dough needs to reach at least 90°C (195°F).
13. Leave the bread in the tin for 10 minutes, then turn out onto a serving plate. Spoon over the glaze, a spoonful at time, then leave to cool for a further 30 minutes before slicing or tearing apart.

TOFFEE APPLE

Food writers are fond of 'love letters' to foodstuffs. The best I can muster for toffee apples is a poison pen letter. I hate them. So why devote a chapter to them? Well I love toffee, I love apples, just not together in their toffee apple form where they bring out the worst in each other. Chewing a mouthful of leathery, grey apple skin along with tart, crunchy fruit flesh and razor-like shards of sugar shell is not my idea of fun. Just one of those masticatory challenges would be plenty, my mouth can't cope with all three. It's not a multitasker. Instead, these recipes offer a more relaxed eating experience. The apples deliver their slightly tart contrast to the sweet toffee, either baked to soft collapse or incorporated into fillings or cake batter. And the toffee is mostly present as sauces flavoured with either caramelised sugar, 'toffee-ed' condensed milk or brown sugars. Hard caramel is represented, but in easier-to-eat incarnations. And if you still want to challenge your chops, you could always eat the wooden stick.

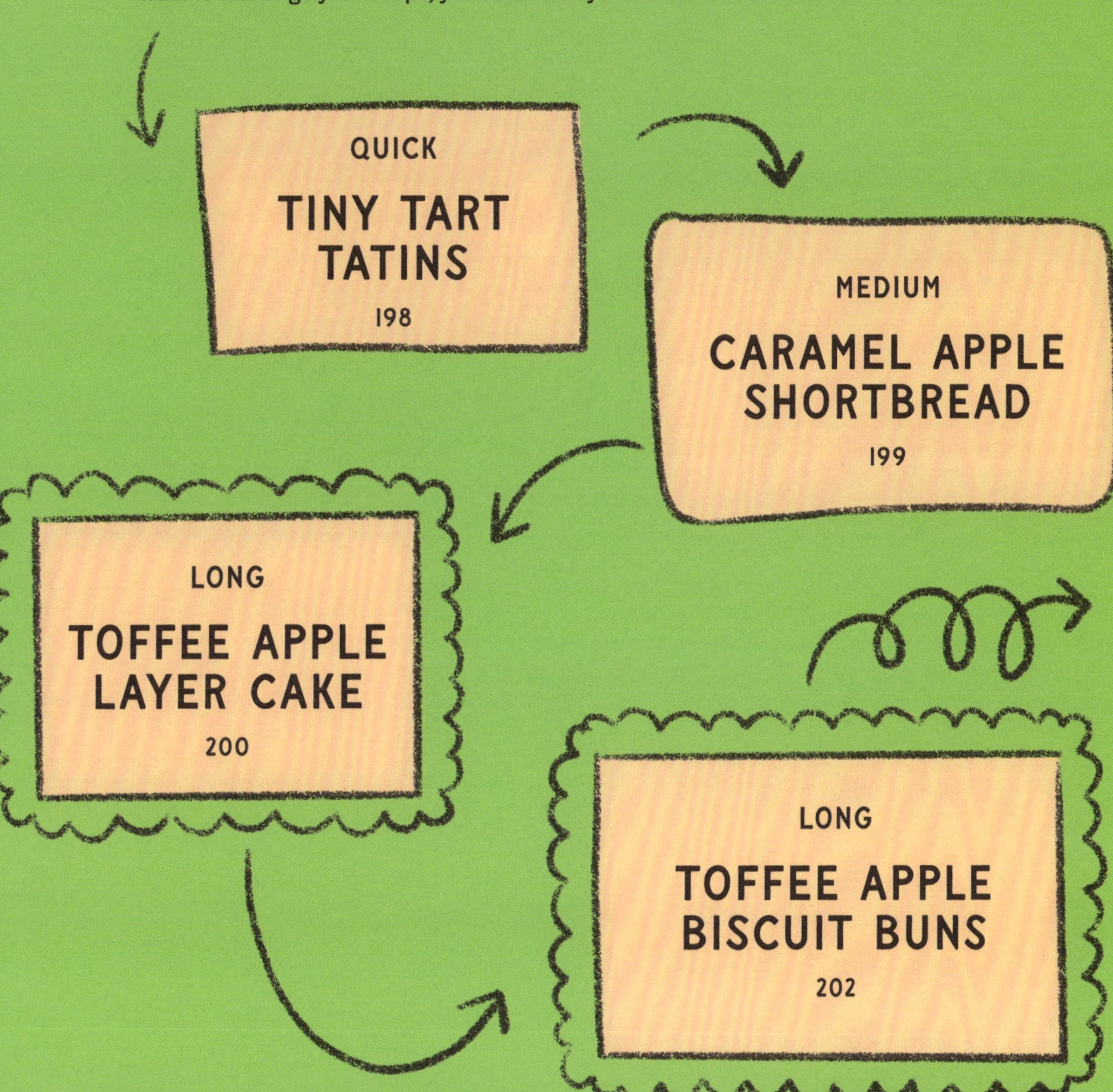

TINY TART TATINS

Hands on **30 minutes**
Ready in **40 minutes**

MAKES
6 mini tarts

EQUIPMENT
12 or 6 cup muffin tin (pan)

Flat baking sheet

If you're looking for an authentic Tarte Tatin recipe, this isn't it. The apples aren't slowly caramelised with sugar and butter in a cast-iron pan by a pair of French sisters. But if you're looking for crisp, flaky pastry, upside-down baked apples and a slick of sweet, buttery sauce, this does the job quickly and deliciously. And if you're outraged the name suggests they're at all authentic, firstly, here's a paper bag to breathe into, and secondly, imagine how cross you'd be if I'd called them Tat Tatins.

3 eating apples (Granny Smith or Braeburn)

Pinch of salt

320g (11 oz) packet ready-rolled puff pastry

Full quantity of Sticky Toffee Sauce (page 189)

1. Set the oven to 175°C fan (375°F/gas 5) and cut six 12-cm (5-inch) squares of baking paper.
2. Peel the apples and core with a corer to make a neat hole. Halve the apples horizontally and sprinkle the tiniest pinch of salt over each dome.
3. Sit a square of baking paper over a muffin cup, press an apple half into it, flat side up, and flatten the excess paper against the top of the tin. Repeat with the other apple halves.
4. Cut out six 8–9-cm (3–3½-inch) discs of pastry and lay one over each apple half. Use a fork to lightly press the rim of the pastry onto the tin to seal the edge. Poke a small slit through the centre of the pastry with a knife to allow the steam to escape.
5. Bake on the second shelf down for 20 minutes or until the centre of the pastry is as puffed and golden brown as the edges.
6. For decoration, roll the excess pastry to 2–3mm (⅛ inch) thick and cut out nine 2.5-cm (¾-inch) discs – the wide end of a piping nozzle is perfect for this – then poke a hole in the centre of each one with a chopstick. You need six discs, but make nine so you have spares. Using a knife, cut at least six stalk and leaf shapes. Arrange them, with the discs, on a flat baking sheet. Bake on the rung below the tarts for 10 minutes or until puffed and lightly golden. When cool, re-open the central holes in the discs with the chopstick, slot a stalk and leaf piece in, then sit on top of the tarts when needed (step 9).
7. While the tarts bake, make the Sticky Toffee Sauce (page 189).
8. Once the tarts are baked, invert a flat baking sheet over the muffin tin. Holding both the tin and tray with oven-gloved hands, flip upside down so the tarts are pastry-side down on the baking sheet. Lift off the muffin tin and remove the baking paper.
9. To serve, plate up the tarts individually and pour a generous amount of sauce into the cored centre of each apple and top with a decorative pastry piece. Serve with extra sauce.

CARAMEL APPLE SHORTBREAD

Hands on **55 minutes**
Ready in **1 hour 40 minutes**

MAKES
12–16 squares

EQUIPMENT
20 x 30-cm (8 x 12-inch) brownie tin (pan)

Digital thermometer

This is caramel shortbread who went on a wellness retreat. They took away some lovely ideas about eating more fruit and nuts, but then got hungry on the drive home and ate a packet of Rolos. The addition of slightly bitter walnuts to the shortbread and the almost-wholesome, apple-studded caramel make this a delightfully balanced bake when it comes to flavour. But, unless you can smuggle one into your next gong bath, it's completely useless for your spiritual equilibrium.

SHORTBREAD BASE

200g (7 oz) plain (all-purpose) flour or 265g (9⅓oz) gluten-free plain (all-purpose) flour + ½ tsp xanthan gum

50g (3½oz) cornflour (cornstarch, omit if using gluten-free flour)

45g (1½oz) dark brown soft sugar

45g (1½oz) granulated sugar

75g (2⅔oz) walnuts

160g (5⅔oz) salted butter

APPLE FILLING

4 eating apples (Granny Smith or Braeburn)

210g (7½oz) salted butter

125g (4½oz) caster (superfine) or granulated sugar

75g (2⅔oz) light brown soft sugar

1 x 397-g (14 oz) can sweetened condensed milk

¼ tsp sea salt flakes

CHOCOLATE TOPPING

100g (3½oz) milk chocolate + 2 tsp vegetable oil

100g (3½oz) white chocolate + 2 tsp vegetable oil

1. Set the oven to 165°C fan (350°F/gas 4) and line the brownie tin with baking paper.
2. To make the shortbread base, combine the flours and sugars in a bowl.
3. Very finely chop or food process the walnuts to the size of rice grains. Add to a dry frying pan (skillet) on a medium-low heat and stir to toast evenly. As soon as they smell toasty and nutty, turn off the heat and add the butter to melt in the residual heat.
4. Scrape the walnuts into the bowl and mix to make a dough. Using the back of a spoon, press the dough into the brownie tin in an even layer.
5. Bake in the middle of the oven for 30 minutes.
6. While the shortbread bakes, peel, core and chop the apples into 1-cm (⅓-inch) pieces to give 350g (12⅓oz) of prepared fruit. Add 10g (⅓oz) of butter to the frying pan with the apples. Put on a medium heat and cover with a lid. When the fruit starts to release its juices, lift the lid to allow the moisture to evaporate. Don't let the apples brown – stir occasionally. When soft, but not collapsed, remove from the heat.
7. Start the caramel 10 minutes before the base is baked or once it's out of the oven so the filling can be poured as soon as it's ready. To a heavy-bottomed pan, add the remaining butter, the sugars and condensed milk, then stir over a medium-low heat. When everything is blended, turn up the heat to medium. Any remaining sugar grains will dissolve as the mixture heats. Stir continuously as the mixture heats up to a controlled bubble. You will smell the milk solids caramelising and the caramel will thicken and deepen in colour. Keep at that low boil for 5 minutes or until it reaches 120°C (250°F). Remove from the heat and stir in the salt flakes.
8. Scatter the cooked apples over the base, then pour over the hot caramel filling. Leave to cool for 15 minutes.
9. Once the caramel is firm enough to take the topping, melt the chocolates and oil in separate microwave-safe or heatproof bowls. Pour the milk and white chocolates over the caramel, then swirl into each other. Chill in the freezer for 30 minutes.
10. Cut the finished slab into 12–16 squares. Store in an airtight container at room temperature for up to 3 days.

TOFFEE APPLE LAYER CAKE

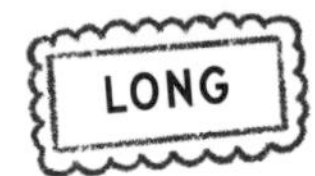

Hands on **1 hour 45 minutes**
Ready in **2 hours 40 minutes**
plus 24 hours for straining yogurt

SERVES 12
Makes one 18-cm (7-inch) four-layer cake

EQUIPMENT
Two 18-cm (7-inch) cake tins (pans)

This is one of the chapter's long recipes, so you know there's work involved, but this brown-butter apple cake, sandwiched with caramel apples and a sharp yogurt frosting is more than worth the effort. You can save a bit of time by swapping yogurt for cream cheese frosting, but what you can't sidestep is the apple prep: with dried, fresh and pureed fruit, there will be peeling. The reward, however, is a cake so appley it'll start charging you a monthly subscription and move all its functions around after every software update.

YOGURT FROSTING

1kg (2lb 3 oz) full-fat plain yogurt, strained overnight to approximately 500g (17½ oz) – use 450g (16 oz) for the recipe

170g (6 oz) salted butter, softened

170g (6 oz) icing (confectioners') sugar

APPLE PURÉE

800g (1lb 12 oz) peeled and cored cooking apples (from about 4 large apples)

APPLE CAKE

80g (2¾ oz) dried apple rings

120g (4¼ oz) salted butter

360g (12⅔ oz) apple purée (see above)

4 large (US extra-large) eggs

200g (7 oz) light brown soft sugar

1 tsp ground cinnamon

Pinch of salt

100g (3½ oz) plain (all-purpose) flour or 120g (4¼ oz) gluten-free self-raising flour

20g (¾ oz) cornflour (cornstarch, omit if using gluten-free flour)

100g (3½ oz) ground almonds (almond meal)

1½ tsp baking powder (omit if using gluten-free flour)

PREPARE THE YOGURT FOR THE FROSTING

1. Using the quantities given here, prepare the yogurt for the frosting (page 222). Start this the day before making the cake, straining the yogurt for 24 hours. If you've forgotten to do this, use cream cheese frosting instead.

MAKE THE APPLE PURÉE

2. Add the chopped apples to a dry frying pan (skillet), cover with a lid and put on a medium heat. When the fruit starts to soften and break down, remove the lid to allow the moisture to evaporate. Stir the apple so the purée thickens and doesn't burn. After 30 minutes, the apples should have reduced by half and become a thick purée. Scrape 360g (12⅔ oz) of the purée into a bowl and set aside. Store any leftover purée, then wipe out the frying pan for step 5.

MAKE THE APPLE CAKE

3. Set the oven to 175°C fan (375°F/gas 5), line the bases of the cake tins with discs of baking paper.
4. Finely chop the dried apple rings to 2-mm (1⁄16-inch) pieces, then add to the apple purée bowl.
5. To the clean frying pan, add the butter and put on a medium-low heat. Swirl it around the pan to melt; the solids will sink to the bottom as the liquid bubbles on the surface. When the bubbles die down to a foam, it's a good indication the milk solids are golden brown. If so, remove from the heat. Pour onto the dried and pureed apple, mix and leave to cool.
6. To a stand mixer or large bowl, add the eggs, sugar, cinnamon and salt. Beat until thick and mousse-like. This will take up to 5 minutes.
7. Add the flours, ground almonds and baking powder to a small bowl and mix together.
8. Add the butter and apple to the eggs by sliding it down the side of the bowl to avoid deflating the frothy mix.
9. Scatter one-third of the flour / almonds into the bowl and fold together with the apple and the eggs. Add the rest of the flour / almonds in two more goes, and stop mixing as soon as everything is evenly combined.

TOFFEE APPLE TOPPING

4 eating apples (Braeburn or Granny Smith)

200g (7 oz) granulated sugar

50g (1¾ oz) double (heavy) cream

10. Divide the batter equally between the two lined cake tins and bake in the middle of the oven for 35 minutes. A metal skewer will come out clean when they are baked. Test the cakes in at least two places in case you hit a patch of wet apple and it looks uncooked.
11. Leave the cakes in their tins for 5 minutes before turning out onto a wire rack.

MAKE THE YOGURT FROSTING

12. Using the overnight strained yogurt, make the frosting (page 222).

MAKE THE TOFFEE APPLE TOPPING

13. Peel, core and cut the apples into 1.5-cm (½-inch) pieces.
14. Make a dry caramel with the sugar (page 227) and pour most of it onto a heatproof non-stick liner to make a large disc of hard caramel. Leave a thin layer of caramel in the pan, don't scrape it clean.
15. To the caramel pan, add the cream and apples. Put back on a medium heat and gently warm to dissolve the caramel into the cream and soften the apples. When the fruit has gone slightly translucent and is covered in a light glaze of caramel, remove from the heat and cool.

ASSEMBLE THE CAKE

16. When completely cool, split each cake in two so you have four layers (page 9). Set the first layer on your cake plate and cover with frosting. Spoon one-third of the softened toffee apple pieces over the top. Place the second layer of cake over the first. Repeat with the next two layers of cake, finishing with the fourth cake placed upside down so the top is flat. Use a large palette knife to spread a thin coating of frosting over the top and sides of the cake to trap the crumbs, then chill for 15 minutes to set that layer. Use the remaining frosting to give the cake a generous second coat. Crack the discs of hard caramel into shards and use to decorate the top of the cake. The caramel shards will eventually dissolve from being in contact with the moisture in the frosting, so add them just before serving.

TOFFEE APPLE BISCUIT BUNS

Hands on **1 hour 25 minutes**
Ready in **3 hours**

SERVES 9

EQUIPMENT

Large 30 x 40-cm (12 x 16-inch) baking sheet

9 wooden lolly (popsicle) sticks

Digital thermometer

DOUGH

160g (5⅔oz) warm water (no warmer than 35°C/95°F)

25g (1 oz) granulated sugar

1 tsp fast-action dried yeast

250g (9 oz) strong white bread flour

¼ tsp salt

½ tsp ground cinnamon

15g (½oz) sunflower oil or any other flavourless oil

BRAMLEY BISCUIT SPREAD

250g (9 oz) peeled and cored Bramley apples (or other cooking apples)

100g (3½oz) light brown soft sugar

200g (7 oz) digestive biscuits (graham crackers), page 215

100g (3½oz) cold salted butter (dairy or plant-based)

TO ASSEMBLE

150g (5¼oz) peeled and cored Bramley apples (or other cooking apples)

Ingredients continued overleaf

These spirals of cinnamon dough, filled with Bramley biscuit spread, dipped in red caramel and served on a stick are like eating a toffee apple, only nice. The Bramley biscuit filling is inspired by the popular concept of turning a biscuit into a spread. This one is a combination of wheaty digestives and Bramley cooking apples for a deliciously sharp contrast in a sweet, buttery spread. The recipe makes double the amount of spread needed for the buns; you can use the extra as a pie filling under some fresh apples, spread it on toast or eat it with a spoon.

MAKE THE DOUGH

1. To a large bowl, add the warm water and sugar then sprinkle the yeast over and mix.
2. Add the flour, salt, cinnamon and oil and mix with a table knife to form a ragged dough. Follow the instructions on page 212 to use the pull-and-fold kneading method or knead the dough by hand for 12 minutes or in the mixer for 10 minutes, until the dough is smooth and elastic.
3. Cover and leave to proof until doubled in size.

MAKE THE BRAMLEY BISCUIT SPREAD

4. Peel, core and chop the apples as small as you have time for, then add to a frying pan (skillet) with the sugar. Cook on a medium heat until the apples have broken down to a pulpy purée.
5. Add the purée to a food processor, roughly break the biscuits in and blitz to start breaking them down.
6. Add the cold butter in cubes and run the processor until the mixture is completely blended; it will look like smooth peanut butter. Set aside until needed for constructing the buns.

MAKE THE BUNS

7. Finely chop the Bramley apples.
8. Tip the dough onto a floured work surface and knock all the air out of it with your knuckles. Flour the dough and roll out to a 25 x 45-cm (10 x 18-inch) rectangle, the short edge running left to right.
9. Spread half the Bramley biscuit spread over the dough, leaving a border free of filling at the far short edge. Scatter the finely chopped fresh apples over the biscuit spread. Moisten the clear edge of dough with a little water, then roll up from the near short edge into a 25-cm (10-inch) long 'sausage'. Smooth along the wet edge to seal. Using a strong thread or flavourless dental floss, garrotte the rolled dough into nine spiral slices.

Continued overleaf

'TOFFEE' CARAMEL

200g (7 oz) granulated sugar

60g (2 oz) water

10g (1/3 oz) golden syrup or glucose syrup

Red food colouring (optional)

10. Set the spirals on a lined baking sheet 3cm (1 inch) apart from their neighbours, giving each one a light squashing to flatten slightly. If the tails of the spirals are loose, slightly stretch and tuck under the buns to stop them unravelling as they expand in the oven.
11. Loosely cover the spirals with a piece of lightly oiled baking paper or cling film (plastic wrap) and leave to proof until the dough is light and puffy and the buns have grown slightly (see page 213, step 7); at room temperature this usually takes 30 minutes.
12. Set the oven to 200°C fan (425°F/gas 7).
13. Bake in the middle of the oven for 20 minutes or until the buns have puffed and their surface is an even golden brown. Use a probe thermometer to check the internal temperature of the dough is at least 90°C (195°F), then leave to cool on the tray.
14. When completely cool, push a wooden lolly stick into the side of each bun so they can be picked up like a cartoonish lolly.

MAKE THE 'TOFFEE' CARAMEL

15. Now, start the caramel. Add the sugar, water, syrup and colouring, if using, to a heavy-bottomed pan and put on a low heat to dissolve the sugar. Do not stir, just leave it to get on with its thing. (See the instructions for making a wet caramel for more information, page 228.)
16. When the sugar has dissolved, turn the heat up to medium and wait for it to reach 150°C (300°F), then remove from the heat.
17. Either spoon the caramel over the buns or carefully tilt the pan, dip one side of the spiral flat into the caramel and then set back down, caramel side up, on the lined baking sheet.
18. These buns are best eaten within 4 hours while the 'toffee' caramel is still crunchy.

BEST (ENTIRELY MADE UP) APPLE VARIETIES TO DIP IN TOFFEE

BUTTERY BETTY

SWIMMING GALA

PINK JAZZ GRANNY

SWEET REVENGE

RED BIFFIN

COXLESS FOUR

DELICIOUS LADY

ROYAL GUSSET

REVEREND WHISTY'S COMFORT

MABLE'S PIPPIN

JONABITE

GORDON'S BENNET

FOUNDATION RECIPES

ROUGH PUFF PASTRY

Hands on **15 minutes**
Ready in **55 minutes**

MAKES
Enough for one 25-cm (10-inch) square of pastry

While a great portion of this book is devoted to bakes that are enjoyably time consuming, even I have my line in the sand. Full puff pastry not only crosses that line, it spits at my feet and disrespects my mother. I'm not a fan. This might say more about my pastry skills than anything else, but I've never found it to be superior in taste or texture to a well-made rough puff. So here's how to make rough puff well.

225g (8 oz) plain (all-purpose) flour

150g (5¼ oz) fridge-cold salted butter

6–7 tbsp fridge-cold water

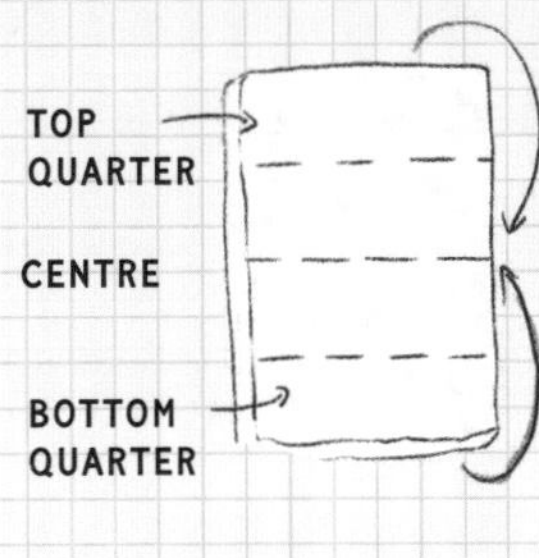

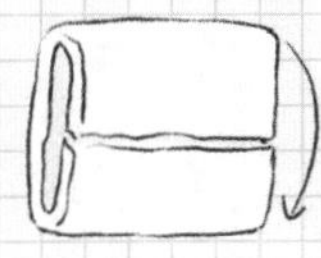

TIPS
Keep your butter right at the back of the fridge where it's coldest. If it's a hot day, chill the mixing bowl and grater in the fridge before using.

1. Add the flour to a large bowl and coarsely grate the butter into it. Dip the butter block in the flour after every few grates to help stop the shreds clumping together.
2. Using a table knife, toss the shredded butter around in the flour – keep your hands out so the butter stays as cold as possible.
3. Sprinkle in 6 tablespoons of cold water, then mix it in with a table knife to form rough clumps. Add a little more water if there is still a lot of unmixed dry flour. Now, use your hands to pull the clumps into a shaggy ball.

ROLL AND FOLD #1

4. On a lightly floured work surface, pat the dough into a vague oblong and roll to 20 x 10cm (8 x 4 inches) and 2cm (¾ inch) thick. Fold the top quarter of dough down to the centre and the bottom quarter up to the centre. Now fold both halves together so you have four thick layers. This is known as a book fold. Wrap the folded pastry in a plastic bag and use a pen to mark this as 'Roll and Fold #1'. Chill the pastry in the freezer for 10 minutes.

ROLL AND FOLD #2

5. Remove the pastry from the freezer and unwrap it. Before you start rolling backwards and forwards, press directly down with your rolling pin along the full length of the pastry to make gentle ridges. Flattening it roughly first makes it easier to roll out the pastry evenly. Roll to 25 x 15cm (10 x 6 inches) and repeat the book fold. Wrap and mark this as 'Roll and Fold #2'. Chill in the freezer for 10 minutes.

ROLL AND FOLD #3

6. Repeat the process and chill in the freezer for 10 minutes.

ROLL AND FOLD #4

7. Repeat the process and chill in the freezer for 10 minutes. After this final chill, the pastry is ready to be used as your recipe requires. Alternatively, wrap the pastry tightly and keep it in the fridge for up to 24 hours, or freeze it for later use.

CHOUX PASTRY

Hands on/ Ready in **25 minutes**

MAKES
Enough for 12–14 golf ball-sized profiteroles

Making choux pastry that works perfectly every time relies on remembering three things. Firstly, be accurate with the definitive measurements you're given. Secondly, unfortunately, no recipe can give a definitive measurement when it comes to adding the eggs – you'll have to judge it. And lastly, don't open the oven door too early. So, the egg thing is very much a game of chicken, which is apt. Too much and the pastry is too runny to puff. Too little and the pastry is too tight to puff. There are several reasons why there's no reassuring, definitive quantity for how much egg to use: flour can hold different amounts of moisture; you may have boiled off more water than you realise in the first stage; all eggs are different sizes. Yes, it's incredibly annoying not to just read 'add 30g of egg', but follow the recipe and I'll tell you exactly what to look for.

35g (1¼ oz) plain (all-purpose) flour or 20g (¾ oz) gluten-free plain (all-purpose) flour + 15g (½ oz) gluten-free self-raising flour

50g (1¾ oz) boiling water

17g (⅔ oz) salted butter

1 large (US extra-large) egg (although you won't need all of it)

1. Weigh the flour into a bowl and have it to hand.
2. Into a heavy-bottomed pan, weigh the boiling water, then add the butter.
3. Put the pan on a medium-low heat and bring the water gently to just boiling point – you don't want a fast boil that evaporates everything you've carefully measured.
4. As soon as little bubbles break most of the water's surface, turn off the heat and tip in all the flour. With a rigid spatula or a wooden spoon, immediately beat the flour vigorously into the liquid until it pulls away from the sides of the pan and forms a ball of dough.
5. Tip the dough into a large mixing bowl and spread it out thinly to cool.
6. Crack the egg into a jug (pitcher) and break it up well with a fork.
7. When the dough is cool enough to be able to stick your finger in, start adding the egg. Begin by pouring in one-third of the egg and, using a hand mixer, start beating. At this point the mix will look like a terrifying cross between cottage cheese and scrambled egg, but just keep beating and the egg will blend with the dough to make a stiff, smooth paste. Add a little more egg if you're struggling to beat it smooth. To give you more control and a better feel for the consistency of the paste, swap to using a wooden spoon or rigid spatula. From this point, look for signs the choux is getting to the right consistency. Add the egg one teaspoon at a time, beat it in and then watch for two things when the paste falls off your spoon / spatula: you're looking for a 'reluctant drop' – it should drop and hang off the spatula due to its weight and gravity. If you have to shake the paste to make it hang, it needs more egg – and then you need to look at the shape the paste leaves hanging on the spatula – you're after a smooth 'V', if the 'V' has ragged edges it needs a tiny bit more

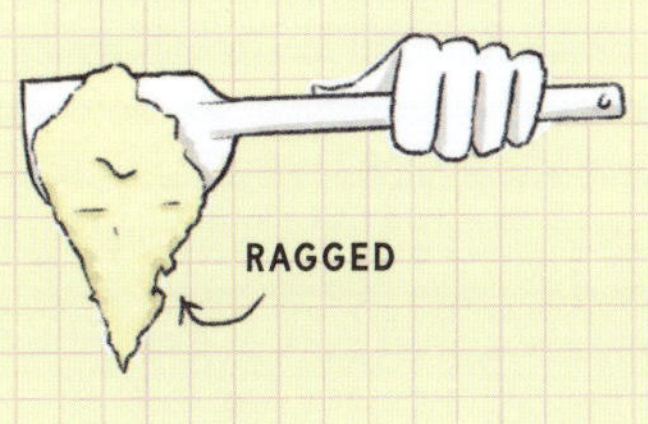

egg. Keep adding tiny amounts of egg and testing the paste until you have a coquettishly reluctant drop and a pleasingly smooth 'V'. You can also blob a teaspoon's worth on a lined baking sheet; if the consistency is right, there shouldn't be any spread. When it is right, you will, almost certainly, have some leftover egg. *PLEASE don't be tempted just to chuck it in thinking that it's a crime to waste it, it's a worse crime to ruin an entire batch of choux. Make a tiny leftover egg omelette instead.

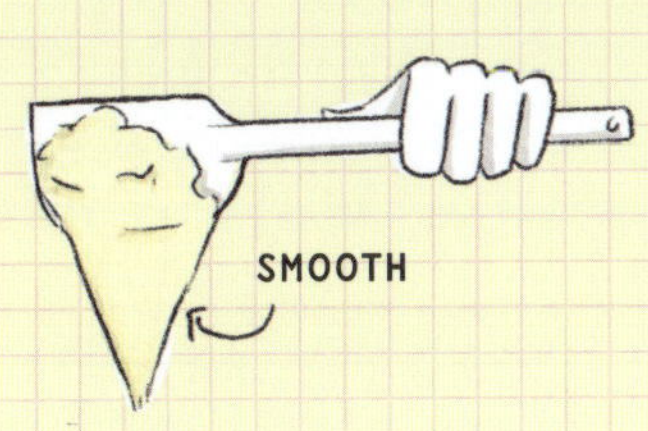

8. When you're happy with the consistency, pipe the choux and bake as the recipe requires. Just remember not to open the oven door early. A quick drop in temperature before the pastry has crisped enough to support itself means that the steam inside each bun will cool and won't be able to keep the shapes puffed up. The choux buns will collapse – and maybe so will you, not the outcome you wanted.
9. As a rule of thumb, small choux buns or profiteroles bake in the middle of the oven for 30–35 minutes at 175°C fan (375°F/gas 5). I don't open the door until at least 28 minutes.

GLUTEN-FREE

There's very little difference when making gluten-free choux, the results are just as crisp and structurally sound as the gluten version. Make the recipe as per the gluten version, look for the same signs regarding the amount of egg to add, but just bear these few things in mind:

1. Use the mix of gluten-free plain (all-purpose) and self-raising flours as stated in each recipe. The raising agent and xanthan gum pre-mixed in the self-raising flour give extra lift and structure in the absence of gluten.
2. Make sure your water isn't boiling too fiercely; a gentle bubble is all that's needed. If it's too hot, the flour will seize before you can mix it to a smooth dough.
3. Unsurprisingly, the gluten-free choux is slightly less elastic than the gluten version, so when checking for the 'reluctant drop' and the smooth 'V', if you're not sure whether to risk a touch more egg, err on the side of caution and don't.

WHOOPS!

Unfortunately, if you've added too much egg and your paste is runny, the diagnosis is terminal for that batch. Adding flour cannot save it and baking a runny paste will only yield sad little whoopee cushions of pastry. But just because your choux can't hold itself together, there's no need for you to fall apart. If ingredients, time and commitment allow, make another batch and don't repeat the mistake. Or, for now, just make pancakes. Add a dash of milk and a little baking powder for thick, fluffy pancakes or add extra milk until you have the consistency of single (light) cream and make thin crêpes.

SWEET SHORTCRUST PASTRY

Hands on **5 minutes** with a food processor or **10–15 minutes** by hand. Ready in **40–45 minutes** for gluten or **15 minutes** for gluten-free

MAKES
Enough for 20 small jam tarts or 12 deep-filled mince pies or one deep 21-cm (8½-inch) tart with leftovers

A good sweet shortcrust pastry recipe is literally the foundation of many a wonderful thing to bake and eat, so here's mine. It's easily adaptable to be gluten-free and plant-based and the results are light, crisp and – like this intro – nice and short.

250g (9 oz) plain (all-purpose) flour

2 tsp baking powder*

50g (1¾ oz) icing (confectioners') sugar

125g (4½ oz) baking block or salted butter (dairy or plant-based), cold from the fridge

20g (¾ oz) / 4 tsp cold water

GLUTEN

1. To a food processor, add the flour, baking powder (if using), icing sugar and baking block / butter and blitz to a fine breadcrumb-like texture.
2. Add the cold water and blitz again until the pastry forms larger crumbs.
3. Tip them onto the work surface and, working the pastry as little as possible, use your hands to press the crumbs into a clump, then into a thick disc.
4. Wrap the pastry in cling film (plastic wrap) or baking paper and chill in the fridge for 30 minutes, then use as your recipe requires.

---

*The addition of baking powder gives the pastry a light, biscuity structure, but you can leave it out when you want a closer, shorter texture. Throughout this book, the recipes specify whether or not to include it.

250g (9 oz) gluten-free self-raising flour

50g (1¾ oz) icing (confectioners') sugar

125g (4½ oz) baking block or salted butter (dairy or plant-based), cold from the fridge

30g (1 oz) / 2 tbsp egg white

GLUTEN-FREE

1. To a food processor, add the flour, icing sugar and baking block or butter and blitz to a fine breadcrumb-like texture.
2. Add the egg white and blitz until the crumbs come together as a smooth ball of pastry.
3. Use straight away as your recipe requires. Unlike gluten pastry, there's no need to chill before using. When cold, this pastry is brittle and unworkable but soft and easy to handle at room temperature. There's no gluten to go tough, so you can re-roll this pastry as much as needed. If it tears when lifting, patch it up in the tin and it will bake back together.

250g (9 oz) gluten-free self-raising flour

¼ tsp xanthan gum

50g (1¾ oz) icing (confectioners') sugar

125g (4½ oz) plant-based baking block or salted butter, cold from the fridge

20g (¾ oz) / 4 tsp cold water

PLANT-BASED GLUTEN-FREE

Make as the gluten-free pastry, but with the addition of the extra xanthan gum and the given quantity of cold water instead of egg white.

WITHOUT A FOOD PROCESSOR

Add the dry ingredients to a bowl, mix well, then grate in the baking block or butter. Rub the fat into the flour until sandy in texture. Add the water or egg white and mix in with a table knife. Pull the crumbs together to form a clump then knead once or twice to make a disc. Chill for 30 minutes if gluten or use straight away if gluten-free.

FILO PASTRY

Hands on **1 hour 10 minutes**
Ready in **1 hour 40 minutes**

MAKES
15 circular sheets of pastry, enough for a 20-cm (8-inch) baklava (page 31)

If you'd like to spend time trying something new out of curiosity or just for the hell of it, you could do worse than make filo. Naked potholing would be a lot worse. This method makes it relatively easy to achieve the paper-thin layers of filo because you roll them simultaneously in a stack rather than stretching one single sheet, inch by inch, over a tabletop.

170g (6 oz) strong white bread flour

1/4 tsp salt

80g (2 3/4 oz) water

1/2 tsp white wine vinegar or cider vinegar

1/2 tbsp olive oil

FLOUR FOR ROLLING

75g (2 2/3 oz) cornflour (cornstarch)

75g (2 2/3 oz) strong white bread flour

1. To a large bowl, add the flour and salt and mix.
2. Make a well in the centre of the flour and pour in the water, vinegar and oil. Using a table knife, mix to a ragged dough and then pull the dough together into a ball.
3. Knead for 10 minutes, then rest in a covered bowl for 30 minutes.
4. Divide the dough into 15 equal pieces (approximately 17g/2/3 oz each) and roll into neat balls. Cover the balls loosely with a large piece of cling film (plastic wrap).
5. Flour the work surface with plenty of the rolling flour and roll each ball to a disc of 10-cm (4-inch) diameter. As you make them, stack the discs into three piles of five with at least a tablespoon of rolling flour dusted in between each disc. Put the stacks, as you make them, under the cling film with the remaining balls.
6. Working with one stack of five at a time, generously flour the work surface and the top of the stack and start rolling them out as a whole. Roll out from the middle of the stack, rather than backwards and forwards over the whole disc, rotating the stack after each roll so it grows into an even circle.
7. As the discs grow, all layers need to be constantly checked and re-floured so they don't stick together. After every few rolls, pull back one half of a disc, re-flour and fold back, then pull back the other half, re-flour and fold back. Keep rolling and re-flouring until the discs reach at least 30cm (12 inches) in diameter. At this size the sheets should be thin enough to read newspaper print through. If it isn't, keep rolling. If you're too young to know what a newspaper is, can you read a TikTok caption through it?
8. Place the stacks on top of each other as they're fully rolled, under the cling film so they don't dry out. Use straight away or wrap well and freeze until needed.

ROLL AS A WHOLE

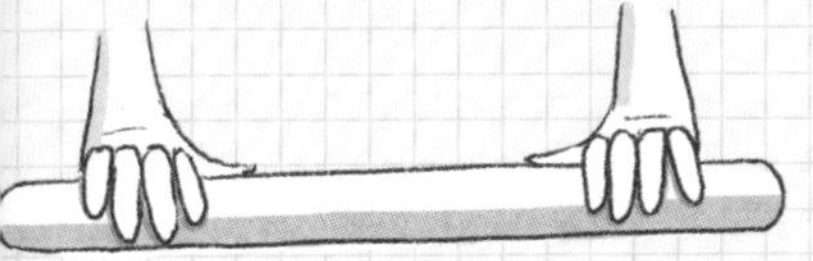

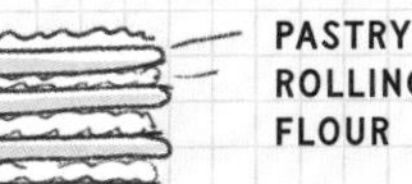

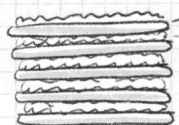

ROLL OUT FROM THE CENTRE

PULL-AND-FOLD KNEADING METHOD

Hands on **15 minutes**
Ready in **2 hours 25 minutes**

I haven't kneaded a loaf since I read Dan Lepard's beautiful book on bread making, *The Handmade Loaf.* It details a method of making dough that completely revolutionised my bread making. Instead of trying to knead and wrestle the dough as soon as it's mixed, resting times (to allow the flour to hydrate and the gluten to develop) are combined with gentle pulling and folding to stretch the gluten as it forms. The result is bread with the texture of a traditionally kneaded dough, light and springy with chewy resistance, but without having to thrash it around like you're a dominatrix in a baker's cap.

This is my take on Dan's method: it wasn't a deliberate departure, it just emerged over the years due to my inability to follow instructions and retain information. Resting, pulling and folding takes longer than traditional kneading but bread making is not a quick process; if you've committed to making a yeasted dough you're in for the long haul and an extra 35 minutes isn't going to break the time bank. Particularly when it's mostly hands-off time in which you can prepare other aspects of the recipe or just stare out the window wondering where you can buy a baker's cap.

MAKE THE DOUGH

1. Using the quantities given for the recipe you're making: weigh the warm water / liquid into a large bowl, sprinkle the yeast over and swirl around a few times to start dissolving it. Add the flour and salt, then pour the oil down the side of the bowl into the water rather than onto the dry ingredients. Using a table knife, stir and scrape the contents into ragged clumps. Keep mixing. The dough should form a rough ball easily using the knife, but you can pull it together with your hands towards the end if needed. Scrape the dough up into a ball, pour a teaspoon of oil into the bowl, then return the dough and roll it in the oil. Cover the bowl and set a timer for 15 minutes.

PULL AND FOLD #1

2. When the timer goes off, do the first pull and fold. (I pull and fold the dough in the bowl to save a bit of cleaning, but you can do it on the work surface if you prefer, returning it to the bowl for its rests.) Hold the dough in place with one hand. With the other hand, take a section of dough, placing your fingers under and your thumb on top, and pull it gently out to the side to stretch it. During the first 15-minute rest, the gluten will start to develop and the dough will feel a bit chewing-gummy but it won't be very strong. Pull it gently to get the most stretch you can without it snapping then fold the end back into the centre and push it lightly down. Work your way around the ball of dough, pulling out and stretching each section and folding it back in. You'll probably work your way full circle around the bowl in seven or eight pulls. Cover the bowl and set the timer for another 15 minutes.

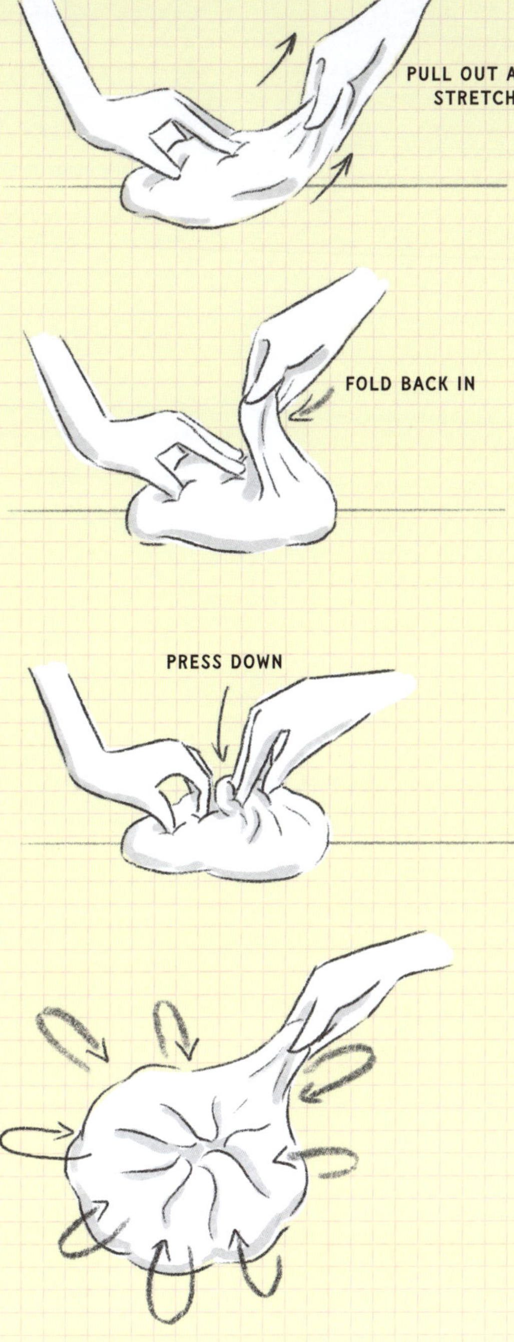

PULL AND FOLD #2

3. Repeat the same pull-and-fold process. You'll notice this time that the dough is much stretchier and easier to pull than the first time – this is because both resting and handling have developed the gluten further. Cover and set the timer for the last 15-minute rest.

PULL AND FOLD #3

4. Repeat the pull-and-fold process. This time you should be working with a dough that is really happy to stretch when you pull it and feels nicely elastic. This is the final pull and fold. Re-oil the bowl with a teaspoon of oil and turn the dough upside down so all the tucks are hidden underneath.

FIRST PROOF

5. Cover the bowl and leave for its first proof to double in size; this takes between 1 and 2 hours depending on the type of dough and the ambient temperature of the room.

SHAPE AND SECOND PROOF

6. Tip the dough out of the bowl. Depending on the make up of the dough, the recipe will tell you whether or not to flour the work surface. Flatten the dough down – known as knocking back – and shape according to the recipe, then leave it for its second proof, which is usually much shorter than the first.

IS THE DOUGH READY TO BAKE?

7. I find the best way to check a dough has finished its second proof is to gently prod it and watch how it responds. If the dough springs back quickly and the indentation fills in completely, you need to leave it for longer. It's ready to bake when the prodded indentation fills slowly but not completely, leaving a slight depression on the surface. Bake as directed in your recipe.

VANILLA MINI BISCUITS

Hands on **15 minutes**
Ready in **1 hour 10 minutes**

MAKES
Approximately 50 mini biscuits

EQUIPMENT
Large 30 x 40-cm (12 x 16-inch) baking sheet

125g ($4\frac{1}{2}$ oz) plain (all-purpose) flour or gluten-free self-raising mix

$1\frac{3}{4}$ tsp baking powder (omit if using gluten-free flour)

60g (2 oz) icing (confectioners') sugar

60g (2 oz) salted butter, plant-based butter or baking block, at room temperature

2 tsp water

1 tsp vanilla extract

Was there ever a biscuit dough that could be all things to all people? If all people want an extra day at the weekend and a wrinkle-free forehead, these will disappoint. However, if they want a light, crunchy, buttery vanilla biscuit that's just as good when it's plant-based and gluten-free, here's the recipe.

1. To a food processor, add the flour, baking powder, sugar and butter, then blitz to fine crumbs. Add the water and vanilla, then pulse until everything comes together as a ball of soft dough. If you don't have a food processor, combine the dry ingredients in a large bowl. Coarsely grate in the butter, then rub it into the dry ingredients with your fingertips. Add the water and vanilla, then mix in with a table knife to form ragged clumps. Pull everything together into a ball of dough with your hands – stop handling it as soon as it's formed so it doesn't get overworked and tough.
2. Roll the dough between two sheets of lightly floured baking paper to a thickness of approximately 5mm ($\frac{1}{4}$ inch). Chill the rolled-out dough on a flat baking sheet in the fridge for at least 30 minutes.
3. Set the oven to 150°C fan (325°F/gas 3) and line the baking sheet with baking paper.
4. Cut the firm dough into 1-cm ($\frac{1}{3}$-inch) strips and then cut those strips into 1-cm ($\frac{1}{3}$-inch)-ish squares.
5. Place the squares a little apart on the baking sheet to allow for their slight spread.
6. Bake in the middle of the oven for 16 minutes or until they lose their unbaked sheen and turn matt. They should stay pale and rather than turning golden, keep an eye on them and turn the temperature down if the biscuits start to colour.
7. Leave to cool completely on the tray before lifting them.
8. Use straight away or store in an airtight container for up to 1 week.

For a chocolate version, remove 10g ($\frac{1}{3}$ oz) of the flour and replace it with 10g ($\frac{1}{3}$ oz) of unsweetened cocoa powder.

DIGESTIVE BISCUITS

Hands on **20 minutes**
Ready in **1 hour 10 minutes**

MAKES
24–28 x 6-cm (2⅓-inch) round biscuits

EQUIPMENT
Two flat baking sheets

It's testament to the digestive biscuit's (graham cracker's) humble deliciousness that even being named after a murky biological process doesn't put anyone off eating them. But is it really worth making your own? Well, when they're as embarrassingly easy to make, and as light and buttery as these are, I would say the answer was alimentary, my dear Watson.

150g (5¼ oz) wholemeal bread flour or gluten-free brown bread flour

100g (3½ oz) plain (all-purpose) flour or gluten-free plain (all-purpose) flour

25g (¾ oz) oat bran or gluten-free oats

70g (2½ oz) light brown soft sugar

½ tsp bicarbonate of soda (baking soda)

130g (4½ oz) salted butter, at room temperature

4 tsp water

1. To a food processor, add the flours, oat bran, sugar, bicarbonate of soda and butter and pulse to a sandy consistency. If you don't have a food processor, add the dry ingredients to a large bowl, coarsely grate the butter over and rub in with your fingertips.
2. Add the water and pulse the processor until everything comes together as a ball of dough. By hand, add the water to the bowl, mix in with a table knife then bring the crumbs together with your hands, gently pressing and squeezing until you have formed a ball of dough.
3. Flatten the dough slightly into a thick disc and wrap in baking paper or cling film (plastic wrap) and chill in the freezer for 15 minutes.
4. Set the oven to 175°C fan (375°F/gas 5) and line the baking sheets with baking paper.
5. Between two sheets of very lightly floured baking paper, roll the disc of dough to 4mm (⅛ inch) thick and use a 6-cm (2⅓-inch) round cookie cutter to press out the biscuits. Re-use the offcuts by stacking them on top of each other, covering with the paper and re-rolling them.
6. Arrange the biscuits on the lined baking sheets slightly apart (they don't really spread) and prick them over with a fork.
7. Bake in the middle of the oven for 17 minutes or until lightly golden and sandy-looking and very slightly risen.
8. Leave on the sheet for 5 minutes before transferring to a wire rack to cool completely. Use straight away or store in an airtight container for up to 1 week.

FRENCH MERINGUE

Hands on/Ready in **20 minutes**

MAKES
12 x 5-cm (2-inch) diameter meringue mounds

I'm not a fan of meringue for meringue's sake. Sorry, no offence, meringue, whatever nationality you are, but I find you just too sweet. However, as a component part of a recipe – off-setting a sharp fruit curd in a meringue pie (pages 134–143), lightening a rhubarb mousse (page 172) or topping a minty ice cream (page 182) – your billowy clouds of sweet air are perfect, and very welcome. As a general rule, for every egg white you need to use 55g (2 oz) of white caster (superfine) or granulated sugar, a tiny pinch of salt and a pinch of cream of tartar. The cream of tartar helps keep the whipped meringue stable.

2 large (US extra-large) egg whites

Pinch of salt

1/8 tsp (or a large pinch) cream of tartar

110g (3¾ oz) white caster (superfine) or granulated sugar

1. To a clean, grease-free stand mixer or a large bowl, add the egg whites, salt and cream of tartar.
2. Start beating the egg whites. As soon as they hold stiff peaks, begin adding the sugar, one teaspoon at a time, using an actual teaspoon rather than a teaspoon measure. Leave 10–15 seconds between each teaspoon. With each addition, you'll see the meringue become thicker and glossier.
3. When all the sugar has been added and the meringue is holding stiff peaks, use as the recipe requires.

FOR BAKING INDIVIDUAL MERINGUES

Preheat the oven to 100°C fan (210°F/gas ¼). Pipe or spoon mounds of meringue onto a baking sheet lined with non-stick baking paper. Bake in the middle of the oven for 1 hour 20–30 minutes, or until the meringues are dry enough to lift from the paper. When they are, turn off the heat, leave the meringues on their baking sheet in the oven, and prop the door open using the handle of a wooden spoon or similar. Leave the meringues in the oven to cool completely then eat or store in an airtight container, for up to two weeks, until needed.

*Which sugar you use is not critical; caster (superfine) sugar has smaller grains and dissolves more quickly than granulated, but unless you're whisking this by hand that won't make any difference. My advice is to use what you have in the cupboard.

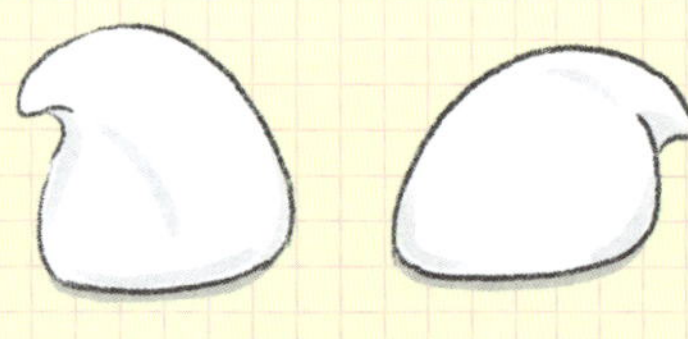

SOFT PEAKS

STIFF PEAKS

SNEAKY PEAKS

PLANT-BASED FRENCH MERINGUE

Hands on/Ready in **25 minutes**

MAKES
12 x 5-cm (2-inch) diameter meringue mounds

I haven't included a vegan Italian meringue recipe because, frankly, I can't get one to work, and this no-cook French meringue is so stable that I haven't felt the need to pursue one. This works well and tastes good, so job done. The general rule is for every 40g (1⅓ oz) of aquafaba (equivalent to one large egg white) use 60g (2 oz) of caster (superfine) or granulated sugar, ⅛ teaspoon of cream of tartar and a pinch of salt.

80g (2¾ oz) chickpea (garbanzo bean) aquafaba*

¼ tsp cream of tartar

Pinch of salt

120g (4¼ oz) white caster (superfine) or granulated sugar**

1 tbsp vanilla extract

1. Whip the aquafaba until it holds stiff peaks. If this is your first time, be warned, it takes substantially longer than whipping egg whites. If you have a powerful stand mixer, it's likely to be up to 5 minutes, with a hand mixer possibly 10 minutes or longer. And as for doing it by hand, well, I wouldn't even consider it.
2. When the aquafaba is holding stiff peaks, add the cream of tartar and salt and whip them in. The cream of tartar is essential to stabilise the meringue; leave it out and the structure will be noticeably weaker and very likely to collapse.
3. Add the sugar one teaspoon at a time, leaving 10 seconds between each addition so the meringue doesn't deflate.
4. When all the sugar has been added, add the vanilla and beat briefly to mix in. Use as the recipe requires.
5. The quantities given here make 12 x 5-cm (2-inch) meringue mounds or piped nests, which bake in the middle of the oven at 100°C fan (210°F/gas ¼) for 1 hour 45 minutes–2 hours. Alternatively, this meringue can be blow torched, making it a good egg-free alternative to the Italian meringue topping for the Mint Chocky Road (page 182).

---

*The aquafaba from some brands of beans seems to whip up better than others, so try a few different ones to find what works best for you. Aquafaba from various beans – cannellini (white), kidney and butter (lima) beans – can also be whipped up, but I've found chickpea works best for a stable meringue.

**As with egg French meringue, white caster (superfine) or granulated sugar both work well, so just use what you have.

ITALIAN MERINGUE

Hands on/Ready in **25 minutes**

MAKES
Enough to generously top a 20-cm (8-inch) pie

EQUIPMENT
Digital thermometer

It's a great irony that while Italian meringue is the most stable version you can make, it's the method most likely to drive you to collapse. At first glance it seems like the baking equivalent of simultaneously patting your head, rubbing your tummy, juggling fire and balancing a table on your chin. But once you get your head around the stages involved, they're not that demanding and the results are worth it. I recommend a stand mixer, but if you're using an electric hand mixer, use a heavy ceramic mixing bowl or one you can anchor to the work surface – you won't have a free hand to hold it still while you pour in the syrup and beat the eggs. So, get everything ready, read the recipe before you start, deep breath, and good luck. Or should I say, buona fortuna.

165g (5¾ oz) granulated sugar

50g (1¾ oz) water

10g (⅓ oz) / ½ tbsp golden syrup or glucose syrup

3 large (US extra-large) egg whites (or 120g/4¼ oz from a carton) – make sure the egg is room temperature

Pinch of salt

¼ tsp cream of tartar

1. To a heavy-bottomed pan, add the sugar and shake gently so the granules lie in a flat layer. Pour the water into the centre of the sugar so it slowly moistens but doesn't disturb the granules. Add the syrup then put the pan on a low heat so the sugar slowly dissolves but doesn't bubble. Don't stir it, do nothing more than swirl the pan very occasionally to check if there are still granules of sugar visible. Once the sugar has dissolved, switch off the heat and start the meringue.
2. To a stand mixer, add the egg whites, salt and cream of tartar and beat until the egg whites hold stiff peaks then stop the machine.
3. Put the sugar on a medium-high heat, and when it reaches 120°C (250°F) immediately start the mixer on high and trickle the hot sugar onto the meringue in a very thin stream. Don't pour it in too quickly or the meringue will collapse. Avoid pouring it onto the fast-moving beaters in case it flings the sugar around.
4. Keep the beaters going for 5 minutes, or up to 10 minutes if you're using a hand mixer. The meringue will steadily become really thick and glossy and firmly hold its shape.
5. Switch the beaters off and when completely cool use as the recipe requires. It's best used within a few hours but at a push you can cover it tightly with cling film (plastic wrap) and keep in the fridge for a day.

WHOOPS!

If your meringue suddenly deflates when adding the syrup, it was probably added too fast and the weight of the sugar collapsed the structure of the egg white.

If the meringue stays floppy even after the sugar has been carefully and slowly trickled in and beaten for 5 minutes, the meringue was probably not beaten sufficiently before the syrup was added. Make sure the egg whites are holding stiff peaks before adding the hot syrup.

MARSHMALLOW

Hands on **30 minutes**
Ready in **up to 2 hours**

MAKES
32 x 3-cm (1-inch) cubed marshmallows

EQUIPMENT
20 x 30-cm (8 x 12-inch) brownie tin (pan)

Digital thermometer

It isn't important to make your own marshmallows, but if I only stuck to doing things that were important, my day wouldn't be that full. Making your own marshmallows means you can flavour them however you want, rather than just vanilla or pink. Add liquid flavourings with the gelatine, in place of the vanilla, or after that step beat in freeze-dried fruit powders for a sharp, fresh contrast to the pillowy sweetness. This method uses Italian meringue; if you haven't made it before, see opposite for more info.

25g (3/4 oz) cornflour (cornstarch)

25g (3/4 oz) icing (confectioners') sugar

250g (9 oz) granulated sugar

70g (2 1/2 oz) water

20g (3/4 oz) / 1 tbsp golden syrup or glucose syrup

5 sheets of gelatine

2 large (US extra-large) egg whites (or 80g/2 3/4 oz from a carton), at room temperature

1/4 tsp cream of tartar

Pinch of salt

45g (1 1/2 oz) / 3 tbsp boiling water

1 tbsp vanilla extract

1. Line the brownie tin with non-stick baking paper. Combine the cornflour and icing sugar, then generously sift a good dusting over the paper.
2. To a heavy-bottomed pan, add the sugar and shake gently so the granules lie flat. Pour the water into the centre of the sugar so it slowly moistens but doesn't disturb the granules. Spoon the syrup into the centre of the sugar. Put the pan on a low heat so the sugar slowly dissolves but doesn't boil. Don't stir it. Do nothing more than swirl the pan very occasionally to check if there are still granules of sugar visible. When all the sugar has dissolved, switch off the heat.
3. To a small bowl, add the gelatine leaves and enough cold water to cover them. Set aside to soak for 10 minutes.
4. Add the egg whites, cream of tartar and salt to the stand mixer. Beat until the egg whites hold stiff peaks, then stop the machine.
5. Put the sugar pan on a medium-high heat. When it reaches 120°C (250°F), start the mixer on high and slowly pour the hot sugar over the meringue in a very thin stream. Avoid pouring it onto the fast-moving beaters in case it flings molten sugar around the kitchen.
6. Once the sugar is added, keep the beaters going while you scoop the gelatine sheets from their soaking water and pour it away. Return the sheets to the bowl and pour over the boiling water from the kettle. Add the vanilla and stir to melt everything together. If the gelatine sheets don't fully dissolve, warm the bowl in the microwave for a few seconds. Trickle the gelatine into the meringue and beat for a further 2–3 minutes. The marshmallow mixture should be thick and glossy.
7. Pour the warm marshmallow mixture onto the dusted baking paper and use a palette knife to spread it level in the tin.
8. Leave to set at room temperature for 1–2 hours, then heavily dust the top of the marshmallow with cornflour / sugar. Don't try to speed up the setting time by refrigerating it, as chilling makes marshmallow weep rather than set firm. Use a sharp knife to cut into pieces – the size and shape is up to you – and toss in more cornflour / sugar to stop them sticking to each other. Store in an airtight container at room temperature.

PASTRY CREAM

Hands on **15 minutes**
Ready in **45 minutes**

MAKES
Enough to fill
15–18 profiteroles

If you've never made crème pâtissière because it sounds daunting, start calling it pastry cream and it will feel more approachable. Then when someone tells you pastry cream is really just thick custard, it will seem entirely doable... Pastry cream is really just thick custard.

This recipe makes a medium firm, pipable pastry cream perfect for filling profiteroles. Where a firmer consistency is needed for other recipes in this book, the amount of cornflour is increased and cream is beaten in after cooling. The cooking method for both is the same. Follow the instructions below with the recipe-specific quantities to make the required pastry cream.

20g (¾ oz) cornflour (cornstarch)

25g (¾ oz) granulated sugar

1 large (US extra-large) egg

½ tbsp vanilla extract

200g (7 oz) whole (full-fat) milk

40g (1⅓ oz) unsalted butter, room temperature

1. Combine the cornflour, sugar, egg and vanilla in a medium bowl until lump free.
2. To a heavy-bottomed pan, add the milk and put on a medium heat. Bring it just up to the boil then trickle into the cornflour and egg mix, whisking continuously until all the hot milk has been combined.
3. Pour back into the pan and put on a medium-low heat. Stir continuously to stop lumps forming as the custard thickens. I start with a spatula to scrape the base and get into the corners and then swap to a whisk as it starts to thicken. Recipes with more cornflour will get quite stiff as they heat so you'll need to whisk vigorously as it thickens. Bring it just up to the boil so a bubble or two breaks the surface. Taste to check the chalkiness of the cornflour has cooked out; if not, keep cooking until it has gone.
4. Remove from the heat. Immediately add the butter and stir into the custard; the butter will melt and blend in, making it smooth and glossy. For thicker custards you will have to whisk quite hard.
5. Scrape into a large, shallow bowl and press baking paper or cling film (plastic wrap) directly over the surface of the hot custard so a skin doesn't form as it cools. The thinner you can spread the custard the faster it will cool. Put it in the fridge to chill.
6. When the custard is firm and cool, give it a very brief beat, just a couple of seconds, to make it smooth. Use as the recipe requires.
7. For thicker pastry creams, use a stand or hand mixer to beat the cool, firm custard to break it up – it will look horribly lumpy. Add the cream (the amount is given in the specific recipe) and beat until it comes together, stopping as soon as the pastry cream is thick and smooth. Use as your recipe requires.

PLANT-BASED / EGG-FREE PASTRY CREAM

Hands on **15 minutes**
Ready in **45 minutes**

You can make this pastry cream vegan friendly by using plant-based milk, cream and coconut oil. If you just need to avoid eggs, you can swap the milk and cream for dairy versions. Here I use coconut oil as a substitute for dairy butter because it adds a rich creaminess without any of the weird aftertastes from some plant-based butters. However, if you don't want to use coconut oil, you can swap for a plant-based butter (not a soft spread) of your choice.

40g (1⅓oz) cornflour (cornstarch)

25g (¾oz) granulated sugar

½ tbsp vanilla extract

240g (8½oz) plant-based milk or whole (full-fat) dairy milk

50g (1¾oz) coconut oil, unsalted plant-based butter or dairy butter

100g (3½oz) plant-based whippable double (heavy) cream or dairy double (heavy) cream

1. To a heavy-bottomed pan, add the cornflour, sugar, vanilla and 50g (1¾oz) of the milk and mix until lump free. Whisk in the remaining milk and add the solid coconut oil; it will melt in during cooking.
2. Put the pan on a medium heat and stir continuously to stop lumps forming as the custard thickens. A stiff spatula is good for scraping the base and getting into the corners and for vigorously beating the very thick cooked custard. Bring just up to the boil so a bubble or two breaks the surface. Taste to check the chalkiness of the cornflour has cooked out; if not, keep cooking until it has gone.
3. Scrape into a large bowl and press baking paper or cling film (plastic wrap) directly over the surface of the hot custard so a skin doesn't form as it cools. Put it in the fridge to chill.
4. When the custard is firm and cool, add it to a stand mixer / large bowl / food processor and beat until it becomes a smooth paste. Don't panic if it doesn't come together, it will when you add the cream. Add the cream and beat, stopping as soon as the pastry cream is thick and smooth.
5. Use as your recipe requires.

CREAM CHEESE FROSTING

Hands on **15 minutes**
Ready in **30 minutes**

MAKES
Enough to sandwich and cover an 18-cm (7-inch) four-layer cake

280g (10 oz) salted butter*

150g (5¼ oz) icing (confectioners') sugar

2 tsp vanilla extract

350g (12⅓ oz) full-fat cream cheese

The secret to this classic, creamy frosting working every time is don't use an electric mixer; this risks overbeating the cream cheese until it releases its water, making it runny and unsalvageable.

1. Soften the butter for a few seconds at a time in the microwave until it has the consistency of yogurt.
2. Sift the icing sugar into a large bowl, add the very soft butter and vanilla, then mix together. The butter should be soft enough to do this by hand.
3. To a separate bowl, add the cream cheese and gently break up to smooth out any lumps. A spoonful at a time, fold the cream cheese into the butter and sugar.
4. When all the cream cheese has been incorporated, chill for 15 minutes to firm the frosting slightly, then use as your recipe requires.

YOGURT FROSTING

Hands on **15 minutes**
Ready in **24 hours 30 minutes**

MAKES
Enough to sandwich and cover an 18-cm (7-inch) four-layer cake

1kg (2lb 3 oz) full-fat plain yogurt

170g (6 oz) salted butter*

170g (6 oz) icing (confectioners') sugar

A sharper take on Cream Cheese Frosting, but not a quicker one. You need to start straining the yogurt 24 hours before making the frosting. Use a 4% fat natural yogurt, rather than a thick Greek one, for the best yogurty flavour and sharpness.

1. The day before, suspend the yogurt in a muslin cloth or a fine jelly bag over a large bowl (I tie mine to a wooden spoon) to strain out the watery whey. It can sit out on the side overnight; there's no need to refrigerate it. After 24 hours, the yogurt should weigh approximately 500g (17½ oz).
2. In a large bowl, soften the butter for a few seconds at a time in the microwave until it has the consistency of (unstrained) yogurt. Sift the icing sugar onto the butter and then mix in until smooth.
3. One large spoonful at a time, fold 450g (16 oz) of the room-temperature strained yogurt into the butter and sugar until smoothly incorporated.
4. Chill for 15 minutes to firm the frosting, then use as your recipe requires.

---

*If you prefer, you can use unsalted butter but do add a small pinch of salt which will balance the sweetness and make the flavour fuller.

PEARL SUGAR

Hands on **20–30 minutes**
Ready in **30–40 minutes**

MAKES
75g (2⅔oz)

Pearl sugar, also known as nibbed sugar, is small, dense chunks of solid white sugar used to decorate bakes like panettone or kanelbullar. It looks pretty but, as the nibs don't dissolve fully in a batter, it also gives a delicious sweet crunch within things like Liege waffles. It's not readily available to buy in supermarkets but that's ok because it's really easy to make your own version from bog-standard granulated sugar. Stored in an airtight container, a batch will last a very long time – unless you end up casting all your pearl sugar before swine. (Lucky swine.)

75g (2⅔oz) granulated sugar

1 tsp water (plus extra, if needed)

1. Add the sugar to a non-stick frying pan and put on a very low heat. Add the water, and chop it into the sugar to dampen it just enough that the granules stick together to form craggy clumps. If the sugar isn't clumping, add more water, ¼ teaspoon at a time. If you've added too much water and the grains of sugar are dissolving, mix in more sugar.
2. When all the sugar has clumped, in various sized clusters, keep it on a very low heat to dry out and solidify the pieces. Make sure it never gets hot enough to caramelise the sugar. The damp sugar will be a silvery grey; as it dries out it will return to a bright white. This can take up to 30 minutes, just keep an eye on the crystal-like clumps. Stir or shake the pan every now and again so they heat evenly. When the sugar has all returned to white, remove the pan from the heat and leave to cool.
3. Store the cooled pearl sugar crystals in an airtight container at room temperature until needed and then use as your recipe requires.

PLANT-BASED GANACHE

Hands on **10 minutes**
Ready in **40 minutes**

MAKES
Enough to sandwich and cover an 18-cm (7-inch) four-layer cake

This is a really simple recipe you can knock up with store cupboard ingredients. And I mean genuine store cupboard ingredients: a can of plain beans, oil and chocolate. That is if you haven't eaten all the chocolate from the store cupboard when you had that really difficult day. The recipe uses the magical emulsifying properties of lecithin in the aquafaba to blend the oil and chocolate together, so you don't need any sort of cream. I use half 70% dark (bittersweet) chocolate, which is usually plant-based anyway (although check the pack), and half plant-based milk chocolate so the ganache isn't too intense, but you can try whatever combination you like. Using mild olive oil gives a delicious depth of flavour, but it is expensive so you can swap for a sunflower oil which will work perfectly.

230g (8 oz) cannellini (white) bean aquafaba

175g (6¼ oz) mild olive oil or sunflower oil

175g (6¼ oz) plant-based 'milk' chocolate

175g (6¼ oz) dark (bittersweet) chocolate (70% cocoa)

1. To a large microwave-safe bowl, add the aquafaba and oil and mix together to emulsify the two.
2. Chop up both chocolates, add them to the liquids and microwave in 15-second bursts, just long enough to melt the chocolate. Stir until the chocolate has fully melted and blended with the oil and aquafaba, then pour into a separate large bowl to set. If you don't have a microwave, sit the bowl over a pan of hot water to melt everything together.
3. The ganache needs to cool only to about 18°C (64°F) for it to firm up to a pipable, spreadable consistency. You can put it in the fridge to chill but keep checking it regularly; it will go from 'worryingly runny' to 'perfectly firm' very quickly. Try and avoid letting it chill too hard to spread otherwise you'll have to rewarm it gently and wait for it to set again. Use as soon as it's a soft, spreadable consistency.
4. If you want a good shine on the finished ganache, dip a palette knife into just-warm water and stroke it over the surface to smooth it. Re-dip the knife before each stroke.

WHOOPS!
If at any point the ganache splits, where the fats separate from the solids, just boil the kettle and stir in some hot water, one teaspoon at a time, to re-emulsify the mixture. This rescue will also work for dairy-based ganache, should it suffer a similar fate.

CHOCOLATE FUDGE FROSTING

Hands on **15 minutes**
Ready in **45 minutes**

MAKES
Enough to sandwich and cover an 18-cm (7-inch) four-layer cake

The best thing about this icing, apart from how good it tastes on a cake, is it makes you feel amazing even after the sugar crash. And that's because calmly overcoming failure is an essential step in the recipe. As you beat the cooled chocolate mix, the fats start to separate and look like an absolute horror show. But all you need to know is beating in a few teaspoons of humble tap water will emulsify everything back into a thick fudgy spread. When you use this newly acquired resilience in the face of future challenges, just remember it all started with chocolate fudge icing.

25g (1 oz) dark brown soft sugar

100g (3½ oz) light brown soft sugar

200g (7 oz) sweetened condensed milk

150g (5¼ oz) milk chocolate

200g (7 oz) salted butter

4 tsp (approximately) water, for beating when cool

1. Chop the chocolate as finely as you can be bothered so it melts faster.
2. To a heavy-bottomed pan, add all the ingredients, except the water. Put on a very low heat and stir slowly as everything warms and melts.
3. When the mixture is evenly blended, turn the heat up slightly. Keep stirring so nothing burns and bring it up to a gentle boil. Keep it gently bubbling for 2 minutes, or, if you have a thermometer, until it comes up to 115°C (240°F). This is the 'soft ball' stage of heating sugar: at this temperature the sugar structure changes, making the frosting thicker and more fudgy in consistency.
4. Remove from the heat, scrape the hot icing into a bowl and leave to cool and firm up. To speed the cooling, put the bowl in the fridge but don't let the icing go much below 20°C (70°F) or it will be too firm to beat at the next step. If you're not in a rush, just leave it on the side.
5. When the icing has firmed to a consistency similar to peanut butter, start beating it. It will almost instantly start to separate, the oils pooling in the base of the bowl. Just add ½ teaspoon of water at a time and carry on beating. The water helps to re-emulsify the fat with the chocolate; after just a few additions, the icing will come back together. Beat for a further minute until it is thick and pale. Set aside at room temperature until needed.
6. If the icing feels stiff when it comes to using it, a few seconds in the microwave will loosen it enough to make it easily spreadable so it won't tear a delicate cake.

TEMPERING CHOCOLATE

To create the decorations for the Chocolate Mountain Mudslide (page 16) and Black Forest Floor (page 58), you'll need the snap, shine and strength of tempered chocolate. On an average day, you're unlikely to need to temper much chocolate, but if you fancy having a go, this is the most straightforward way. This method melts the chocolate at the lowest possible temperature to keep it 'in temper', warming it to the point it's liquid and workable but not hot enough to destroy its original crystal structure. If you heat chocolate above a certain point, the crystals in the cocoa fat break down and when it sets again those crystals reform in a different way, making the chocolate dull, bendy and sticky. Shiny and strong versus dull and sticky? We should all aim to stay in temper.

1. Start by chopping the chocolate very finely. This is time consuming but it will make life easier in the long run. You can use a grater or a food processor with a grater attachment, but the static produced by hand grating and the washing up produced by the food processor generally point me back to a knife and chopping board.
2. Add most of the chopped chocolate to a metal bowl (one large enough to sit on top of the pan, not in it), saving 1–2 tablespoons in a separate small bowl.
3. Boil the kettle, half fill the pan and sit the metal bowl over the hot water. The pan doesn't need to be heated, the residual heat should be enough to melt the chocolate; only put it on a very low heat if the water cools so much the chocolate stops melting.
4. The chocolate will start to melt immediately; just keep mixing the melted and unmelted together. Keep a digital thermometer in the bowl so you can always see what temperature it is. The goal is to melt all the chocolate without going over its 'in temper' temperature. Different chocolates have different temperatures up to which they are 'in temper':
   70% dark (bittersweet) chocolate: 32°C (90°F)
   Milk chocolate: 30°C (86°F)
   White chocolate: 28°C (82.5°F)
5. If the chocolate is getting too hot too quickly, lift the bowl off the pan and stir to cool it slightly. If you do go over the temperature by a degree or so, don't panic, just sprinkle in a little of the chocolate you've held back. This not only brings the temperature down, you're also adding more tempered chocolate with unbroken cocoa fat crystals and these encourage the rest of the chocolate to reform properly. It's like sitting the naughty kid next to the good kid and hoping the good rubs off. Only this actually works.
6. Use straight away as your recipe requires.

DRY CARAMEL

Hands on/Ready in **10 minutes**

There are two ways to make caramel, wet and dry. Dry caramel is simply sugar heated in a pan so it liquefies then caramelises from 160°C (320°F). A wet caramel on the other hand (please don't get any on your hand) uses water to dissolve the sugar so it's liquid before it's heated to caramelising temperature. But let's start with the dry one, firstly, because it matches my sense of humour, and secondly, as it's easier and far less prone to failure, it also matches my sense of laziness.

1. Weigh the required amount of sugar into a heavy-bottomed pan* and put on a medium-low heat. Keep an eye on it; if you see any smoke or bubbling turn the heat down.
2. After 2–3 minutes, you'll notice the sugar granules at the edges of the pan have started to liquefy. Use a heatproof spatula to drag back the top layer of granules and check the bottom layer has also started to melt. When it has, gently mix the liquid sugar together with the clumps of uncaramelised sugar to even out the heat. (Don't panic, you can stir a dry caramel as much as you like. It's a wet caramel you must leave alone, but more on that later.)
3. From this point, the sugar will continue to liquefy and then caramelise to a rich amber colour as it heats. It doesn't need continuous stirring, just give it the occasional mix if areas of undissolved, uncaramelised sugar need mixing into the liquid caramel.
4. When all the sugar granules have dissolved and the caramel is the colour you want, remove from the heat. Bear in mind the sugar will carry on caramelising for a time in the pan while it holds residual heat. The more often you make this, the more you will get a clearer sense of what depth of colour you want and how long to leave it caramelising.
5. Use as your recipe requires.

WHOOPS!

If your caramel bubbles or foams, it's got too hot, it's on its way to burning and it'll end up tasting bitter. Unfortunately you can't unburn caramel, you just have to prevent it from happening. Keep a close eye on it while it's caramelising; if you see any bubbles start to break the surface, turn the heat down or remove the pan so it can cool and stir slowly to dissipate the heat.

---

*Throughout this book there are a lot of heavy bottoms, I like heavy bottoms and I cannot lie. With regards to a pan, the 'heavy bottom' really means a thick bottom that disperses the heat evenly across the whole pan base. A heavy-bottomed pan is useful for heating anything that needs even, gentle cooking: curds, pastry creams, etc. For a reliable caramel, I'd say one is essential, eliminating hot spots that burn the sugar or cold patches that leave it unmelted.

WET CARAMEL

Hands on/Ready in **20 minutes**

As the name suggests, this version involves liquid. Water is added to the sugar so it dissolves to a liquid state before it reaches caramelising temperature. It's a trickier way to make caramel because it's temperamental; if you stir it or heat it too quickly or there's a sugar grain out of line, it can crystallise rather than caramelise the whole pan. So why bother? Well, there are a couple of reasons. It's useful to know how to make the wet version. If you want a really pale caramel (to stick a croquembouche together), this method makes it easier to stop the sugar caramelising too fast because it heats more slowly than the dry. And, although neither of these are caramel because they are not heated to 160°C (320°F), it's the same principle used to make the hard crack red 'toffee' on the Toffee Apple Biscuit Buns (page 203), and as the starting point for Italian Meringue (page 218) and Marshmallow (page 219). So don't be put off. Remember a few key points and you shouldn't have a problem. The first rule of wet club is don't stir: that agitates the crystals in the sugar and just reminds them they would rather be a white solid than an amber liquid; a swirl of the pan every now and then is all it needs, otherwise leave it mostly alone. Second rule of wet club: I told you not to stir. Third rule: get a bit of help. Add some glucose syrup or golden syrup; these both contain inverted sugars which help prevent the crystals in the dissolved sugar reforming and crystallising the lot.

For 200g (7 oz) granulated sugar use 60g (2 oz) water and 20g (¾ oz) / 1 tbsp golden syrup or glucose syrup. (The amount of water doesn't need to be too precise as it will evaporate by the time the sugar caramelises.)

1. To a clean and dry heavy-bottomed pan, add the sugar and shake gently so the sugar lies flat.
2. Pour the water into the centre of the sugar so it slowly moistens but doesn't disturb the granules. Add the syrup then put the pan on a low heat so the sugar slowly dissolves but doesn't boil. Don't stir it, do nothing more than swirl the pan very occasionally to check if there are still granules of sugar visible.
3. When all the sugar has dissolved, turn up the heat slightly and look for the colour slowly changing from a clear liquid to pale gold to rich amber as it continues to heat. A thermometer isn't necessary for caramel as you are just going by colour.
4. When it has reached the colour you want, remove the caramel from the heat.
5. Use as your recipe requires.

WHOOPS!

If, for whatever reason, your sugar and water solution does crystallise into a white flaky, granular mass, firstly, I'm not going to judge you and, secondly, it's not the end of the world. Don't throw it away. Crystallised sugar can still be made into caramel. But you will need time, so weigh up whether saving a couple of hundred grams of sugar is worth your time. All you have to do is add more water to the crystallised sugar in the pan, but I mean a lot more. For 200g (7 oz) of sugar add about 200g (7 oz) of boiling water and 1 tablespoon of golden or glucose syrup. Put on a medium heat to slowly dissolve all the crystallised sugar into the water. When it's all liquid, bring it up to a gentle boil, don't stir it, just wait patiently for the water to evaporate. Once the water has boiled away, the sugar will gradually heat up to 160°C or 320°F and start caramelising and you can take it from there.

What's the difference between caramel and toffee?

It's particularly confusing when a lot of things we assume to be made from toffee turn out to be made from caramel. For example, despite being called toffee apples, it's usually a hard caramel not a dairy-based toffee covering those unfortunate fruit orbs. Conversely, caramel or millionaire's shortbread is usually made from a boiled condensed milk toffee not a caramel. But the sticky nitty gritty is: caramel is sugar heated to 160°C or 320°F from which point it caramelises, giving it its toasted flavour and amber colour, and then dairy is added if you're making a sauce. Toffee is sugar cooked with dairy (butter, cream) and its toasted flavour and amber colour come not from the sugar being caramelised, but from the dairy proteins browning in the heat (the maillard reaction) and, if used, from the brown sugar. Toffee is cooked to between 140°C or 284°F (soft crack) and 155°C or 311°F (hard crack), not hot enough to caramelise the sugar, but hot enough to alter its structure so it's firm or solid when cooled. So in terms of making them the processes are different but the outcomes are similar; both are sweet and brown with a deep, rich, toasted flavour.

SALTED CARAMEL SAUCE

Hands on/Ready in **20 minutes**

MAKES
Enough to fill a 330-ml (11-fl oz) jar

EQUIPMENT
Sterilised glass jar with lid

Being self-sufficient in making your own salted caramel sauce, dairy or plant-based, opens up a whole host of impressive-but-secretly-quite-simple recipes, so it's definitely worth trying. As the saying doesn't quite go, teach a person to fish and they can feed themselves for life, teach a person to make salted caramel sauce and they can be happy for life.

225g (8 oz) granulated sugar

200g (7 oz) double (heavy) cream

¼–½ tsp table salt

1. Add the sugar to a heavy-bottomed pan and start making a dry caramel (page 227).
2. While the sugar heats, weigh the cream into a small jug (pitcher) or, if you don't have a microwave, a separate small pan.
3. While there are some clumps of sugar visible in the caramel, heat the cream to just boiling point. Ideally you want the cream to be hot just as all the sugar has caramelised, but a few degrees here or there for the cream won't matter – your priority is not allowing the caramel to go too dark.
4. When you're happy with the depth of colour in the caramel, switch off the heat and pour a small amount of cream into the pan – about 2 tablespoons is ideal, but you don't have to measure it. The cream will hiss and bubble as it's added, so swirl it carefully around the pan, but don't stir it. Once the cream has dissolved into the caramel, add a similar amount of cream again and repeat the swirling to mix. If you add too much cream too quickly, the caramel will almost certainly harden into a lump that will take forever to dissolve over a low heat. Even if this feels slightly slow, trust me – it's much quicker than stirring patiently for an extra 15 minutes.
5. As the caramel in the pan gets closer to a runny sauce, you can add greater amounts of cream at a time – keep swirling it in. If the sauce has cooled down too much for the cream to be easily incorporated, put it back on a very low heat. If the sauce isn't fully blended after all the cream has been added, use a heatproof spatula to squash any thick, gloopy caramel against the bottom out from the centre to the sides. Avoid stirring in circles as this tends to gather lumps and stick them together.
6. When you have a smooth sauce, stir in up to ½ teaspoon of your preferred salt – start with a small pinch and add more to taste. Sea salt flakes give an occasional crunch and burst of salty flavour, however I prefer the uniformity of easily dissolved, cheap-as-chips table salt.
7. Leave the sauce to cool in the pan for 10 minutes so that it doesn't crack the clean jar. Pour the sauce into the jar, then once it reaches room temperature, seal with the lid.
8. Store at room temperature in the cupboard (rather than in the fridge) so that it is spreadable when needed. Sugar is a preservative so it keeps perfectly unrefrigerated.

PLANT-BASED SALTED CARAMEL SAUCE

Hands on/Ready in **20 minutes**

MAKES
Enough to fill a 330-ml (11-fl oz) jar

EQUIPMENT
Sterilised glass jar with lid

This delicious dairy-free alternative is slightly paler than the dairy version, because it doesn't contain the milk solids that brown when added to the molten sugar, but it's every bit as deeply rich in caramel flavour. Because plant-based creams have a lower fat content than dairy, plant-based butter is added to give the lusciously thick saucy consistency you're after.

225g (8 oz) granulated sugar

125g (4½ oz) plant-based double (heavy) cream

75g (2⅔ oz) plant-based butter (not soft spread)

¼–½ tsp table salt

1. Follow the instructions for the dairy version opposite, but once you've added all the plant-based cream and have a smooth sauce, stir in the plant-based butter.
2. If the finished, room-temperature sauce ends up too thick, too much of the liquid from the cream has boiled off. If you want a runnier sauce at room temperature, gently warm the caramel to loosen it up and stir in an extra 1–2 tablespoons of cream and leave to cool. If the finished, room-temperature sauce is too runny, put it back in the pan and bubble it for 5 minutes to boil off any excess liquid so it's thicker when cool.

LEMON CURD

Hands on **15 minutes**
Ready in **45 minutes**

MAKES
Enough to fill a 330-ml (11-fl oz) jar

EQUIPMENT
Sterilised glass jar with lid

This is a deliciously buttery and bright lemon curd, thickened with cornflour (cornstarch) and whole egg, rather than multiple yolks which, to my tongue, can make curds overpoweringly eggy and, to my wallet, expensive. It is as good for filling a cake or a pie as it is spread on toast or licked off a spoon while you stare blankly into an open fridge, wondering, 'Does this count as eating more fruit?'

100g (3½ oz) granulated sugar (add more to taste)

5g (⅕ oz) / ½ tbsp cornflour (cornstarch)

1 large (US extra-large) egg

80g (2¾ oz) lemon juice (from 2 or 3 lemons)

Yellow food colouring (optional)

100g (3½ oz) unsalted butter

Micro pinch of salt

1. To a small bowl, add the sugar and cornflour, then mix. Add the egg, whisking until there are no lumps, then pour through a fine-mesh sieve (strainer) into a heavy-bottomed pan. Discard any stringy eggy bits that are left in the sieve.
2. Add the lemon juice to the pan, put on a medium-low heat and stir continuously until the curd thickens. Taste the curd. If it's too sour, add more sugar a little at a time. If there's any chalkiness from the cornflour, cook for a little longer until it has gone. Add the yellow food colouring now, if using.
3. Remove the pan from the heat and stir in the butter until completely melted and emulsified with the curd. Add a micro pinch of salt to balance the flavours. Use as your recipe requires or scrape into a sterilised jar, leave to cool to room temperature and then seal and store in the fridge.

IF YOU DIDN'T ASK FOR LEMONS,
TELL LIFE, NEXT TIME,
YOU'D PREFER THE MONEY

ANY JAM CURD

Hands on **10 minutes**
Ready in **40 minutes**

MAKES
Enough to fill a 330-ml (11-fl oz) jar

EQUIPMENT
Sterilised glass jar with lid

Having the super power (yes, it is) to turn any jam into a luscious, buttery curd is such a handy, hacky way to gussie up a bake. With just 10 minutes of preparation (and a bit of cooling time) you've got a quick and delicious filling for a pastry, a tart or a cake, one that's just a bit more glamorous than a skim of jam but requires no tedious fruit preparation beyond opening a jar.

170g (6 oz) ready-made jam (jelly or preserve)

10g (4 tsp) cornflour (cornstarch) – if your jam is very runny use 12g (1½ tbsp)

50g (1¾ oz) water

1 large (US extra-large) egg

Squeeze of lemon juice or citric acid (optional)

80g (2¾ oz) unsalted butter

Micro pinch of salt

1. Add the jam to a heavy-bottomed pan and break it up a bit. If you want a smooth curd, press the jam through a sieve (strainer) first to catch any seeds or skin, but make sure you prepare enough to still have 170g (6 oz) of sieved jam in the pan.
2. Add the cornflour and water to a small bowl and mix until there are no lumps, then whisk in the egg. Pour through a fine-mesh sieve (strainer) into the jam pan and discard any stringy eggy bits that are left.
3. Mix everything in the pan so the egg is well incorporated with the jam, then put over a medium heat.
4. Keep stirring the curd as it cooks; it will take about 5 minutes to thicken. Taste as you go. If there is some chalkiness from the cornflour, cook it for a further minute or two until that's gone. If you want the curd to taste a bit sharper, add a squeeze of lemon or a little citric acid at this point.
5. Remove from the heat and stir in the unsalted butter. When the butter has melted into the curd, add the tiniest pinch of salt to balance the flavours. Pour into a bowl and chill in the fridge until you need it for your recipe or pour into a very clean jam jar and keep in the fridge.

PLANT-BASED / EGG-FREE ANY JAM CURD

15g (½ oz) cornflour (cornstarch)

100g (3½ oz) aquafaba or water (see note below)

170g (6 oz) ready-made jam (jelly or preserve)

Squeeze of lemon juice or citric acid (optional)

80g (2¾ oz) unsalted plant-based butter or coconut oil

Micro pinch of salt

1. Add the cornflour to a heavy-bottomed pan and mix to a smooth slurry with a little of the aquafaba or water. When there are no lumps, add the rest of the aquafaba or water to the pan.
2. Add the jam to the pan and mix well before putting on a medium heat.
3. Follow the above steps 4–5 as per the egg-based recipe.

NOTE ON AQUAFABA

You can use water rather than aquafaba, but egg-free fruit curds can start to separate when kept in the fridge, whereas the lecithin from the beans helps the fats stay emulsified for a better texture for longer. If you're using the curd straight away as a filling for a cake or tart, water will be fine. I use the aquafaba from cannellini beans (white beans) as it smells less than chickpea (garbanzo bean) water, but either works.

INDEX

THANKS

Firstly, the team at Murdoch, Céline, Lisa, Sarah, Amelia and Bonnie without whom there wouldn't be a book in which to thank them. It's been an absolute dream working with you, a really good dream, not the sort where you're naked on the toilet in an exam and your teeth are falling out.

Annie Rigg and your team, Caitlin MacDonald and Lu Cottle, for making my recipes look so good and for gifting me the chance to swan about while you worked your cinnamon buns off in a heatwave.

Mowie Kay for your stunning photography and cool head in the aforementioned heatwave.

Jon Stefani for going above and beyond the remit of most agents by actually answering my emails and for mopping up when I get an attack of 'idearrhoea'.

Dr Chintal Patel for your abundant kindness and support and for your help in getting this book ball rolling.

Mallika Basu for your generous guidance in keeping me appreciating, not appropriating.

Ivan Day for the Food History Jottings blog and its fascinating Battenberg deep dive.

Euan, I couldn't have done any of this without you, I wouldn't have wanted to do any of this without you (and for seeing the funny side when I told 20 million people I was married to Peter Capaldi).

Hal and Peter, my funny, kind children and (only sometimes quite rude) in-house bake testers.

My parents, all three of them, thanks for everything and sorry for all the mess.

Lal Siroky for being my dearest, longest-serving friend, and for christening a potato peeler 'a poteeler', a name that still has the power to reduce me to hysterics 35 years on.

Sarah Irons for not just your friendship but also your patient scientific advice on matters of density, mass and volume.

Kay Brophy for your never-ending positivity and all those pub-based counselling / egging-on sessions.

Alexis Strum for being the best and funniest multi-hyphenate, emotional support pop star I could wish for.

Anna Christoforou for the friendship, the food and the funnies.

Amy Beashel for your counsel, encouragement and unapologetic delight in being a fellow pun lovin' criminal. Whenever I filo, you bake me feel seen and curd.

Katy Rink for printing and championing my work and for coaxing me on to pursue the next steps, I wouldn't have done half of it without your gentle shoves.

Marjorie Hall for kindly sharing not just your love and warmth with me and family, but also your Bakewell Tart secret (ground rice, page 23), I'm grateful for both.

Finally, *The Great British Bake Off*, without your sustained and emphatic rejection of my charms, I wouldn't have got cross enough to fully commit to my pudding pusher calling. It all goes to show, everything happens for a raisin.

ABOUT THE AUTHOR

Baking across social media and Substack as The Caketoonist, Tat Effby has built up a combined following of over 600k fans of her idiot-proof recipes and idiotic humour. Her fans include both culinary luminaries and comedy legends. As a cartoonist, Tat's work has appeared in national publications such as the *Guardian*, the *Observer*, *Private Eye* and the *Oldie*. As a baker, Tat was relentlessly rejected by *The Great British Bake Off* for years. So instead of the tent, she took all her pent-up cake energy to social media and started sharing her dry sense of humour and moist sense of cake. Her videos, a frothy confection of detailed instructional recipes and very stupid jokes, have been watched over 90 million times.

Published in 2026 by Murdoch Books, an imprint of Allen & Unwin

Murdoch Books UK
Ormond House
26–27 Boswell Street
London WC1N 3JZ
Phone: +44 (0) 20 8785 5995
murdochbooks.co.uk
info@murdochbooks.co.uk

Murdoch Books Australia
Cammeraygal Country
83 Alexander Street
Crows Nest NSW 2065
Phone: +61 (0)2 8425 0100
murdochbooks.com.au
info@murdochbooks.com.au

For corporate orders and custom publishing, contact our business development team at salesenquiries@murdochbooks.com.au

Publisher: Céline Hughes
Project Editor: Lisa Pendreigh
Design Manager: Sarah Odgers
Cover and Layout Design: Double Slice (Amelia Leuzzi and Bonnie Eichelberger)
Photographer: Mowie Kay
Illustrator: Tat Effby
Food and Prop Stylist: Annie Rigg
Production Manager: Natalie Crouch

Murdoch Books Australia acknowledges the Traditional Owners of the Country on which we live and work. We pay our respects to all Aboriginal and Torres Strait Islander Elders, past and present.

EU Authorised Representative: Easy Access System Europe, Mustamäe tee 50, 10621 Tallinn, Estonia, gpsr.requests@easproject.com

ISBN 978 1 76150 117 3

A catalogue record for this book is available from the British Library

A catalogue record for this book is available from the National Library of Australia

Colour reproduction by Splitting Image Colour Studio Pty Ltd, Wantirna, Victoria
Printed in China by C&C Offset Printing Co., Ltd.

RECIPE NOTES
Both metric and imperial measurements are used in this book.

Follow one set of measurements throughout, not a mixture, as they are not interchangeable. (See the housekeeping notes on page 8.)

Eggs are always UK large or US/Aus extra-large, unless specified otherwise.

Butter is always unsalted, unless specified otherwise.

Citrus fruits are always unwaxed.

All spoon measurements are level, unless specified otherwise. Tablespoon measures are 15ml (3 teaspoons).

You may find oven cooking times vary depending on the oven and oven setting you are using. The recipes in this book are based on fan-assisted (convection) oven temperatures. For non-fan-assisted ovens, as a general rule, set the oven temperature to 20°C (25–50°F) higher than indicated in the recipe.

IMPORTANT: Those who might be at risk from the effects of salmonella poisoning (the elderly, pregnant women, young children and those suffering from immune deficiency diseases) should consult their doctor with any concerns about eating raw eggs.

10 9 8 7 6 5 4 3 2 1

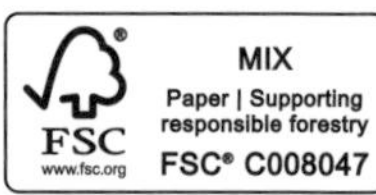